Risking Enchantment

JEANIE WATSON

Risking Enchantment

Coleridge's Symbolic
World of Faery

University of Nebraska Press
Lincoln and London

Acknowledgments for the use of previously published material appear on page
xi.

The paper in this book meets the minimum requirements of American National
Standard for Information Sciences—Permanence of Paper for Printed Library
Materials, ANSI Z39.48–1984.

Publication of this book was assisted by a grant from The Andrew W. Mellon
Foundation

For Melissa and Michael

Contents

Acknowledgments

This book has a very personal, as well as scholarly, history—a history I see in terms of the people associated with places where I have lived and worked, with each segment of personal and professional history making its own contribution to my thinking and my way of reading Coleridge.

My interest in the Romantic period began in Carol Russell's senior high English class; a particular love of Coleridge's poetry dates from Clement Goode's courses at Baylor University in the early 1960s. Dr. Goode taught me to read poetry and opened up for me the world of poetry as an exploration of life. Moments of illumination that occurred as I wrote a paper on "The Rime" and studied "Frost at Midnight" with Stu Rosenbaum and Keith Lovin became the core of my present reading of these poems.

Teaching experiences and conversations with colleagues have made essential and inextricable contributions to the history of this book. At Stonehill College, I struggled with my Romantics students into an understanding of the *Biographia* and "Eolian Harp" and "Kubla Khan." At Gustavus Adolphus College, Claude Brew and I developed interpretations of "The Rime" and "Christabel," and I owe my introduction to the *Four Quartets* to him. Through a Gustavus sabbatical, granted by Dean Robert Karsten, and the generous recommendation of Carolyn Heilbrun, I spent 1980–81 as a Visiting Scholar at Columbia University. There I began writing the first draft of what would—through several evolutions—become RISKING ENCHANTMENT. Conversations with Professor Heilbrun and Carl Woodring brought in the strands of androgyny and Coleridge's use of music.

Summer research grants from Marshall University in 1982 and 1983 and from Rhodes College in 1984 enabled me to work at the British Library and participate in Wordsworth Summer Conferences at Grasmere, where I read a portion of the initial draft of the "Christabel" section of the book and began friendships with a number of Coleridge colleagues. The last draft greatly benefited from Uli Knoepflmacher's recommendations for paring down during a National Endowment for the Humanities Summer Seminar at Princeton in 1986. J. Robert Barth, in particular, has been a friend and encourager along the way. He and Anthony J. Harding both read the final draft, making excellent suggestions for which I am grateful. I also want to thank Ben Oliver for his careful reading of the manuscript and for his support and friendship.

Other people, in numerous places and over time, have given the encouragement and friendship that have made it possible for me to write this book over a good number of years and through a series of new jobs and life circumstances. I feel very fortunate in my friendships and in the ways in which the personal and the professional have reinforced each other. I especially thank Karen Kornell, Linda and Robby Faust, Deborah Downs-Miers, Florence and Don Ostrom, Judy Mohraz, Woody Wooden, Phil Pittman, David Goslee, Carole Levin, Jim McGavran, Mary Briscoe, Jennifer Brady, Miriam Banks, Gerald Duff, Marjorie and Walt Herbert, Jan Dawson, Ken Roberts, and Ed Kain. I am grateful to all these people and to many, many others—and to the academic institutions at which I have worked.

I want also to thank Gail Stroud at Rhodes for typing the first drafts and to acknowledge that without Dotty Secor at South-western and her incredible patience and good cheer at the computer, this book would have been next to impossible.

Finally, I want to thank Stu, who has always been there for me, both in and out of marriage, and our children, Melissa and Michael, with the hope that they will always risk enchantment.

Portions of this book first appeared in *Christianity and Literature*, *Cithara*, and *Prose Studies*. I am grateful to these journals for their permission to reprint parts of the following essays: "Seeing Through the Glass: From Secular to Sacred Story," *Christianity and Literature* 37.1 (1987): 45–53; "Coleridge's 'Love': Symbolic Analogate of Love," *Cithara* 27.1 (1987): 29–39; "Coleridge's Androgynous Ideal," *Prose Studies* 6.1 (1983): 36–56.

Abbreviations Used for the Works of Coleridge

AR	*Aids to Reflection*
BL	*Biographia Literaria*, ed. Engell and Bate
BL Shawcross	*Biographia Literaria*, ed. Shawcross
C	"Christabel," in *The Complete Poetical Works*
C&S	*On the Constitution of Church and State*
CL	*The Collected Letters*
CN	*The Notebooks*
DN	"Destiny of Nations," in *The Complete Poetical Works*
EH	"The Eolian Harp," in *The Complete Poetical Works*
Friend	*The Friend*
KK	"Kubla Khan," in *The Complete Poetical Works*
Rime	"The Rime of the Ancient Mariner," in *The Complete Poetical Works*
RM	"Religious Musings," in *The Complete Poetical Works*

Abbreviations

SM	*The Statesman's Manual*
TL	*Hints towards the Formation of a More Comprehensive Theory of Life*
TT	*The Table Talk*

INTRODUCTION

"Habituated *to the Vast*"

*A*lthough *Coleridge* was well aware of the late eighteenth-and early nineteenth-century strictures against fairy tales, he himself did not agree with them. As a boy, he read fairy stories voraciously; as a father, he repeated them to his children; and when he came to write "Christabel," one of his most compelling yet, even now, most puzzling works, what he wrote was a fairy tale. Many years after it was composed—Part I in 1797; Part II in 1800—Coleridge wrote in the *Biographia Literaria* that the poem "pretends to be nothing more than a common Faery Tale" (*BL* 2: 238). Although "Christabel" embodies his most overt and fully developed use of the fairy tale genre with its narrative elements and characters and motifs, this genre and the concept of Faery, in general, provide texture, allusion, points of reference, and a symbolic language in Coleridge's poetry throughout his writing career—this, despite the fact that fairy tale literature was antithetical to the prevailing rationalistic atmosphere of the late eighteenth and early nineteenth centuries. In poems as early as the exuberant, youthful "Songs of the Pixies" (1793) and as late as the mature and meditative "Garden of Boccaccio" (1828), fairy songs can be heard in the gardens of Coleridge's imagination, bringing at times the pleasurable visions of "The Eolian Harp" and at others the painful moans and screams of the terrified lost child in "Dejection." In part, perhaps, because of his own childhood reading of fairy tales and other chapbook literature of the imagination, Coleridge associates the world of Faery with the realm of imagination and Spirit, with the willingness to suspend disbelief and participate in mystery.

The argument of this book has several interrelated components: (1) The burden of Coleridge's poetry, early and late, is an exploration of the possibilities available to the human spirit for intuitive spiritual knowledge and for growth and participation in the Reality of Spirit—possibilities that must inevitably be played out within the limitations imposed by the fallen world. (2) This exploration rests on a bedrock belief that the world is by nature consubstantial—and therefore symbolic. (3) The symbolic character of existence is conveyed in Coleridge's poetry through symbolic metaphors and symbolic story. (4) The concept of Faery is one of those symbolic metaphors, and where the traditional genre of fairy tale is transformed by the poet into a tale of Faery, this tale becomes a symbolic story; the terms "Faery" and "tale of Faery," as used in this study, thus denote a heightened, symbolic use of the genre. (5) Coleridge uses these tales of Faery—whether they occur as brief moments of spiritual encounter or as entire narratives—as appropriate vehicles for the exploration of the possibilities of knowledge of and participation in Spirit, which he sees as the soul's task in the world.

A number of things follow from the argument. If Faery is a symbolic metaphor of Spirit, the two must be significantly and fundamentally "like." And if they are "like" and if traditional folk fairy tales have the ability in the imagination of an artist like Coleridge to be transformed into tales of Faery, then a genre that is ordinarily secular in import and narrative can be used to convey the sacred story of Spirit. Both the secular and sacred tales are about invisible things, things mysterious and inexplicable in the empirical and analytical mode of our daily existence but perfectly true and perceivable and understood—"known"—at another, equally valid, level of existence. Further, therefore, the secular Other World of fairy tale—a once-upon-a-time and outside-time kind of place—entered through the hearer's or reader's imaginative participation, can become the "Land of Faery": in Coleridge's definition, a "mental space," in which there is a "marvellous independence or true imaginative absence of all particular place & time—it is neither in the domains of History or Geography, is ignorant of all artificial boundary" (*CN* 3: 4501)—a realm entered through and as an act of the symbolic imagination. Thus tales of Faery, in Coleridgean terms, are themselves symbolic acts of the imagination, acts of symbolic encounter that occur first as the poet creates the tale and again as the reader re-creates, in imaginative participation, the unfolding of the tale. Traditional fairy tales have always had to do with growth and development, with maturation, and with relationship and love. Similarly, Coleridge's tales of Faery function symbolically within this tradition as instances of symbolic encounter and experience which allow for and actively encourage the individual spirit's participation in the Love that is God.

The poems and parts of poems that I call tales of Faery and discuss within that context range from declarative assertions about the nature of the world we live in and the role of the human spirit within that world to a variety of narratives which begin, in effect, with a "what if" hypothesis and end by carrying out the implications of that hypothesis, whether in full or fragmentary form. What if, for example, the soul were afraid to journey into mystery? What if there were no return from the journey? Or what if one were to return, only to find no companionship, no human relationship of love to give expression to one's new-found intuitive knowledge of Love? Under what conditions can existence in Faery be sustained in a fallen world? These and other questions and their possible answers are implicit in the stories Coleridge tells in his poems. Stories and tales and moments within stories become significant because they ask the fundamental questions of existence

3

and because they can function symbolically as entrances into Faery.

The roots of Coleridge's sense of the symbolic significance of story can be seen in the intensity of his own childhood response to the reading of imaginative literature and the certainty behind the early connection he makes between those experiences and the spiritual realities of the universe. Coleridge is very conscious that his own awareness of the reality of Spirit and mystery was fostered throughout his childhood by his reading of fairy tales, legends, Eastern tales, and the like. It is an interesting fact that the genres we have for the most part relegated to children's literature—and thus tend to dismiss as irrelevant to mature, adult concerns—are the very ones that Coleridge chooses to exploit to their fullest potential as vehicles for exploring the meaning of life. A sense of Coleridge's attitude toward and statements about fairy tales and related stories serves as a useful introductory argument, attesting to their significance in his thinking and writing.

Born in 1772, Coleridge grew up at a time when fairies and fairy stories in general were under suspicion. Although French literary fairy tales had begun entering the English market as early as 1699 and were extremely popular in the early and mid-eighteenth century,[1] these, as well as local superstitious tales of fairies and goblins, were increasingly thought to be, at best, "prejudicial nonsense" (Kilner viii) or, at worst—following the lead of John Locke's theories of human development and education—extremely harmful fare, especially for children.[2] So influential were Locke's ideas that in 1803, Lucy Aiken could write in her *Poetry for Children* that fairy tales were no longer a danger to children, since the "'wand of reason' had banished 'dragons and fairies, giants and witches' from the nursery."

Banishment of the fairies had been attempted long before the end of the eighteenth century—and with as little ultimate success.[3] Chaucer's Wife of Bath said that in King Arthur's day, Britain was full of fairy folk, now driven away by the friars. The fairies, however, knew how to bide their time, live with country people, and wait for their reemergence in the English Renaissance at the hands and in the lands of Shakespeare's *Midsummer Night's Dream*, Spenser's *Faerie Queene*, Drayton's *Nymphidia*, and a host of lesser works.[4] The Renaissance world of fairies was a crowded one, filled with "bull beggars, spirits, witches, urchens, elves, hags, fairies, satyrs, pans, fauns, sylens, pit with the cansticke, tritons, centaurs, dwarfes, giants, imps, calcars, conjurors, nymphs, changlings, incubus, Robin good-fellowe, the spoorne, the mare, the man in the oke, the hell waine, the fierdrake, the puckle, Tom Thombe, hob goblin, Tom tumbler, boneless, and other such bugs," to give only Reginald Scot's list of creatures used at the time to frighten children and to people superstitious stories (152–53). This motley tribe originated as part of the oral tradition, lived partly in legend and romance (Christian, Arthurian, or otherwise), partly in prose, partly in ballad; it fed on simple superstition and existed in common faith and communal story; it inhabited the imaginative world of the fabulous. It was never truly banished; instead, in the rationalistic seventeenth and eighteenth centuries, it stepped sideways, out of the mainstream of legitimate, suitable moral literature and into the "Other World" of the chapbook, in the process becoming universally available.

Chapbook literature encompassed everything, and it was this "pedlar's pack"—as Harvey Darton calls it—of "all the popular literature of four centuries in a reduced and degenerate form" that helped fill young Samuel Taylor Coleridge's days of childhood reading:

> When it dawned on the moralists, in and after the Blue-Stocking Age, that chapbooks were low, they had a very wide hostile field to survey: nothing less than a universal library, which was at the same time a sub-history of English literature. The good godly books were in it, as has been said, both those meant for children and those above their heads. The lives of those who wrote them—Bunyan's, for instance—were likewise in it. Jumbled in the pack were things for half a dozen other types of mind: *Mother Shipton* . . . Cocker's *Spelling Book* (first published in the seventeenth century) and *Arithmetic* (1660), *Joe Miller's Jest Book* (Miller lived, less eminent in life than in name, about 1684–1738), *George Barnwell* (adapted from Lillo's play of 1731 and from the older facts), *Bampfylde Moore Carew* (the mid-eigh-

teenth-century vagabond), *The Wandering Jew* (whose story in England goes back as far as Roger of Wendover, in the thirteenth century), *Fair Rosamund, Jane Shore, John* or *Tom Hickathrift*, several *Jacks*—housebuilders, giant-killers, climbers and others—*Dick Whittington*, various chapters of Arthurian legend, *Fortunatus, Friar Bacon, Friar Rush* ("full of pleasant mirth and delight for young people" as early as 1620), *The Friar and the Boy, Dr Faustus, Mother Bunch's Closet newly broke open* (advice to maidens and wives), *The Wise Men of Gotham*, . . . *Dorastus and Fawnia* (based—in England—on Greene's *Pandosto*), *Don Quixote, Francis Drake* and later admirals, alphabets, *Robin Hood, Tom Thumb*, practically all the known Middle Age Romances, *Robinson Crusoe* and his shadow, *Philip Quarll*, Perrault's fairy-tales (usually singly), Aesop, Dr. Watt's *Divine Songs*; anything and everything. The list could be trebled without repetition. (81–82)

It should be noted that major components of this extremely popular chapbook literature were the fairy tales (both native English tales like *Jack the Giant-Killer* and French tales like *Beauty and the Beast*), medieval and Arthurian romance, and Bunyan's *Pilgrim's Progress*. Coleridge, like many other child and adult readers, surely must have absorbed these stories without making strict genre distinctions,[5] the lack of distinction abetted by the illustrations to the stories: "From about 1700 or so the small woodblocks," used for illustration, "became ubiquitous. . . . Whether through loans or through direct copying and recutting, the same 'cuts' appear constantly in different books issued by different publishers. George, Guy, Bevis, giants, dying Christians, boars, dragons, fiddlers were interchangeable figures, and historical propriety, or fidelity to the detail of any one text, did not matter" (Darton 74). We should not be surprised if generic lines tended to blur, if fairies sometimes aided but other times thwarted Christian knights, if the Edenic world seemed a fairy "once upon a time." Taken together, these tales of the imagination provide an Other World that exerts the appeal of a strong and compelling reality.

Coleridge attests to the strength of this imaginative world's appeal for him, even at an extremely young age. Of the years October 1775 to October 1778, he writes to Thomas Poole: "These three years [ages three to six] I continued at the reading-school—

because I was too little to be trusted among my Father's School-boys. . . . I took no pleasure in boyish sports—but read incessantly." Coleridge continues:

> My Father's Sister kept an *every-thing* Shop at Crediton—and there I read thro' all the gilt-cover little books that could be had at that time, & likewise all the uncovered tales of Tom Hickathrift, Jack the Giant-killer, &c, &c &c &c—/—and I used to lie by the wall, and *mope*—and my spirits used to come upon me suddenly, & in a flood—& then I was accustomed to run up and down the church-yard, and act over all I had been reading on the docks, the nettles, and the rank-grass. —At six years old I remember to have read Belisarius, Robinson Crusoe, & Philip Quarle [Quarll]—and then I found the Arabian Nights' entertainments—one tale of which (the tale of a man who was compelled to seek for a pure virgin) made so deep an impression on me (I had read it in the evening while my mother was mending stockings) that I was haunted by spectres, whenever I was in the dark—and I distinctly remember the anxious & fearful eagerness, with which I used to watch the window, in which the books lay—& whenever the Sun lay upon them, I would seize it, carry it by the wall, & bask, & read—. My Father found out the effect, which these books had produced—and burnt them. —So I became a *dreamer.* (*CL* 1: 179)

Coleridge's reading list includes the most popular chapbooks available—"all the gilt-cover little books that could be had at that time"—fairy tales, *The Arabian Nights*, *Robinson Crusoe*, and all the rest. When one considers a five-year-old reading alone, hour after hour, stories from the *Arabian Nights* and fairy tales like "Blue Beard," one would be surprised if the effect were not imaginatively intense—and such was indeed the case. In *The Friend*, Coleridge explains: "Among my earliest impressions I still distinctly remember that of my first entrance into the mansion of a neighboring Baronet, awfully known to me by the name of THE GREAT HOUSE, its exterior having been long connected in my childish imagination with the feeling and fancies stirred up in me by the perusal of the Arabian Nights' Entertainments." And in a note, he elaborates:

> As I had read one volume of these tales over and over again before my fifth birth-day, it may be readily conjectured of what sort these fancies and feelings must have been. The book, I well remember, used to

lie in a corner of the parlour window at my dear Father's Vicarage-house: and I can never forget with what a strange mixture of obscure dread and intense desire I used to look at the volume and *watch* it, till the morning sunshine had reached and nearly covered it, when, and not before, I felt the courage given me to seize the precious treasure and hurry off with it to some sunny corner in our playground. (*Friend* 1: 148)

Despite (or, more likely, because of) the "mixture of obscure dread and intense desire" with which the child Coleridge responds to these fairy tales of the imagination, the book becomes a "precious treasure." And the reading hardly lacks in moral instruction. In fact, just the opposite is the case. Of the years October 1779 to October 1781, Coleridge declares, "I read every book that came in my way without distinction" (*CL* 1: 210); but as he reflects on these years, he makes a precise connection between his reading of fairy tales and his ability to accept with delight, unmixed with "incredulity," the vastness of the story of the stars:

My father was fond of me, & used to take me on his knee, and hold long conversations with me. I remember, that at eight years old I walked with him one winter evening from a farmer's house, a mile from Ottery—& he told me the names of the stars—and how Jupiter was a thousand times larger than our world—and that the other twinkling stars were Suns that had worlds rolling round them—&. . . I heard him with a profound delight & admiration; but without the least mixture of wonder or incredulity. For from my early reading of Faery Tales, & Genii &c &c—my mind had been habituated *to the Vast*—& I never regarded *my senses* in any way as the criteria of my belief. I regulated all my creeds by my conceptions not by my *sight*—even at that age. (*CL* 1: 210)

Then, going in the face of a century of Lockean philosophy and strictures against fairy tales, Coleridge confidently continues:

Should children be permitted to read Romances, & Relations of Giants & Magicians, & Genii?—I know all that has been said against it; but I have formed my faith in the affirmative.—I know no other way of giving the mind a love of "the Great," & "the Whole."—Those who have been led to the same truths step by step thro' the constant testimony of their senses, seem to me to want a sense which I pos-

sess—They contemplate nothing but *parts*—and all *parts* are necessarily little—and the Universe to them is but a mass of *little things*.—
It is true, that the mind *may* become credulous & prone to superstition by the former method—but are not the Experimentalists credulous even to madness in believing any absurdity, rather than believe
the grandest truths, if they have not the testimony of their own senses
in their favor?—I have known some who have been *rationally* educated, as it is styled. They were marked by a microscopic acuteness;
but when they looked at great things, all became a blank & they saw
nothing—and denied (very logically) that any thing could be seen;
and uniformly put the negation of a power for the possession of a
power—& called the want of imagination Judgment, & the never
being moved to Rapture Philosophy. (*CL* 1: 210)

It is precisely this imaginative comprehension of "the Great"
and "the Whole"—the comprehension of the world of Spirit—
which consumes Coleridge's entire intellectual and practical life
and which he tries to pass on to his children, using the same means
that had functioned so effectively for him—fairy tales. That Coleridge's son Hartley was reading or being read fairy tales by the age
of six is testified to by a letter to Coleridge from Charles Lamb,
who, with his sister Mary, had been selecting books for Hartley.
Lamb was convinced that "wild tales" (a popular name for fairy
tales and other imaginative stories) which encouraged the imagination were better for children than the currently prolific moral
tales, epitomized by the writing of Mrs. Barbauld, Mrs. Trimmer,
et al. On 23 October 1802, Lamb writes to Coleridge, complaining:

"Goody Two Shoes" is almost out of print. Mrs. Barbauld's stuff has
banished all the old classics of the nursery; and the shopman at
Newbery's hardly deigned to reach them off an old exploded corner of
a shelf, when Mary asked for them. Mrs. B.'s and Mrs. Trimmer's
nonsense lay in piles about. Knowledge insignificant and vapid as
Mrs. B.'s books convey, it seems, must come to a child in the *shape* of
knowledge, and his empty noddle must be turned with conceit of his
own powers when he has learnt that a Horse is an animal, and Billy is
better than a Horse, and such like; instead of that beautiful Interest
in wild tales which made the child a man, while all the time he
suspected himself to be no bigger than a child. Science has succeeded
to Poetry no less in the little walks of children than with men. Is there

9

no possibility of averting this sore evil? Think what you would have been now, if instead of being fed with Tales and old wives' fables in childhood, you had been crammed with geography and natural history?

Still fuming, Lamb concludes: "Damn them! I mean the cursed Barbauld Crew, those Blights and Blasts of all that is Human in man and child" (Lamb 1: 326).

Coleridge's daughter Sara, "on the eve of Christmas Eve, 1802, was born a child of nature and of faerie destined paradoxically to be a scholar and an editor." Beginning thus, Carl Woodring, in his essay "Sara *fille*: Fairy Child," places the "studious, wistful, agile, beautiful" child Sara—whose "beauty was one of her gifts from another land"—directly within a fairy tale, living in the "picturesque kingdom of Greta" near the "giant Wordsworth" and in the large house at Greta where Sara, growing up, "did not have enough of Catherine Morland in her to discover any wicked wizards or witches in the cupboards." "Everything," says Woodring, "points to Sara as Cinderella, with the maligned absent father as the fairy godmother" (211–12).

In her *Memoir*, Sara Coleridge recalls a visit to her father in 1808 at the Wordsworths' house at Allan Bank. While personal circumstances made much of the month-long visit painful,[6] one of her primary recollections of the time is that because of crowded conditions at the house, "I slept with him, and he would tell me fairy stories when he came to bed at twelve and one o'clock. I remember his telling me a wild tale, too, in his study, and my trying to repeat it to the maids afterwards" (1: 18). Sara's later hearing of tales of witches and goblins, as well as more approved fare, had an effect on her quite similar to the one Coleridge himself had experienced as a child. In both cases, the effect seems to have had to do at least as much with an extreme personal sensitivity as with the particular story:

> I remember well that nervous sensitiveness and morbid imaginativeness had set in with me very early. During my Grasmere visit I used to feel frightened at night on account of the darkness. I then was a stranger to the whole host of night-agitators, ghosts, goblins, demons,

burgers, elves, and witches. Horrid ghastly tales and ballads, of which crowds afterwards came in my way, had not yet cast their shadows over my mind. And yet I was terrified in the dark, and used to think of lions, the only form of terror which my dark-engendered agitation would take. My next bugbear was the Ghost of Hamlet. Then the picture of Death at Hell Gate in an old edition of Paradise Lost, the delight of my girlhood. Last and worst came my Uncle Southey's ballad horrors, above all the Old Woman of Berkeley. Oh, the agonies I have endured between nine and twelve at night, before mama joined me in bed, in presence of that hideous assemblage of horrors, the horse with eyes of flame! I dare not, even now, rehearse these particulars, for fear of calling up some of the old feeling, which, indeed, I have never in my life been quite free from. What made the matter worse was that, like all other nervous sufferings, it could not be understood by the inexperienced, and consequently subjected the sufferer to ridicule and censure. My Uncle Southey laughed heartily at my agonies. Even mama scolded me for creeping out of bed after an hour's torture, and stealing down to be in the parlour, saying I could bear the loneliness and the night-fears no longer. But my father understood the case better. He insisted that a lighted candle should be left in my room, in the interval between my retiring to bed and mama's joining me. From that time forth my sufferings ceased. (1: 24–26)

Understanding Sara's fears, the father's remedy was not the cessation of storytelling but, rather, a lighted candle. Certainly, the effects of a vivid imagination seem not to have done eternal damage. Sara went on to write her own fairy tale for children, *Phantasmion*, which was published in 1837,[7] though it is evident that even at that date, fairy tales had not gained unqualified acceptance. In a letter to Arabella Brooke (29 July 1837), Sara writes: "In these days, to print a Fairy Tale is the very way to be *not read*, but shoved aside with contempt. I wish, however, I were only as sure that *my* fairy tale is worth printing, as I am that works of this class are wholesome food, by way of variety, for the childish mind. It is curious that on this point Sir Walter Scott and Charles Lamb, my father, My Uncle Southey, and Mr. Wordsworth were all agreed" (Sara Coleridge 1: 181–82).

Fairy tales are wholesome food for the child's spirit, and the effect that Coleridge identifies with a child's fairy tale experience—that of the imaginative comprehension of the wholeness and unity of Spirit—is evident in his daughter as well as himself. In language that echoes her grandfather's own comments about the cosmic and metaphysical significance of fairy stories, Edith Coleridge says of her mother:

> There is a third province of human nature beside those of the intellect and the moral sense,—that of the spiritual, where the pure spirit of Sara Coleridge breathed freely, as in an "ampler ether, a diviner air." In these regions she wandered hand and hand with her father, whose guidance she willingly followed, with a just confidence in his superior wisdom, yet with no blind or undiscriminating submission. He, like herself, was but a traveller through the heavenly country, whose marvels they explored together; and the sun of Reason was above them both to light them on their way. (Sara Coleridge 2: 30)

Coleridge's life occupation was that of "traveller through the heavenly country," and the Land of Faery provided an important and integral terrain for many of his travel stories. Given the abundance of biographical, autobiographical, and literary evidence of Coleridge's interest in Faery and fairy tales, one would expect an equal abundance of related critical commentary, but such has not been the case. It is, therefore, one of the purposes of this book to begin to fill this critical lacuna and to explore the ways in which telling tales of Faery gives Coleridge a language and a set of genre conventions for expressing his most important concerns.

Tales of faery are symbolic stories that present the Reality of Faery—which is also the Reality of Spirit and Wholeness and the Reality of Love. At the same time, Coleridge's tales of Faery present the reality of the fallen world: the world of division, incomplete perception of Wholeness, and distortion or failure of love. These stories, then, are about the ways Love is known and made manifest in a fallen world and the ways in which Love is denied. Further, tales of Faery, since they *are* symbolic, provide the reader with occasions of symbolic encounter with Faery/Spirit/Love.

The first chapter, "The Symbolic World and the Land of Faery," discusses the ways in which the concept of Faery and the genre of fairy tale function as appropriate means of presenting Coleridge's consubstantial universe—how, in other words, tales of Faery become instances of imaginative symbolic experience, functioning within the fallen world to convey the reality of Love. The use of fairy imagery and allusion is so profuse in Coleridge's poetry that it can go almost unnoticed critically or be easily dismissed, seeming to serve in merely decorative or conventional—and thus insignificant—ways. And except for some brief acknowledgment that "Christabel" is indeed a fairy tale, this is what has happened. However, the pervasiveness of a particular kind of language in the work of a poet like Coleridge argues for the significance of that language as an expression of the concerns of the poet's mind and heart, and such is the case with Coleridge's language of Faery.[8] Further, fairy imagery and allusion are part of the language of Faery, certainly, but not really its most important part. Instead, since Faery is itself a metaphor for Spirit, and since this metaphorical relationship represents this world's relationship to the world of Spirit, symbolic metaphors—especially as they work in mutual reinforcement of each other—constitute the true language of Faery. When the symbolic imagination interweaves in song the generative androgynous union of lovers within the blossoming fairy arbor, Faery is present. The first chapter, then, answers these questions: why does Coleridge place so much of his poetry in the world of Faery, and through what metaphors and genre conventions does he do so?

In Coleridge's work, Faery can appear as a brief moment in either poetry or prose; in works that are, on the whole, of slight literary merit; or in more substantial works ostensibly concerned with matters far away from Faery: occasional poems, conversation poems, political and philosophical and theological poems, or prose theory.[9] Chapter 2, "On the Borders of Faery," looks first at some moments of encounter with Faery in just such a wide range of poems. Wherever the symbolic imagination fuses and intertwines metaphors of Spirit, Faery is present. The last part of the chapter looks at "Kubla Khan" and "The Rime," in each of which Coleridge has expanded the brief moment, the moment "out of time," into a longer tale of Faery. In these poems of mystery, the borders of Faery are crossed and recrossed, and the reader is encouraged to risk enchantment.

Chapter 3, "Romantic Faery Tales of Love," examines five narratives—"Love," "The Dark Ladié," "The Night-Scene," "Alice du Clos," and "The Three Graves"—each of which, in its entirety, constitutes a tale of Faery. All are love stories. All use the closely related traditional genres of fairy tale and ballad as a way of presenting the possibilities of love and Faery along with the limitations of the fallen world. The fallen world is an inescapable reality of the human condition, but there can and must be moments in which the individual human spirit and lovers united in love participate in the Oneness of Spirit and Love. Faery affirms the reality of the wholeness that may no longer always be perceived—and yet exists. These five narratives present the human spirit's present predicament and various possible "resolutions."

Finally, Chapter 4, " 'Christabel': 'In a World of Sin,' " takes up Coleridge's most complex poem to show how reading it as the fairy tale Coleridge asserts that it is—and as the symbolic story it also most assuredly is—can give new insight into its meaning and the continuing fascination it elicits. "Christabel" is the "hardest" of the three mystery poems because it asks the hardest questions, because it insists simultaneously on the reality of Spirit and the "world of sin," and because, in it, a fairy tale heroine—who also represents each of us as readers—does not come to her rightful happy ending.

Three final comments: First, there is obviously no *one* way to approach Coleridge's poetry. His intellect and psyche and the poems themselves are too complex for such a reductive reading, as the critical literature—as well as common sense—demonstrates. My discussion of his poetry in terms of Faery is not meant in any way to suggest that this is the only lens that will bring things into focus. At the same time, Coleridge's poetry is rich with faery language and narrative, and I do intend to suggest that because his language of faery becomes a symbolic language—denoting instances of symbolic experience—incorporating into our critical awareness a consideration of his poetry as tales of Faery helps us see one important way in which Coleridge tries to make sense of the multiplicity of the world. The tale of Faery allows him to present the joy of Oneness. It gives him a way to bring or manifest order, if only for a moment of insight and illumination. And because the tale of Faery as symbolic story is an artistic form, it provides a safe vehicle—at least for a time—for the exploration of the irrational in human experience and the exploration of the darkness and mystery of Mystery, hidden yet really and symbolically present and available.

Second, I am aware that this study does not deal with Coleridge's poetry and prose in strict chronological fashion, particularly as the prose functions as theoretical counterpoint for the poetry. It would be absurd to say that chronology does not matter, that poems or philosophy written late in a career could just as easily have been written at an earlier stage. Life experience, artistic development, intellectual enthusiasms, disappointments, friends, lovers, and time provide context and texture for belief and literary production and action—or their lack. Still, it is true for Coleridge that the central concerns are present both early and late. What is the fundamental nature of God and of human existence? What does it mean for the soul to exist in a fallen world? What can we affirm? What are the limits of affirmation? What does the world mean, and how do things fit together? For Coleridge, there is a determined and felt belief in harmony and in the Oneness of God which is the mystery and unifying force of all creation, and this often in the face of personal doubt, insecurity, and despair— no easy faith. While in some obvious ways Coleridge's poetry reflects its chronology, there are other ways—because the central concerns remain central—in which the poems can be seen to be playing off one another, shedding light on or exploring alternative solutions to the central questions of existence. In the same vein, later theoretical analysis may throw a broader light on an insight existent earlier in a poem's intuitively right image.[10] I have tried to avoid deliberately misleading or inaccurate chronological conflation, but I have also used Coleridge's own texts as commentary on each other, a practice he himself follows and encourages.

Finally, the quotations from T. S. Eliot's *Four Quartets*: I have for many years been struck by Coleridgean echoes in the *Quartets*—words, phrases, intuitions, and vision. Coleridge believed in the affinity of minds of a certain sort and says, for example, of his intuitive understanding of Plato: "Plato's works are preparatory exercises for the mind. He leads you to see, that propositions involving in themselves a contradiction in terms, are nevertheless true; and which, therefore, must belong to a higher logic—that of ideas. They are self-contradictory only in the Aristotelian logic, which is the instrument of the understanding. I have read most of the works of Plato several times with profound attention, but not all his writings. In fact, I soon found that I had read Plato by anticipation" (*TT*, 30 Apr. 1830). Just as Coleridge could read Plato "by anticipation"—that is, by his own intuitive understanding of Plato—so, I think, he would read Eliot and Eliot reads him.[11]

CHAPTER ONE

The Symbolic World and the Land of Faery

*O*ur *first question* might well be "why Faery?" The answers, the reasons behind Coleridge's engagement with the Land of Faery—the literary and cultural movements of the times, the influence of his friends and contemporaries and literary ancestors, Coleridge's own personal history and psyche, as well as the questions of psychology, philosophy, and theology that occupied him— are as multifaceted as his own complex personality. As we have seen from Coleridge's own description of the importance of fairy tales to him as a child, the whole range of explanations for "why Faery?" was present from the beginning. Each of the parts of the explanation necessarily interacts with the others to form the whole. For example, although we might well expect a poet who considers the author of *The Faerie Queene* to be the most musical of the poets of genius to take seriously the poetic possibilities inherent in the Land of Faery, nevertheless, the literary tradition that includes such fellow travelers in Faery as Spenser and Shakespeare cannot in and of itself provide a sufficient explanation for Coleridge's lifelong journey in the Perilous Land. Certainly, these and other writers of significance help validate Coleridge's interest as a legitimate one—fairy queens and elves and magic do not necessarily have to be put away in the toy cupboards of one's childhood. Indeed, given Coleridge's voracious childhood reading of the fairy tales, romances, and legends contained in chapbook literature—along with the more "acceptable" literary classics—it becomes difficult to imagine enough cupboards with locks secure enough to hide from remembrance Robinson Crusoe, Jack the Giant Killer, Tom Hickathrift, Dick Whittington, Robin Hood, and all the rest, not to mention the tales of the *Arabian Nights. Mother Bunch's Closet newly broke open* was a closet filled to bursting, spilling its treasures into Coleridge's child and adult consciousness alike. And as we can all attest, books read and reread with vivid attention and self-absorbtion in childhood can never truly be put away. The images in the mind, the feelings of horror and delight, the wonder, and the sense of *realness* never entirely go away. At the very least, Coleridge's frequent and intense early journeys into the Land of Faery give him an intimate and unquestioning familiarity with its varying terrains and its inhabitants, customs, pleasures, and dangers.

Coleridge feels at home in Faery, and to some extent this accounts for his easy, sometimes almost habitual or unselfconscious allusions to the elves and fairy arbors of the Other World. Another strand of explanation lies in various literary manifestations of the late eighteenth-century vogue for elves and fairies: such works as Collins's "Ode on the Popular Superstitions of the Highlands of Scotland," Gray's "The Bard," Warton's "Ode to Fancy," Beattie's "The Minstrel," and Robert Burns's songs and poems, plus the ballad revival in Britain and renewed interest in folk stories of all kinds. The traditional oral genres of ballads and folk and fairy tales, filled with superstitions, magic, fairy glens, and supernatural occurrences, comprise a vital backdrop for the questions of value and taste, convention and genre, that occupy the conversation, theory, and poetry of Coleridge and his literary contemporaries and friends. Sara Coleridge says that on the question of the value of fairy tales, "Sir Walter Scott and Charles Lamb, my father, My Uncle Southey, and Mr. Wordsworth were all agreed" (1: 182).

Their agreement evidences itself in various ways: remarks in letters, reminiscences of childhood, and literary endeavors. Sara's "Uncle Southey" contributed one of the best-known fairy tales in children's literature, the story of "The Three Bears." Although it contains no elves or fairies, and few readers now are aware that contemporary versions of the story derive from Southey's literary tale, "The Three Bears" occupies a firm place in the core of the fairy tale canon.

Charles Lamb's first book for children was *The King and Queen of Hearts* (1805), based on the nursery rhyme. Darton describes Lamb's *Adventures of Ulysses* (1808) as a "refreshing oasis in a moral desert" (199). *Mrs. Leicester's School* followed in 1809 and *Prince Dorus* in 1811. *Tales from Shakespeare*, written with his sister Mary and published in two volumes in 1806 (but dated 1807), received high praise. The *Critical Review* for May 1807 reads: "We have compared these little volumes with the numerous systems which have been devised for riviting attention at an early age . . . and we do not scruple to say, that unless perhaps we except *Robinson Crusoe*, they claim the very first place, and stand unique, without rival or competition." *Felissa; or, The Life and Opinions of a Kitten of Sentiment*, billed as "an autobiography of a cat who could trace her ancestry to Puss in boots," has also been ascribed to Charles Lamb (*Osborne* 1: 252).

Wordsworth's contribution is particularly relevant to Cole-ridge's views. The ease with which we can imagine conversations between the two poets about their childhood reading of tales of Faery aids our understanding of the sympathy of sensibility that could result in Wordsworth's contributions to "The Rime" and Coleridge's completion of Wordsworth's initial efforts on "The Three Graves." The account in Book Five of *The Prelude* of Words-worth's own childhood reading and its significance for his moral growth and its relation to the natural world provides a glowing testimonial to romance and Faery and a useful parallel to Cole-ridge's own claims for tales of Faery:

Oh, give us once again the wishing-cap
Of Fortunatus, and the invisible coat
Of Jack the Giant-killer, Robin Hood,
And Sabra in the forest with St. George.
The child whose love is here, at least doth reap
One precious gain—that he forgets himself.   ([1805] 5.364–69) [1]

Tales of Faery, explains Wordsworth, take the child outside his self-circumscribed world and enable him or her to develop a sympathy with larger realities. Similarly, Coleridge says: "From my early reading of Faery Tales, & Genii &c &c—my mind had been habituated *to the Vast*" (*CL* 1: 210). The core concern of Book Five of *The Prelude* is an evaluation of current educational theory and the proliferation of moral tales to the extinction of the literature Wordsworth had read as a child. Wordsworth's position is never in doubt:

Thanksgivings from my heart that I was reared
Safe from an evil which these days have laid
Upon the children of the land—a pest
That might have dried me up body and soul.   ([1805] 5.226–29)

He acknowledges that in the child of the present time—"child, no child, / But a dwarf man"—"the moral part / Is perfect, and in learning and in books / He is a prodigy" ([1805] 5.323–25). This child is skilled and learned in science, astronomy, geology, history: "He sifts, he weighs, / Takes nothing on trust" ([1805] 5.337–38). This is the "*rationally* educated" child of Coleridge's description (*CL* 1: 210). But the end result of this sort of education, avows Wordsworth, is a child who, separated from the nurture of the natural world, lives "a life of lies" ([1805] 5.350).

Wordsworth then contrasts his own childhood, in which he was free to receive Nature's blessing and instruction and free to read the books that help mediate terrifying natural occurrences. As an example, Wordsworth tells of seeing, as a very young child, the raising of a drowned man from Esthwaite Lake, potentially an extremely frightening experience for a child. "And yet," he says,

> no vulgar fear,
> Young as I was, a child not nine years old,
> Possessed me, for my inner eye had seen
> Such sights before among the shining streams
> Of fairyland, the forests of romance—
> Thence came a spirit hallowing what I saw
> With decoration and ideal grace,
> A dignity, a smoothness, like the words
> Of Grecian art and purest poesy.   ([1805] 5.473–81)

Immediately following this example, Wordsworth describes a "precious treasure," *The Arabian Nights*. His sense of the book's being both a "precious treasure" and "scarcely earthly" parallels Coleridge's description exactly, though Coleridge's sense of "anxious and fearful eagerness" (*CL* 1: 179) is not present:

> I had a precious treasure at that time,
> A little yellow canvass-covered book,
> A slender abstract of the *Arabian Tales*;
> And when I learned, as now I first did learn
> From my companions in this new abode,
> That this dear prize of mine was but a block
> Hewn from a mighty quarry—in a word,
> That there were four large volumes, laden all
> With kindred matter—'twas in truth to me
> A promise scarcely earthly.   ([1805] 5.482–91)

It is difficult to imagine any child calling the moral tales of the late eighteenth century a "precious treasure," a "dear prize," or "a promise scarcely earthly." Wordsworth reads his father's "golden store," takes the volumes with him when he goes fishing, "devouring as I read" ([1805] 5.503, 511). These romances, legends, and fairy tales read in childhood—"wholesome food," as Sara Coleridge names them—become constant "friends" for life. They feed the hidden appetite of the soul, help direct the soul to works of love, and prepare the child to "see into the life of things" (*Poetical Works*, "Tintern Abbey" 49).

Earlier in Book Five, Wordsworth calls "ballad-tunes" the "Food for the hungry ears of little ones / And of old men who have survived their joy" ([1805] 5.211–13). Sir Walter Scott's *Minstrelsy of the Scottish Border* (published in 1802–03, five years after Wordsworth and Coleridge's *Lyrical Ballads*) was undoubtedly the second most important ballad book—after Percy's *Reliques* (1765)—of the ballad revival in Britain. Preceded in his efforts by such ballad collectors and imitators as Percy, Joseph Ritson, David Herd, Thomas Evans, and John Pinkerton, Scott—subsequent to the publication of *Minstrelsy*—became the center of a large school of ballad men: Robert Jamieson, James Hogg, C. K. Sharpe, William Motherwell, Allan Cunningham, and others.

Several points of intersection between Scott and Coleridge are of interest here. First, both write imitation ballads that combine ballad and romance—*The Lay of the Last Minstrel, Marmion, The Bride of Triermain*, "The Rime of the Ancient Mariner," "Christabel," "Love," and "The Dark Ladié," for example. Both read fairy tales and romances as children; as adults, both were still interested in fairy tales and the elements and traditions of Faery. Recalling his early reading, Scott says: "In the intervals of my school hours I had always perused with avidity such books of history or poetry or voyages and travels as chance presented to me—not forgetting the usual, or rather ten times the usual, quantity of fairy tales, eastern stories, romances, etc." ("Memoir" 27). Scott also shares Coleridge's love of Spenser and his childhood disregard for genre distinctions: "But Spenser I could have read forever. Too young to trouble myself about the allegory, I considered all the knights and ladies and dragons and giants in their outward and exoteric sense, and God only knows how delighted I was to find myself in such society" ("Memoir" 28). Scott's poetry and fiction are full of fairy mythology, and his introduction to "The Tale of Tamlane" in *Minstrelsy* is an essay, "Fairies of Popular Superstition." In the course of this essay, Scott attempts definitions of "elf" and "faerie," traces their appearance in various cultures, discusses the incorporation of fairies into the world of chivalry, notes their relationship with classical fables by retelling the story of Orfeo, and relates the negative role given to fairies by Christianity and the literary role given them in the Renaissance. Finally, he discusses popular beliefs concerning fairy folk. "The Tale of Tamlane" is itself a ballad tale of Faery. In 1823, upon receiving a copy of Edgar Taylor's translation of the Grimms' *German Popular Stories*, Scott writes Taylor, praising the "wild Fairy interest in [the tales] which makes me think them fully better adapted to awaken the imagination and soften the heart of childhood than the good-boy stories which have been in later years composed for them. . . . Our old wild fictions like our own simple music will have more effect in awakening the fancy & elevating the disposition than the colder and more elevated compositions of more clever authors & composers" (*Letters* 7: 312; 16 January 1823). Finally, of course, in the Scott-Coleridge relationship, there is the "Christabel" episode, in which Scott is taken to be the author of the poem.

In a certain way, then, Coleridge's interest in the oral traditions of folk and fairy tales and ballads can be seen as participation in a larger cultural and literary re-discovery of folk traditions and stories, a participation fed by his childhood reading and his fascination with the supernatural, magic, and the occult: "I am, & ever have been," he says, "a great reader—& have read almost every thing—a library-cormorant—I am *deep* in all out of the way books" (*CL* 1: 260). To place Coleridge in this way gives an important literary/historical context for his poetry of Faery. It helps explain how Coleridge and his interests are like others who are also concerned to reintroduce the faculty of imagination in an overt way, but it does not account for the uniquely Coleridgean transformation of folk fairy tales and ballads into tales of Faery. Coleridge is not a ballad collector. He does not write "The Three Bears." He does not simply relate a rural tale. Instead, he *is* the author of "Christabel" and "Rime of the Ancient Mariner" and "Kubla Khan," poems of incomparable mystery and power. His tales of Faery are not fairy tales in the usual sense—though he does use many of the conventions of the traditional fairy tales; rather, his tales of Faery are about the Land of Faery and the human spirit's existence in Faery.

The Land of Faery is a state of being, a mental/emotional construct, an act of creation. In Faery, contraries are reconciled, diversity unified. Faery is the home of the soul before the Fall; it is the Garden, the place of Oneness with Spirit. But the Garden also held the Snake and the Forbidden Fruit—possibilities for disorder, division, irrationality. Faery is the desire of the heart, but the Land is perilous indeed. As Coleridge's tales of Faery grow more complex, they inevitably shift from fairy tale to ballad, from the happy ending to the tragic. At the most fundamental level, Coleridge writes stories about existence in Faery because he knows the Land so well. It is the place of the soul's journey, the place where nightmare is as possible as vision, where the truths of the psyche sleep, where one can encounter the One.

Thomas McFarland's comments on the sense of longing in Romanticism are relevant here. In describing Wordsworth's and Coleridge's lives and works as "diasparactive," McFarland quotes Peter Brown's *Augustine of Hippo*: "If to be a 'Romantic' means to be a man acutely aware of being caught in an existence that denies him the fullness for which he craves, to feel that he is defined by his tension towards something else, by his capacity for faith, for hope, for longing, to think of himself as a wanderer seeking a country that is always distant, but made ever-present to him by the quality of the love that 'groans' for it, then Augustine has imperceptibly become a 'Romantic.'" Noting that "the sense of longing—which is an inner form of the perception of reality as diasparactive—saturates Romanticism," McFarland briefly cites examples of symbols for that which is longed for—"Novalis's 'blaue Blume' or Goethe's 'Land wo die Zitronen blühn.' The land where the lemon trees bloom is congruent with Brown's 'country that is always distant' (and both to the 'kingdom which has no end' so ardently sought by Augustine [*De civitate Dei* 22.30])" (7). Romantic preoccupation with the medieval and the oriental are attempts to remove this "always distant country" in terms of time and space. "Alternatively," observes McFarland, "the sought-for realm could be removed in space, in time, and in reality as well: a faery land forlorn, approached across perilous seas. In this latter manifestation especially, the apprehension of the distant country frequently partook of the nature of dream or reverie" (8).

24

Despite the rationalistic times in which he grew up and despite his own extraordinary talent for analysis, whether philosophical, theological, literary, or psychological, Coleridge's sensibility is still and simultaneously that of a person who longs for the "far countrée," a person who is "enchanted," to use Morris Berman's term in *The Reenchantment of the World.* An "enchanted" world assumes a "participating consciousness" for whom modern distinctions between "psychic and material, mind and body, symbolic and literal" do not exist. "Real knowledge [occurs] only via the union of subject and object, in a psychic-emotional identification with images rather than a purely intellectual examination of concepts." The participating consciousness sees the world as a "vast assemblage of correspondences. All things have relationships with all other things, and these relations are ones of sympathy and antipathy. . . . The world duplicates and reflects itself in an endless network of similarity and dissimilarity." "Participation is self and not-self at the moment of experience." It is the ability to "know a thing precisely in the act of identification, and this identification is as much sensual as it is intellectual. It is a *totality* of experience: the 'sensuous intellect.'" "The essence of original participation is the *feeling*, the bodily perception, that there stands behind the phenomena a 'represented' that is of the same nature as me—*mana*, God, the world spirit, and so on. This notion, that subject and object, self and other, man and environment, are ultimately identical, is the holistic world view" (Berman 73–77). The language of alchemy and magic and dreams preserves the reality of the enchanted participating consciousness—as does poetry of symbolic encounter. A central tenet of this language is the notion that "reality is paradoxical, that things and their opposites are closely related, that attachment and resistance have the same root" (82). In the enchanted world, magic and the human psyche and Spirit are inextricably related.

The world enchanted is Coleridge's Land of Faery. In the symbolic world of Faery, Coleridge can explore the psychological and spiritual implications of the soul's existence as participating in God while also inhabiting a fallen state. Faery allows moments of symbolic participatory experience in which contraries are re-solved. At the same time—because the Snake offered the Forbid-den Fruit in the very Garden itself—the potential for division, partiality, and irrationality in the individual human psyche and in the events of human life, human action, and human relationships always presents itself. Coleridge's poetry explores the complexity of emotional and spiritual states, the inter-relationship of love and hate, good and evil, light and shadow. This exploration makes manifest the tension between Coleridge's own often-tortured psyche and his desire for, belief in, and will toward unity and wholeness.[2] The folk genres of fairy tale and ballad, incorporating as they do the participating consciousness of enchantment, peo-pled with spirits and talking animals, filled with objects of sym-bolic significance, already the land of stark emotional realities and experiences of growth—these genres Coleridge transforms into his poetry about the individual spirit's relationship with Spirit and Love in a fallen world.

> I said to my soul, be still, and let the dark come upon you
> Which shall be the darkness of God. ("East Coker," 3)

> We shall not cease from exploration
> And the end of all our exploring
> Will be to arrive where we started
> And know the place for the first time. ("Little Gidding," 5)[3]

The words are Eliot's, but they might as easily belong to Cole-ridge. The knowledge is the same; the sense of necessary darkness the same; the voyage of unceasing exploration carried on from generation to generation, to the sound of "sea voices" that "men-ace and caress" ("The Dry Salvages," 1), the same. And the knowl-edge and the darkness are one, and one with the bird and the fire and the Rose—which are also one.

> These are only hints and guesses,
> Hints followed by guesses; and the rest
> Is prayer, observance, discipline, thought and action.
> The hint half guessed, the gift half understood, is Incarnation.
> Here the impossible union
> Of spheres of existence is actual. ("The Dry Salvages," 5)

Before we voyage with the Mariner, the introductory epigraph of "The Rime" tells us:

> I readily believe that there are more invisible than visible things in the universe. But who shall describe for us their families, their ranks, relationships, distinguishing features and functions? What do they do? Where do they live? The human mind has always circled about knowledge of these things, but never attained it. I do not doubt, however, that it is sometimes good to contemplate in the mind, as in a picture, the image of a greater and better world; otherwise the intellect, habituated to the petty things of daily life, may too much contract itself, and wholly sink down to trivial thoughts. But meanwhile we must be vigilant for truth and keep proportion, that we may distinguish the certain from the uncertain, day from night.[4]

The human mind can never attain complete knowledge of the invisible. In fact, the ordinary notion of attainment is inappropriate for this kind of knowledge: "He, with whom it is present, can as little appropriate it, whether totally or by partition, as he can claim ownership in the breathing air or make an inclosure in the cope of heaven" (*SM* 70).[5] It is not knowledge that one acquires as one acquires the name of plants or the facts of arithmetic; it is knowledge that one *has*: the purpose of the voyage is "to arrive where we started / And know the place for the first time." It is the knowledge of recognition and illumination. "Knowing is recognition" (*CN* 3: 3962), recognition of

> The one Life within us and abroad,
> Which meets all motion and becomes its soul,
> A light in sound, a sound-like power in light,
> Rhythm in all thought, and joyance every where.   (EH 26–29)

The hints and guesses that concern both Coleridge and Eliot and give their poetry much of its power are symbolic knowings of the actuality of "impossible union."

The "place" of impossible union, the place of the soul's origin and arrival, is a place of knowledge that has, for Coleridge, many interfaceted, almost interchangeable names: Absolute Truth, Reason, the Whole, Reality, Spirit, Love, God. The place is also the dwelling place of mystery, since "Absolute Truth is always a mystery" (*CN* 3: 3878). Further, a certain sort of poetry also serves as a dwelling place of mystery. Eliot's *Four Quartets* exemplifies this sort. In like manner, Coleridge's most compelling poetry achieves its power through the successful presentation—or manifestation, or verbal imaging—of the soul's encounter with and participation in mystery. The poems of mystery come to mind immediately, of course—"Kubla Khan," "The Rime," and "Christabel"—but the conversation poems are also fundamentally poems of encounter, and clusters of lines in numerous other poems manifest moments of knowledge as well. Another way to describe these poems and parts of poems is to call them symbolic and to call the moments of encounter moments of symbolic experience.

One obvious problem in writing a poem that in itself functions as a symbol while at the same time presenting an occasion of symbolic experience comes in getting language to work in just that way. What kinds of subjects, images, metaphors, allusions are available to convey such a thing as the mystery that is God? It is the argument of this book that Coleridge, in his poetry of symbolic encounter, uses the Other World of Faery as a metaphor for the dwelling place of mystery. Faery is a place of the mind, a place of knowledge and perception, a place where Spirit and Love are known and experienced. Faery is an act of the symbolic imagination. The "Land of Faery," explains Coleridge, is "mental space"; its geography exists within the imagination and without boundaries: "The marvellous independence or true imaginative absence of all particular place & time—it is neither in the domains of History or Geography, is ignorant of all artificial boundary—truly in the Land of Faery—i.e., in mental space" (*CN* 3: 4501). Specific references to elves and fairies and sprites pervade Coleridge's poetry, and he uses again and again various conventions of the traditional fairy tale genre, as well as its poetic counterpart, the ballad, so that these allusions and structures of narration, taken together, weave an embroidery of fairy threads in and out of the poems. However, this stitchery serves primarily to heighten the more fundamental concept and symbolic metaphor of Faery, which is the garment itself.

Given Coleridge's assumptions and beliefs about the nature of the universe and the task of the individual soul in the world as we know it, the use of Faery as a metaphor for God-Spirit-Love seems almost inevitable. The rest of this chapter is devoted to making this "inevitability" clearer. First, I want to define the nature of symbolic experience and the assumptions surrounding it—for example, the self-grounded nature of Spirit and the consubstantiality of all being, with its symbolic import—and discuss briefly the symbolic metaphors by and through which symbolic experience is conveyed. I do not intend in a few pages a comprehensive exposition of Coleridge's philosophical and theological thought; others have devoted books to this analysis.[6] Nonetheless, some summary will be useful as context for the readings of poems that follow. Second, the Land of Faery itself needs some definition. Coleridge makes use of the conventions of traditional fairy tales, but clearly, he is writing literary tales—and those of a particular sort. By its very nature, Faery itself allows for the genre use and transformations that occur.

The Symbolic World

In almost every instance, Coleridge's writing, whether poetry or prose exposition, grows out of a set of fundamental assumptions and beliefs about the nature of the universe and the place of the human spirit within that universe. Simply put, the essential belief, underlying all else, is Coleridge's belief in the consubstantial nature of existence. This belief has as a corollary the assumption that if the world is consubstantial, it is also symbolic.

> For all that meets the bodily sense I deem
> Symbolical, one mighty alphabet
> For infant minds. (DN 18–20)

Apprehension of Spirit/God/Wholeness/Love by the individual soul occurs then as an intuitive act of self-knowledge, a symbolic encounter made possible by the action of the symbolic imagination. Additionally, symbolic metaphors operate in the world of nature and in the imaginative language of poetry and story to "show forth" or give concrete manifestation to consubstantial Reality. These metaphors most often exist as a complex or interrelated matrix of association and allusion and, as such, provide—in nature and in poetry—an always potent occasion for further symbolic encounter.

The belief in a consubstantial world in which each thing in the physical, temporal world—along a continuum from the simplest flower unfolding to the act of creative imagination in the human mind—is in its essence symbolic of the infinite, transcendent world of Spirit and, therefore, analogous to that Spirit is the fundamental and pervasive assumption of Coleridge's thinking and writing and life. As J. Robert Barth explains: "The 'consubstantiality' of all being . . . is present in [Coleridge's] work . . . not as a formal philosophical tool but rather as an accepted premise underlying his thought. It is rarely discussed by Coleridge but is everywhere present by implication or indirection" (*Christian Doctrine* 19).[7] That this is so accounts for the fact that while Coleridge does change and develop in his thinking—rejecting, revising, refining, reforming—the core concerns never change; they are present from beginning to end. And it is the centrality of his affirmative and assumptive belief in the consubstantiality of all being that provides this basis of continuity, allowing the critic to move among Coleridge's earliest and latest poems and prose with a sense of at-home-ness. R. H. Fogle puts the matter well: "Fundamentally Coleridge's poetry and thought, his early and his later literary life, are one and the same. This is not to blink Coleridge's apparent shifts, such as his great swing from Hartley to idealism; but I affirm here the basic consistency and continuity of Coleridge's development, considering that in his philosophy 'distinction is not division,' that in his mind as in his dialectic he struggled to synthesize oppositions into organic unity, with Wordsworthian confidence that nothing need finally be discarded as irrelevant or irreconcilable" (131).

For Coleridge, the ultimate name for organic unity is God, and the life task of the human soul is to know how fully it symbolizes that Unity. Nature and the poet teach "infant minds" to con the alphabet, then learn to read the Word behind the words. Additionally, both nature and the poet provide the occasion for the soul's knowledge through the forms they create: the icicle in moonlight, the poet in the woven circle. Coleridge views poetry of genius as symbolic and believes, therefore, that this poetry speaks the truth of Spirit, becoming an occasion of encounter with Spirit for the reader—becoming, in other words, an instance of symbolic knowledge at the same time that symbolic knowledge is the true subject of the poem. Further, these symbolic poems deal with the implications of the soul's symbolic knowledge in a fallen world.

In Chapter 12 of the *Biographia*, a series of theses defines the nature of the Absolute Truth of the Spirit and the way in which the mind encounters, or has knowledge of, that Truth. Absolute Truth, or Spirit, Coleridge explains, is immediate: that is, not derived from some other truth. It is "self-grounded, unconditional and known by its own light"; it "*is*, simply because it *is*." And being self-grounded, it is that from which all other truths are derived. By its nature, Spirit is neither subject alone (that which knows) nor object alone (that which is known); it is, rather, that which is the "identity of both." Spirit is the "most original union" of subjective and objective, of infinite and finite. The "ground of existence, and the ground of knowledge of existence, are absolutely identical," and "in the existence, in the reconciling, and the recurrence of this contradiction consists the process and mystery of production and life" (*BL* 1: 264–81).[8] In other words, Spirit is the eternal creative reconciliation of opposing primary principles. This is the mystery, that impossible union which yet *is*, the reconciliation of contradiction.[9]

And how is it that we can know such a mystery? Because we ourselves are also the mystery: "For a mind is a subject that knows itself, or a subject that is its own object" (*AR* 218n). We know by self-knowledge. "Only in the self-consciousness of a spirit is there the required identity of object and of representation; for herein consists the essence of a spirit, that it is self-representative. If therefore this be the one only immediate truth, in the certainty of which the reality of our collective knowledge is grounded, it must follow that the spirit in all the objects which it views, views only itself" (*BL* 1: 278). The "I Am" of each individual spirit—what Coleridge also calls the soul, the self, and self-consciousness—manifests and partakes of the eternal I AM: "We begin with the I KNOW MYSELF, in order to lose and find all self in GOD." In his essay "Reason and Understanding," Coleridge explicitly sets up the relationship between God—that is, eternal and absolute Truth or Supreme Reason—and the individual soul, between the spiritual and the physical, and between Reason and Understanding:

> I should have no objection to define Reason . . . as an organ bearing the same relation to spiritual objects, the Universal, the Eternal, and the Necessary, as the eye bears to material and contingent phaenomena. But then it must be added, that it is an organ identical with its appropriate objects. Thus, God, the Soul, eternal Truth, &c. are the objects of Reason; but they are themselves *reason*. We name God the Supreme Reason; and Milton says, "Whence the Soul *Reason* receives, and Reason is her Being." Whatever is conscious *Self*-knowledge is Reason; and in this sense it may be safely defined the organ of the Super-sensuous; even as the Understanding wherever it does not possess or use the Reason, as another and inward eye, may be defined the conception of the Sensuous, or the faculty by which we generalize and arrange the phaenomena of perception: that faculty, the functions of which contain the rules and constitute the possibility of outward Experience. . . . The understanding of the higher Brutes has only organs of outward sense, and consequently material objects only; but man's understanding has likewise an organ of inward sense, and therefore the power of acquainting itself with invisible realities or spiritual objects. This organ is his Reason. Again, the Understanding and Experience may exist without Reason. But Reason cannot exist without Understanding. (*Friend* 1: 155–56)

Reason—that is, self-conscious knowledge, which can manifest itself only in and through the Understanding—is the means by which a person comes to know invisible realities and spiritual objects.

Again, in *The Statesman's Manual*, Coleridge explains: "By reason we know that God is: but God is himself the Supreme Reason. And this is the proper difference between all spiritual faculties and the bodily senses;—the organs of spiritual apprehension having objects consubstantial with themselves . . . or being themselves their own objects, that is, self-contempletive" (*SM* 68n). This, argues Coleridge, is the consubstantial world in which we live, and that consubstantiality is the reality of our existence: "The life, we seek after, is a mystery; but so both in itself and in its origin is the life we have" (*AR* 234). Within this context, Coleridge's definition of symbol takes on particular clarity and significance: "On the other hand a Symbol . . . is characterized by a translucence of the Special in the Individual or of the General in the Especial or of the Universal in the General. Above all by the translucence of the Eternal through and in the Temporal. It always partakes of the Reality which it renders intelligible; and while it enunciates the whole, abides itself as a living part in that Unity, of which it is the representative" (*SM* 30). Coleridge here is doing much more than distinguishing the use of symbol from that of allegory in a literary mode. The context of the definition is a discussion of Scripture; in the course of the discussion, Coleridge establishes the symbol in a pivotal position in a profoundly religious world view:

> [Scriptural histories] are the living *educts* of the Imagination; of that reconciling and mediatory power, which incorporating the Reason in Images of the Sense, and organizing (as it were) the flux of the Senses by the permanence and self-circling energies of the Reason, gives birth to a system of symbols, harmonious in themselves, and consubstantial with the truths, of which they are the *conductors*. These are the Wheels which Ezekiel beheld, when the hand of the Lord was upon him, and he saw visions of God as he sate among the captives by the river of Chebar. *Whithersoever the Spirit was to go, the wheels went, and thither was their spirit to go: for the spirit of the living creature was in the wheels also.* The truths and the symbols that represent them move in conjunction and form the living chariot that bears up (for *us*) the throne of the Divine Humanity. (*SM* 29)

The symbol is the concrete representation of Divine Truth, made visible through the power of the imagination. The Spirit relies on the body, on the physical world in all its forms, to be its visible sign. The image-forming or re-forming power gives form to form-lessness, providing a symbolic means through which the percep-tion of the Spirit—which is the power of the intuitive creative imagination—can occur. This latter power, the poetic imagina-tion, using the concrete forms themselves as the symbols that they are, intuits the formless Spirit. Thus, we "see into the life of things" (Wordsworth, *Poetical Works*, "Tintern Abbey" 49), that life which is "at once the Soul of each, and God of all" (EH 48). Where we often go wrong is in mistaking the means for the end: "Here then is the error—not in the faculty itself, without which there would be no *fixation*, consequently, no distinct perception or conception, but in the gross idolatry of those who abuse it, & make that the goal & end which should be only a means of arriving at it. Is it any excuse to him who treats a living being as inanimate Body, that . . . we cannot arrive at the knowledge of the living Being but thro' the Body which is its Symbol & outward & visible Sign?" (*CN* 3: 4066).

It becomes clear that for Coleridge the imagination, as "the living Power and prime Agent of all human Perception, and as a repetition in the finite mind of the eternal act of creation in the infinite I AM" (*BL* 1: 304), is also symbolic.[10] That which is encoun-tered—experienced, perceived—is the I AM or the Spirit, itself the active state of the existence of primary principles which are op-posed but are not contradictory and which exist in interpenetra-tion: a mystery that is reenacted by the faculty of imagination, itself a symbol of the transcendent and a means of illuminating the transcendent.

In an analogous way, the poetry created by the symbolic imag-ination and the reader's encounter with it are also reenactments of the mystery. Coleridge succinctly draws together, in a deliberately interwound and interacting pattern, the poet, poetry, poetic imag-ination, and the reader's experience of the poetry:

> What is poetry? is so nearly the same question with, what is a poet? that the answer to the one is involved in the solution of the other. For it is a distinction resulting from the poetic genius itself, which sus-tains and modifies the images, thoughts, and emotions of the poet's

own mind. The poet, described in *ideal* perfection, brings the whole soul of man into activity, with the subordination of its faculties to each other, according to their relative worth and dignity. He diffuses a tone, and spirit of unity that blends, and (as it were) *fuses*, each into each, by that synthetic and magical power, to which we have exclusively appropriated the name of imagination. This power, first put in action by the will and understanding, and retained under their irremissive, though gentle and unnoticed, controul . . . reveals itself in the balance or reconciliation of opposite or discordant qualities: of sameness, with difference; of the general, with the concrete; the idea, with the image; the individual, with the representative; the sense of novelty and freshness, with old and familiar objects; a more than usual state of emotion, with more than usual order; judgement ever awake and steady self-possession, with enthusiasm and feeling profound or vehement; and while it blends and harmonizes the natural and artificial, still subordinates art to nature; the manner to the matter; and our admiration of the poet to our sympathy with the poetry. (*BL* 2: 15–17)

The poet, becoming himself a symbol through his action, creates a Unity, by means of the reconciling power of the imagination. The action of the poet, which "brings the whole soul of man into activity," parallels both the state in which "religion finitely express[es] the *unity* of the infinite Spirit by being a total act of the soul" (*SM* 90, 90n) and "faith [which] is a *total* act of the soul: it is the *whole* state of the mind, or it is not at all!" (*Friend* 1: 315). Thus, the power of the symbolic imagination manifesting itself through the poet results in a corresponding act in the mind of the reader:

To find no contradiction in the union of old and new, to contemplate the ANCIENT OF DAYS with feelings as fresh, as if they then sprang forth at his own fiat, this characterizes the minds that feel the riddle of the world, and may help to unravel it! To carry on the feelings of childhood into the powers of manhood, to combine the child's sense of wonder and novelty with the appearances which every day for perhaps forty years had rendered familiar. . . . And so to represent familiar objects as to awaken the minds of others to a like freshness of sensation concerning them. . . . This is the prime merit of genius, and its most unequivocal mode of manifestation. (*Friend* 1: 109–10)

Through this action the imagination reveals itself, and what is revealed as its mode of being is identical with Coleridge's description of the principle of Absolute Truth he calls Spirit and with the symbol which makes that spirit intelligible. In addition, within this interwoven pattern, the poet's intuitive self-consciousness, analogous—as we have seen previously—with the eternal I AM, constitutes symbolic knowledge. Coleridge makes a distinction between a "spontaneous consciousness natural to all reflecting beings" and a philosophic consciousness which is the "highest and intuitive knowledge" (*BL* 1: 236, 241). This latter is symbolic knowledge that comes, not as a set of external facts or propositions to be discovered through scientific investigation or the discursive analysis of the Understanding but, rather, from within by means of the philosophic imagination—that is, Reason, the intuitive self-consciousness:

> They and they only can acquire the philosophic imagination, the sacred power of self-intuition, who within themselves can interpret and understand the symbol, that the wings of the air-sylph are form-ing within the skin of the caterpillar; those only, who feel in their own spirits the same instinct, which impels the chrysalis of the horned fly to leave room in its involucrum for antennae yet to come. They know and feel, that the *potential* works *in* them, even as the *actual* works on them! In short, all the organs of sense are framed for a corresponding world of sense; and we have it. All the organs of spirit are framed for a correspondent world of spirit; tho' the latter organs are not developed in all alike. But they exist in all. (*BL* 1: 241–42)

What is necessary is the ability to "interpret and understand the symbol."

Symbolic knowledge is intuitive, given to those who actively wait. It is, one might say, an experience of grace. One should no more strive to name—take possession of—the source of the know-ing than one should strive to comprehend for acquisition the work-ing of nature. Of the source of symbolic knowledge, like that of nature, Coleridge says with Plotinus:

> "Should any one interrogate her, how she works, if graciously she vouchsafe to listen and speak, she will reply, it behoves thee not to

disquiet me with interrogatories, but to understand in silence, even as I am silent, and work without words."

Likewise in the fifth book of the fifth Ennead, speaking of the highest and intuitive knowledge as distinguished from the discursive, or in the language of Wordsworth,

The vision and the faculty divine;

he says: "it is not lawful to enquire from whence it sprang, as if it were a thing subject to place and motion, for it neither approached hither, nor again departs from hence to some other place; but it either appears to us or it does not appear. So that we ought not to pursue it with a view of detecting its secret source, but to watch in quiet till it suddenly shines upon us; preparing ourselves for the blessed spectacle as the eye waits patiently for the rising sun." (*BL* 1: 240–41)

The silence and the waiting are the indwelling of the mystery:

I said to my soul, be still, and wait without hope
For hope would be hope for the wrong thing; wait without love
For love would be love of the wrong thing; there is yet faith
But the faith and the love and the hope are all in the waiting.
Wait without thought, for you are not ready for thought:
So the darkness shall be the light, and the stillness the dancing.

("East Coker," 3)

"I . . . am inclined to *wait* for the spirit" (*TT*, 24 Aug. 1833), notes Coleridge. We will have symbolic knowledge of the mystery of Spirit insofar as we are able to wait for its light, patiently and perceptively, in the still darkness. As Coleridge says of the Reason, "the integral *spirit* of the regenerated man": "Each individual must bear witness of it to his own mind, even as he describes life and light: and with the silence of light it describes itself, and dwells in *us* only as far as we dwell in *it*" (*SM* 69–70). Speaking of the relationship of the individual self-conscious Will to the mystery, Coleridge observes: "Here is no room for arguing; but only to know with truth and plainness what we are. When the Will, with a not daring to lift up her eyes in supplication, and substituting the deep desire to supplicate for that of supplication, better prays oftentimes, than the Understanding with all its rhetoric knows how to do—Yet some outward Words we may use, if they come to us, and if we *can*/. I say, *can*: because if the Quiet be great, whether the Quiet of Awe or of Joy, we shall hardly be able to speak, without *fear*—and dread of scattering and scaring away the blessedness, which broods upon us" (*CN* 3: 3927).

The intuitive indwelling is an ongoing experience of grace, of living in mystery. But there are also special instances of illumination, symbolic experiences that may occur as the act of writing a poem which makes intelligible something of the mystery of numinous Reality; or as the aesthetic experience of reading such a poem—that is, interpreting and understanding the symbol; or as an event in the world which we recognize as symbolic encounter; or as simply being able to articulate, give form to, that which we have known as presence.

What we have arrived at with Coleridge is a perception of an extremely comprehensive universe, consubstantial, interconnected, "the parts of which mutually support and explain each other" (*BL* 2: 13); and yet a universe that does not constrict, since its very essence is that of the constant creation of the state of reconciled opposites, the mystery of God itself: "God is a circle, the centre of which is everywhere, and circumference nowhere. The soul is all in every part" (*AR* 252n). In this consubstantial world, we know ourselves as symbols of the mystery and are therefore open to participation with every other symbol of the one Life. The task and joy of the soul is symbolic knowledge, made possible through the act of imagination. Symbolic knowledge "is not only extolled as the crown and honor of a man, but to seek after it is again and again commanded us as one of our most sacred duties. Yea, the very perfection and final bliss of the glorified spirit is represented by the Apostle as a plain aspect, or intuitive beholding of truth in its eternal and immutable source" (*Friend* 1: 104–05).

And here we stop. Because, also with Coleridge, we know that although the "organs of the spirit . . . exist in all" (*BL* 1: 242), those organs are, for the most part, weak and underdeveloped: "On the IMMEDIATE, which dwells in every man, and on the original intuition, or absolute affirmation of it, (which is likewise in every man, but does not in every man rise into consciousness) all the *certainty* of our knowledge depends. . . . A system, the first principle of which is to render the mind intuitive of the *spiritual* in man (*i.e.* of that which lies *on the other side* of our natural consciousness) must needs have a greater obscurity for those, who have never disciplined and strengthened this ulterior consciousness. It must in truth be a land of darkness" (*BL* 1: 243):

> The first range of hills, that encircles the scanty vale of human life, is the horizon for the majority of its inhabitants. On *its* ridges the common sun is born and departs. From *them* the stars rise, and touching *them* they vanish. By the many, even this range, the natural limit and bulwark of the vale, is but imperfectly known. Its higher ascents are too often hidden by mists and clouds from uncultivated swamps, which few have courage or curiosity to penetrate. To the multitude below these vapors appear, now as the dark haunts of terrific agents, on which none may intrude with impunity; and now all *a-glow*, with colors not their own, they are gazed at, as the splendid palaces of happiness and power. But in all ages there have been a few, who measuring and sounding the rivers of the vale at the feet of their furthest inaccessible falls have learnt, that the sources must be far higher and far inward; a few, who even in the level streams have detected elements, which neither the vale itself or the surrounding mountains contained or could supply. (*BL* 1: 237–39)

The few are those who, in silent anticipation, share in the mystery

> At the source of the longest river
> The voice of the hidden waterfall
> And the children in the apple-tree
> Not known, because not looked for
> But heard, half-heard, in the stillness
> Between two waves of the sea.   ("Little Gidding," 5)

But what of the many who, seeing the mists as "the dark haunts of terrific agents," are afraid? "In wonder all philosophy began; in wonder it ends; and admiration fills up the interspace. But the first wonder is the off-spring of ignorance: the last is the parent of adoration. The first is the birth-throe of our knowledge: the last is its euthanasy and *apotheosis*" (*AR* 254). The distance between the first wonder and the last is the distance between the many and the few.

Full humanity, Coleridge argues, implies both physical and spiritual senses. "Do not the eyes, ears, lungs of the unborn babe, give notice and furnish proof of a transuterine, visible, audible atmospheric world? We have eyes, ears, touch, taste, smell; and have we not an answering world of shapes, colours, sounds, and sapid and odorous bodies? But likewise . . . the Creator has given us spiritual senses, and sense-organs—ideas I mean—the idea of the good, the idea of the beautiful, ideas of eternity, immortality, freedom, and of that which contemplated relatively to WILL is Holiness, in relation to LIFE is Bliss. And must not these too infer the existence of a world correspondent to them?" (C&S 176). Coleridge vehemently affirms the existence of this Other World and its accessibility to each human soul:

> Another and answerable world there is; and if any man discern it not, let him not, whether sincerely or in contemptuous irony, pretend a defect of faculty as the cause. The sense, the light, and the conformed objects are all there and for all men. The difference between man and man in relation thereto, results from no difference in their several gifts and powers of *intellect*, but in the will. As certainly as the individual is a man, so certainly *should* this other world be present to him: yea, it is his proper home. But he is an absentee and *chooses* to live abroad. His freedom and whatever else he possesses which the dog and the ape do not possess, yea, the whole revenue of his humanity, is derived from this—but with the Irish Land-owner in the Theatres, Gaming-houses, and Maitresseries of Paris, so with *him*. He is a voluntary ABSENTEE! I repeat it again and again—the cause is altogether in the WILL: and the defect of intellectual power, and "the having no turn or taste for subjects of this sort," are effects and consequences of the alienation of the WILL—*i.e.* of the man himself. (C&S 176–77)

The world that answers to our spiritual senses constitutes the individual's proper home. Its existence gives evidence of that which is peculiarly human.[11] And yet some people voluntarily absent themselves from home, choosing instead to be a stranger in alien lands, to the detriment of their own souls. Spirit, says Coleridge, "implies an act, and it follows therefore that intelligence or self-consciousness is impossible, except by and in a will. The self-conscious spirit therefore is a will; and freedom must be assumed as a *ground* of philosophy" (*BL* 1: 279–80). The spirit of the individual soul comes to understand and participate in the eternal I AM of the Spirit by means of

> the *freedom* which they possess in common, as the common ethereal element of their being, the tremulous reciprocations of which propagate themselves even to the inmost of the soul. Where the spirit of a man is not *filled* with the consciousness of freedom (were it only from its restlessness, as of one still struggling in bondage) all spiritual intercourse is interrupted, not only with others, but even with himself. No wonder then, that he remains incomprehensible to himself as well as to others. No wonder, that in the fearful desert of his consciousness, he wearies himself out with empty words, to which no friendly echo answers, either from his own heart, or the heart of a fellow being; or bewilders himself in the pursuit of *notional* phantoms, the mere refractions from unseen and distant truths through the distorting medium of his own unenlivened and stagnant understanding! To remain unintelligible to such a mind, exclaims Schelling on a like occasion, is honor and a good name before God and man. (*BL* 1: 244)

Eliot's Prufrock possesses, at least, restlessness of spirit; but not heeding the warning of the epigraph to "The Rime," he lives "habituated to the petty things of daily life," becomes too much contracted, and does not dare. The Mariner's restlessness, on the other hand, results in action, which catapults his self-consciousness into an awareness of the world of Spirit which has surrounded and inhered in him all along. On his return from the voyage, however, he finds it appropriate to stop only "one of three," the other two being, perhaps, like Sweeney, oblivious to the meaning of the singing of the nightingales or even to the singing itself: "Human kind / Cannot bear very much reality" ("Burnt Norton," 1).

There is, in fact, very little tolerance for mystery in this world. Even ambiguity makes people uncomfortable. Although consubstantiality is the reality of our existence, so also is the fallen world real. Coleridge is inescapably aware of the immediacy of the fallen world, as his essay "Virtue and Knowledge" would make explicit, even if the very conditions of his own life did not so clearly do so: "O that my readers would look round the world, as it now is, and make to themselves a faithful catalogue of its many miseries! From what do these proceed, and on what do they depend for their continuance? . . . 'It is a wicked world!' . . . [It is] a truth, attested alike by common feeling and common sense, that the greater part of human misery depends directly on human vices and the remainder indirectly" (*Friend* 1: 100–103). In another place, Coleridge acknowledges:

> I have at this moment before me, in the flowery meadow, on which my eye is now reposing, one of its most soothing chapters, in which there is no lamenting word, no one character of guilt or anguish. For never can I look and meditate on the vegetable creation without a feeling similar to that with which we gaze at a beautiful infant that has fed itself asleep at its mother's bosom, and smiles in its strange dream of obscure yet happy sensations. The same tender and genial pleasure takes possession of me, and this pleasure is checked and drawn inward by the like aching melancholy, by the same whispered remonstrance, and made restless by a similar impulse of aspiration. It seems as if the soul said to herself: from this state has *thou* fallen! Such shouldst thou still become, thy Self all permeable to a holier power! thy Self at once hidden and glorified by its own transparency, as the accidental and dividuous in this quiet and harmonious object is subjected to the life and light of nature which shines in it, even as the transmitted power, love and wisdom, of God over all fills, and shines through, nature! But what the plant *is*, by an act not its own and unconsciously—*that* must thou *make* thyself to *become*! must by prayer and by a watchful and unresisting spirit, *join* at least with the preventive and assisting grace to *make* thyself, in that light of conscience which inflameth not, and with that knowledge which puffeth not up. (*SM* 71)

Whether we cease to know our existence as consubstantial because the world is fallen, or whether the Fall is itself a lack of tolerance for living in mystery, the result is all around us.

Coleridge calls the Fall "the creation, as it were, of the non-absolute" (*TT*, 1 May 1830). Within this context, it may be illuminating to think of the world in which we carry on our daily operations and interactions and on which we typically base our assumptions as the world of the Understanding rather than that of the Reason.

> Reason is the knowledge of the laws of the WHOLE considered as ONE: and as such it is contradistinguished from the Understanding, which concerns itself exclusively with the quantities, qualities and relations of *particulars* in time and space. The UNDERSTANDING, therefore, is the science of phaenomena, and their subsumption under distinct kinds and sorts, (*genus* and *species*). Its functions supply the rules and constitute the possibility of EXPERIENCE; but remain mere logical *forms*, except as far as *materials* are given by the senses or sensations. The REASON, on the other hand, is the science of the *universal*, having the ideas of ONENESS and ALLNESS as its two elements or primary factors. . . . The Reason first manifests itself in man by the *tendency* to the comprehension of all as one. We can neither rest in an infinite that is not at the same time a whole, nor in a whole that is not infinite. Hence the natural Man is always in a state either of resistance or of captivity to the understanding and the fancy, which cannot represent totality without limit. . . .
>
> It must not, however, be overlooked, that this insulation of the understanding is our own act and deed. The man of healthful and undivided intellect uses his understanding in this state of abstraction only as a tool or organ: even as the arithmetician uses numbers, that is, as the means not the end of knowledge. (*SM* 59–60, 68–69)

If, however, a person uses the Understanding as the end of knowledge rather than the means, if the Understanding is not infused with the power of imagination, there can be no symbolic experience. For Coleridge, absolute possibility inheres in "the Omnipresent and Absolute" which is the self-conscious Reason, known "only by the intuition and immediate spiritual consciousness of the idea of God, as the One and Absolute, at once the Ground and the Cause, who alone containeth in himself the ground of his own nature, and therein of *all* natures. . . . Here the immediate consciousness decides: the idea is its own evidence, and is insusceptible of all other. It is necessarily groundless and indemonstrable; because it is itself the ground of all possible demonstration. The Reason hath faith in itself, in its own revelations. . . . IPSE DIXIT! So it is: for it is so!" (*SM* 32).

Coleridge would argue that most of us have lost faith in the revelations of Reason; it seems safer to operate on the basis of the Understanding. In this case, we are aware only of a world longed for, seen in vision or dream. A world of metaphysical wholeness, experienced as mystery, once known but now so lost to us that we can speak of it only as "another world," a fantasy fairy world which we ignore or deny or feel as threat or embarrassment. This Other World, for which Faery is actually a metaphor, is the state of infinite possibility, characterized by the creative energy of Spirit, in which all contraries are reconciled and unified through Love. It is the creative ground out of which new forms are continually brought forth—manifestations of the Reality from which they come. We exist there with whole sight. It is the world from which we are fallen; and if it now seems too strange to us through unfamiliarity, the fallen world into which we have moved is all too familiar. Divided into good and bad, masculine and feminine, heaven and hell, the fallen world names and separates, divides into race and class, and sets boundaries. Order that was once harmonious possibility becomes rigid structure. Awesome mystery becomes feared irrationality. There can be no Unity, no Reason, through negation: "It were wiser to seek substance in shadow, than absolute fulness in mere negation" (*Friend* 1: 515). Wholeness cannot come out of negation, which is ultimately static and sterile; rather, the Absolute Truth which is Reason is a continually reconciling and incorporating process. Because we are so accustomed to our fallen world, awareness of wholeness can be achieved only if we allow ourselves the symbolic knowledge of mystery. Through symbolic encounter, Spirit becomes intelligible.

Since the Understanding necessarily contemplates mystery "through a false and falsifying perspective" (*SM* 56), the fallen world insists on division. Furthermore, that division causes such distortion, repression, and falsification of our true reality that we are left with no adequate denotative language with which to articulate the truth of the Reason. Although "the Thoughts of God . . . are all IDEAS . . . incomparably more *real* than all things besides" (*CL* 3: 1195), "as a mystery (Coleridge would add) it is incapable of further definition in the language of the understanding" (*BL* Shawcross 1: lxxxi). Symbol and symbolic story, therefore, become the means of connection, insistent assertions of consubstantiality.

Interestingly, through symbol, the imaginative energy of Spirit *will* intrude, break out, discomfit the structures we have built for our safety: "As every faculty, with every the minutest organ of our nature, owes its whole reality and comprehensibility to an existence incomprehensible and groundless, because the ground of all comprehension: not without the union of all that is essential in all the functions of our spirit, not without an emotion tranquil from its very intensity, shall we worthily contemplate in the magnitude and integrity of the world that life-ebullient stream which breaks through every momentary embankment, again, indeed, and evermore to embark itself, but within no banks to stagnate or be imprisoned" (*Friend* 1: 519). We become aware of this ebullient intrusion in certain works of art that have a quality of "strangeness" about them, a strangeness not simply odd, but powerful and compelling—works that seem to have to do with metaphysical mystery.[12] As the truths of mystery are enunciated, "the soul of man awakes, and starts up, as an exile in a far distant land at the unexpected sounds of his native language, when after long years of absence, and almost of oblivion, he is suddenly addressed in his own mother-tongue" (*SM* 24). It is this intrusion that is the subject of Coleridge's strangest and most compelling poems—"Kubla Khan," "The Rime of the Ancient Mariner," and "Christabel"— and of portions of other poems: "The Eolian Harp," "Love," and "The Night Scene," for example. In each of these poems, Coleridge takes us on a voyage of symbolic encounter with Spirit/Truth/God. And in each case, we must be willing to suspend our disbelief— willing, that is, to live in mystery—which willingness constitutes the symbolic experience.[13]

Those poems which throughout or in part have the quality of arresting strangeness are poems of symbolic encounter: that is, symbolic poems of Faery. In them, Coleridge uses again and again a certain metaphorical cluster of symbols of Spirit: music, androgyny, nature, poetic genius (the symbolic imagination), poetry, the human soul, and Faery. It is obviously not the case that he uses no other symbolic metaphors, and sometimes these particular metaphors are present independently. More often, however, several of them occur together, thus becoming metaphors for each other as well as functioning as symbols of Spirit. Music, with its many different notes producing unified harmony, is an expected and almost inevitable symbol of the Unity of Reality. Androgyny is less expected, perhaps, but entirely apt, as an excellently appropriate image for the reconciliation of opposites that constitutes Love. Nature, comments Coleridge, is God's "amanuensis" (*AR* 200), and nature creates as the poetic genius creates, both of them partaking of and manifesting the I AM of the Creator. Faery, a place of the imagination—or a place of the imagination's truth—provides a prelapsarian Other World appropriate for symbolic encounter. Faery has the unique advantage of having already been given form in fairy tale and the closely related folk ballad. Both usually constitute tales of Faery; both are part of oral tradition (sung or spun tale); and their origin is so uncertain and distant that it becomes simply time past—once upon a time. The conventions of fairy tales give Coleridge a traditional, ready-made language for symbolic speaking that is intuitively right.

To discuss individual symbols of Spirit within the context of Coleridge's consubstantial symbolic universe without reference to other parts of the symbolic cluster would be extremely difficult. Indeed, it is probably definitionally impossible, since each thing that is symbolic of spirit must also have a metaphoric relationship with every other thing symbolic of Spirit. In such a metaphysical universe, densely rich with poetic possibilities, one symbol is best explained by another in an ongoing, complexly interrelated and intrareferential manner. Coleridge himself talks about one symbol in terms of another. For example, by showing nature's relation to poetry, he shows how nature, manifesting as it does the one Life, is a symbol of that Life and an occasion of symbolic knowledge: "We find poetry, as it were, substantiated and realized in nature: yea, nature itself disclosed to us . . . as at once the poet and the poem" (*Friend* 1: 471). Following his discussion in *The Statesman's Man-*

ual of the Bible as a system of symbols consubstantial with the Truth of God (*SM* 29, quoted above), Coleridge continues his "argument" for a consubstantial world by digressing, as he puts it, "to another book, likewise a revelation of God—the great book of his servant Nature. That in its obvious sense and literal interpretation it declares the being and attributes of the Almighty Father, none but the fool *in heart* has ever dared gainsay. But it has been the music of gentle and pious minds in all ages, it is the *poetry* of all human nature, to read it likewise in a figurative sense, and to find therein correspondencies and symbols of the spiritual world" (*SM* 70). Music and poetry and nature and human nature help explain the essence of each other as they declare the "being" of God.

Each of these is a metaphor for each of the others because each is a symbol of God. Coleridge continues his discussion of the reality of the consubstantiality of all Being, summing up, in effect, the whole symbolic system:

> Like can only be known by like: that as Truth is the correlative of Being, so is the act of Being the great organ of Truth: that in natural no less than in moral science. . . .
>
> That, which we find in ourselves, is . . . the substance and the life of *all* our knowledge. Without this latent presence of the "I am," all modes of existence in the external world would flit before us as colored shadows, with no greater depth, root, or fixture, than the image of a rock hath in a gliding stream or the rain-bow on a fast-sailing rain-storm. . . . The fact therefore, that the mind of man in its own primary and constituent forms represents the laws of nature, is a mystery which of itself should suffice to make us religious: for it is a problem of which God is the only solution, God, the one before all, and of all, and through all!—True natural philosophy is comprized in the study of the science and language of *symbols*. The power delegated to nature is all in every part: and by a symbol I mean, not a metaphor or allegory or any other figure of speech or form of fancy, but an actual and essential part of that, the whole of which it represents." (*SM* 78–79)

It is fairly easy to see how creative nature can be "an actual and essential part of that, the whole of which it represents." Evidence is readily apparent to the eye, and Coleridge constantly reiterates, in prose and poetry, the symbolic character of nature. Similarly, music is readily apparent to the ear, and it shares in common with nature a creator and a thing created. It differs from nature, however, in that the creator, though also a symbol of the Creator, is human. Thus, in explaining how music is symbolic, Coleridge equates it with poetry and its creator with the poet, since the creator of the symbolic poem creates form, the poem, through the active reconciliation of polarities—an action which is once again symbolic of spirit: that is, "an actual and essential part, the whole of which it represents." Androgyny acquires form and creative, ongoing existence in the androgynous character of individual persons. Thus the concept and its manifestation in persons provide an entirely apt metaphor for the process of natural creation or poetic creation or the process of poetic genius itself. In each case, the symbol represents—that is, re-presents—Spirit/God/Love as it acts to reconcile and unify.

Each element of the symbolic cluster of metaphors "partakes of the Reality which it renders intelligible; and while it enunciates the whole, abides itself as a living part of that Unity, of which it is the representative" (*SM* 30). Each is individual, yet each is part of a Unity and as such partakes of the reconciling creative energy and process which defines Truth/Spirit/Love. That reconciling creativity—which is the mystery—becomes the mark of each, the reason why the symbols metaphorically enrich the meaning of one another while, at the same time, they singly and together enunciate the wholeness that is Life. Androgyny, a metaphor Coleridge makes use of consciously and intuitively, can serve as a good example of both the interactive and intrareferential nature of symbols and also of that which they represent.[14]

The concept of androgyny is an ancient one, its manifestations multifarious and complexly interrelated in Plato, alchemy, kabbalism, and Jakob Boehme, to name only a few sources. Nevertheless, in each of its strands and manifestations, androgyny has always been associated with reconciliation, strength, creativity, and the gods. Androgyny is an ideal. Its nature is unbounded and characterized by universal vitality and a spirit of reconciliation.

To speak of the androgynous is to speak of an inherent, fundamental, creative wholeness. It is the ongoing reconciliation of opposites. It is the state of energetic existence in which extremes meet without regard for the limitations of the Understanding. The androgynous ideal speaks the language of Sight, distinct from partial sight, which can function only by "setting apart of all pairs of opposites—male and female, life and death, true and false, good and evil" (Campbell 26).

The androgynous nature is characterized by creativity. Absolute masculinity and absolute femininity are, in and of themselves, sterile. It is equally true, however, that what is required is not the obliteration of gender but the reconciliation of the two sexes which yet recognizes the individualizing tendency toward one sex or the other. What is wanted is not annihilation but ongoing creative process: simultaneous difference and identity. In other words, there is unity in duplicity; that is, each sex must be androgynous in a way "which *in* both is the same; but which yet distinguishes them to each other from the rest of mankind" (*CN* 3: 3308). In Coleridge's poetry, the unity in duplicity can be manifested in one character so that the man or woman may be spoken of as an androgynous character or as having an androgynous nature: that is, containing within him- or herself an abundance of both masculine and feminine principles. Or two such persons may come together in a love relationship that merges the two into one. In addition, the erotic, creative energy of such a love relationship may be conveyed by a metaphoric description of nature—or the "androgynous" description may stand alone in the poem without an overt analogue, except that the human love relationship will be implicitly present through sexual imagery. In each of these cases, the reconciliation of Spirit is being symbolized in the unity, the oneness of the androgynous. We conceive this oneness, explains Coleridge, "as the mid-point producing itself on each side; that is, manifesting itself on two opposite poles. Thus, from identity we derive duality, and from both together we obtain polarity, synthesis, indifference, predominance." One half of the duality will, of necessity, predominate; thus, there are two sexes. At the same time, "neither can the antagonists appear but as two forces of one power, nor can the power be conceived by us but as the equatorial point of the two counteracting forces. . . . In Life . . . the two component counter-powers actually interpenetrate each other, and generate a higher third, including both the former" (*TL* 393, 399).

This creative process of Life Coleridge calls "*polarity*, or the essential dualism of Nature, arising out of its productive unity, and still tending to reaffirm it, either as equilibrium, indifference, or identity" (*TL* 391).[15] The ultimate end, argues Coleridge, of these dual tendencies toward individuation and connection is God, what he calls "the highest and most comprehensive individuality" (*TL* 391). Finally, coming full circle, it follows that the creative energy of the Creator is given expression in the person and the symbolic poetry of genius. "The truth is a great mind must be androgynous" (*TT* 1 Sept. 1832), affirms Coleridge. Equally important, the androgynous poet of genius creates not only the work of art itself but also the occasion for the reader's encounter with the work. The reader exists for a time out of time—in the Land of Faery—re-creating in another symbolic act of his or her imagination the vision of the poet.

The Land of Faery

The folk fairy tale is the prose equivalent of the folk ballad. Both were conveyed as oral, communal events, performances of narratives similar in style. A good number of ballads may also be classified as fairy tales. It is not surprising, therefore, that the ballad revival in the late eighteenth and early nineteenth centuries was accompanied by a renewed interest in local legends, folk tales, and folk fairy tales. While some were concerned with collecting the tales and ballads of oral tradition, others—like Coleridge—made use of the oral tradition for their own individual literary purposes, transforming the genre into something much more subtle and complex than the original, while still retaining much that was familiar and recognizable. The character of this transformation can be seen by comparing briefly the traditional oral fairy tales and ballads with the literary romantic fairy tale that sometimes emerges from the imagination of a writer such as Coleridge.

Although exceptions can be found, folk fairy tales in the main have distinctive characteristics in common which, taken together, can be summarized as a sparseness, a clarity of abstraction that heightens and illuminates significance. The narrator of the tale is never part of the tale, never calls attention to him- or herself, tells the tale in an objective manner and an assured tone. The narrator does not explain events or offer interpretation. Nor does the narrator question the authenticity of the events of the tale; supernatural, magical, rationally inexplicable events simply *are*, are true and real. There is little detailed description of setting or of characters. The few details that are given are significant details, details solid, definite, and sharply formed—gold, silver, ring, sword. The world of fairy tales is permanent, imperishable. There is dialogue, but it is limited. The narrative is episodic and repetitive, though often incrementally repetitious. Action is clear and deliberate; the story moves without delay or meditation. The focus is on externals, on the concrete surface. Thus, the inner feelings of characters—their moods, deliberations, and inner conflicts—are not presented. Similarly, character relationships are not explored or analyzed. Rather, they are externalized, made visible through events and objects: the love of the prince for the princess is made real in the wedding ring. Time in fairy tales is "once upon a time"; therefore, time, process, and decay do not exist in the fairy tale, though all parts of the universe—animal, vegetable, mineral—are present and are shown to be interrelated. The characters of folk fairy tales are not individually delineated; they are stock characters with generic or descriptive names like "Jack" or "Beauty." They are types, figures, that can stand symbolically for many things. In keeping with the fairy tale's love of contrasts, characters are almost always unambiguously good or bad. The central character is usually a young person, usually the youngest child, usually isolated. His or her story is one of initiation or maturation. Fairy tale heroes and heroines are wandering journeyers. They are alone but aided by various helpers as they encounter tests and prohibitions and finally achieve success. Folk fairy tales almost always have a happy ending in which those who are good live happily ever after.[16]

Like the folk fairy tale, the literary romantic fairy tale is a subgenre of the quest-romance, whose narrative, according to Northrop Frye, is an episodic "marvellous journey" whose "organizing ideas [are] chastity and magic" and whose typical theme is the "boundary of consciousness, the sense of the poetic mind as passing from one world to another, or as simultaneously aware of both." The typical hero of romance, explains Frye, is one "whose actions are marvellous but who is himself identified as a human being. The hero of romance moves in a world in which the ordinary laws of nature are slightly suspended: prodigies of courage and endurance, unnatural to us, are natural to him, and enchanted weapons, talking animals, terrifying ogres and witches, and talismans of miraculous power violate no rule of probability once the postulates of romance have been established. Here we have moved from myth, properly so called, into legend, folk tale, *märchen*, and their literary affiliates and derivatives." Frye goes on to say that the garden of Eden, the place of innocence, belongs in romance, taking religious or secular—but nonetheless parallel—forms in, for example, *Paradise Lost*, Spenser's Garden of Adonis, and fairy tales. The myths of quest-romance can be sacred or secular: "The flaming sword that keeps the fallen Adam and Eve away from Paradise, in the story of the sleeping beauty . . . is replaced by [a wall] of thorns and brambles" (57, 153, 33, 152). The romantic fairy tale often makes full use of this parallelism so that the secular tale comes to stand for an analogous sacred story.

Though the romantic fairy tale absorbs and makes use of the elements of the folk tale—its style, characters, and narrative structure—it differs in two significant ways. First, of course, there is the fact that it is literary, not oral. There is a written, unchanging text by a single author who selects details and events for his or her own particular purpose and design. The audience is also an individual who, ordinarily, experiences the text in isolation and at his or her own discretionary time and place. The second major difference is that the romantic fairy tale often engages metaphysical, philosophical issues. Its primary concerns are subjective ones, whether emotional, psychological, or existential. The romantic fairy tale takes what was implicit in the folk fairy tale and brings it to the fore, making it the overt matter of the tale. These changes transform the fairy tale in a number of ways, though the changes are not uniformly present in appearance or degree. The narrator is often more visible, offering comment or asking questions. There is more description and discussion of motivation, conflict, and feelings. The romantic fairy tale world does not have the black and white contrast of the folk fairy tales; instead, the color is more often gray, the ending not an entirely happy one. Indeed, as Coleridge's most complex tales of Faery attest, the ending may well be that of ballad tragedy rather than fairy tale's "happily ever after."

What folk fairy tales and romantic literary fairy tales have in common—what is at the core of the fairy tale genre—is the evocation of Faery. While it is possible, with some qualification and overlapping, to give an account of the characteristics of both oral and literary tales, it is much more difficult to define the quality of Faery itself. Faery has to do with tone and atmosphere, with a certain feeling or sense that the tale evokes, an evocation that is possible because there is a corresponding sense or awareness or intuitive knowledge within the hearer of the tale. The "magic" of Faery is "of a peculiar mood and power" (Tolkien 10); tales of Faery are strange and wonderful and, to a large extent, inexplicable. They have a quality of "arresting strangeness" (Tolkien 47–48). In Coleridgean terms, the power of the story is such that we suspend our disbelief; we "cannot choose but hear" (Rime 18). It is the describable elements of tales of Faery that somehow work together to evoke in the story and in us the realm of Faery, but it is Faery that gives the fairy tale the essence of its power.

Coleridge is one of a group of writers—most of whom write in prose rather than verse and almost all of whom write much later—

who may be said to be interested in exploiting the possibilities for metaphysical expression and exploration inherent in a genre whose place of action is the Other World. It is very clear that by the 1840s and 1850s a writer like Dickens can take the world of Faery and the genre of fairy tale and use them for literary purposes. For Dickens, the story itself becomes the means of "evoking the power of sympathetic response that slumbers within each person. That power—the power of imaginative sympathy—humanizes and saves" (Stone 29). The world of Faery is the world of creative imagination, the world of feeling and intuition, the world of imaginative truth. We see this deliberate literary use later in the nineteenth century in George MacDonald's fairy tales and in the twentieth century in the work of J. R. R. Tolkien, to give only two major examples. Although the use of Faery as metaphor for the Other World of imagination and intuition can be secular or religious, it is most often religious—or at the least, highly metaphysical. For Coleridge, Faery becomes a symbol of Spirit, a symbolic metaphor for the intuitive, prelapsarian world of creative imagination. The tale of Faery presents and at the same time provides an occasion for symbolic encounter within a consubstantial world.

Coleridge's appropriation of the folk materials of fairy tales, ballads, romances, and superstitious tales, which culminates most powerfully in "Kubla Khan," "Rime of the Ancient Mariner," and "Christabel," anticipates Dickens and others. But it is exactly contemporaneous with the emergence in Germany of a new literary genre called the *Kunstmärchen*. The term *Märchen*, which originally meant "news" or "gossip" and which is translated into English as "fairy tale," usually refers indiscriminately to both oral and literary fairy tales. The *Oxford English Dictionary* dates the term "fairy tale" to 1750; it probably derived from Countess D'Aulnoy's *Contes de fées*, which was translated into English a year after its publication in 1698 as *Tales of the Fairys* (Opie and Opie 14–15). Since then, "fairy tale" has been used to denote equally folk fairy tales (such as "Jack the Giant-Killer" and the oral stories collected and transcribed by the Grimms) and the literary stories that are either original or adapted from folk tales (such as "Beauty and the Beast"). The term *Kunstmärchen*, there-fore, makes a useful distinction. James Trainer defines *Kunst-märchen* as "a tale embodying folk-motifs but written by sophisti-cated modern authors" (97). Similarly, Jack Zipes—who uses the term "folk tale" for the oral fairy tale and "fairy tale" for the German literary fairy tale—defines *Kunstmärchen* as "a *literary* text which experimented with and expanded upon the stock motifs, figures and plots of the folk tale" (7). The *Kunstmärchen*, then, is a romantic fairy tale, a literary tale that makes use of the much older, traditional, oral folk tale for its own purposes.

The fairy tales Coleridge writes may well be described as En-glish versions of the *Kunstmärchen*, in that he uses the motifs, characters, and plot devices of the oral tradition to create a sym-bolic world. When I use "fairy tale," I mean to refer to all the tales we commonly group together under this term. Additionally, I use the terms "Faery" and "tale of Faery"—and this for several rea-sons. First, Coleridge himself used the spelling "faery." Second, with that spelling I intend to connote a heightened level of the core significance of the genre: that is, the sense of wonder or "strangeness" that is the hallmark of the fairy tale. Tolkien, in agreement with other theorists of fairy tales, says, "Fairy-stories are not in normal English usage stories *about* fairies or elves, but stories about Fairy, that is *Faërie*, the realm or state in which fairies have their being" (9). Coleridge calls the "Land of Faery" a "mental space" (*CN* 3: 4501). Thus, Faery is a state of mind, a place of imagination, a condition of existence and awareness. Tales or parts of tales that give entrance to Faery—that are about that mental space—are, to the extent and for the time they do so, tales of Faery. Faery realms exist in both oral and literary fairy tales.

In coming at the nature of Faery, whether in theoretical dis-cussion or in the language of story, Coleridge and other writers interested in Faery seem to share a common tongue, distinctive and unique, yet familiar to those who speak it. Separated chrono-logically, geographically, and culturally, writers of the language of Faery nevertheless use the same metaphors time and again to describe an imaginative state of existence—the metaphors described above as symbolic metaphors of Spirit. For an understanding of the appropriateness of the tale of Faery for Coleridge's purposes, it may be helpful to see how a number of writers interested in this sort of tale define it and Faery itself. Their comments expand on the implications of Coleridge's own statements, at the same time revealing him as a major influence in their attempts to articulate the nature of Faery.

The quality of Faery itself, the quality that *makes* a fairy tale a fairy tale rather than some other, closely related genre, eludes definition through language. It is a quality more readily experienced or intuited than described. "Fairy tales are perhaps more easily recognized than defined," observes Michael Kotzin (7), an observation the truth of which soon becomes apparent as one reads fairy tale theory. Criticism, whether dealing with definitions of oral or literary fairy tales—not to mention the quality of Faery—reveals a definite reluctance, or inability, to define at all. Interestingly, this definitional "impossibility" becomes one of the chief characteristics of Faery and fairy tale.

Ludwig Tieck expresses it through the character of Anton at the beginning of *Phantasus*: " 'It is difficult,' said Anton, 'to determine what actually makes up a fairy tale and what kind of tone it should possess. We do not know what it is and can give but little account of its genesis. We find it already in existence, everyone adapts it to his own way with something different in mind, and yet almost all prove alike in certain respects, not even the witty ones excepted, which still cannot dispense with that colour, that wonderful tone which resounds within us whenever we as much as hear the word fairy tale' " (qtd. in Trainer 97). Whatever the fairy tale is, we recognize it because of some quality within ourselves.

George MacDonald begins his essay "The Fantastic Imagination" with the same definitional disclaimer: "Were I asked, what is a fairytale? I should reply, *Read Undine: that is a fairytale; then read this and that as well, and you will see what is a fairytale.* Were I further begged to describe the *fairytale*, or define what it is, I would make answer, that I should as soon think of describing the abstract human face, or stating what must go to constitute a human being" (14). Roger Sale, in his *Fairy Tales and After: From Snow White to E. B. White*, asserts that "fairy tale literature is one of the great kinds, a body of stories that do what no other literature does. . . . The term 'fairy tale' is only a convenience since few stories we call by that name contain fairies, elves, leprechauns, or similar creatures. Yet everyone seems instinctively agreed on what the term includes and excludes, even though fairy tales blend easily into related kinds, like myths, legends, romances, realistic folk fables, and cautionary tales" (24). J. R. R. Tolkien concurs:

> Fairy-stories are not in normal English usage stories *about* fairies or elves, but stories about Fairy, that is *Faërie*, the realm or state in which fairies have their being. *Faërie* contains many things besides elves and fays, and besides dwarfs, witches, trolls, giants or dragons: it holds the seas, the sun, the moon, the sky; and the earth, and all things that are in it: tree and bird, water and stone, wine and bread, and ourselves, mortal men, when we are enchanted. . . . The definition of a fairy-story . . . [depends] upon the nature of *Faërie*: the Perilous Realm itself, and the air that blows in that country. I will not attempt to define that, nor to describe it directly. It cannot be done. Faërie cannot be caught in a net of words; for it is one of its qualities to be indescribable, though not imperceptible. . . . A "fairy-story" is one which touches on or uses Faërie, whatever its own main purpose may be: satire, adventure, morality, fantasy. (9–10)

Echoing Tolkien, Max Luthi says that fairy tales present a "universe in miniature"; fairy tale "embraces in its own way the world: nature both dead and living, man and the works of man, and the supernatural." At the same time, "fairy tales are experienced by their hearers and readers, not as realistic, but as symbolic poetry." They are "unreal but they are not untrue; they reflect essential developments and conditions of man's existence" (*Once upon a Time* 25, 66, 70). Similarly, the Opies agree that "although a fairy tale is seldom a tale about fairy-folk, and does not necessarily even feature a fairy, it does contain an enchantment or other supernatural element that is clearly imaginary." On the other hand, "fairy tales are . . . more realistic than they may appear at first sight; while the magic in them almost heightens the realism.

The magic sets us wondering how we ourselves would react in similar circumstances. It encourages speculation. It gives a child license to wonder. And this is the merit of the tales, that by going beyond possibility they enlarge our daily horizon" (18, 20).

To move beyond the daily horizon is to move into Coleridge's "mental space." To allow the mind to move beyond-beneath-through the surface of the "real" world is to allow it to move into a place of imagination in which the truth and significance of the concrete world can be revealed. For the reader of fairy tales, there is the "real" world of everyday life—that is, the knowable, empirical world—and the Other World that one enters as one suspends disbelief in the reality of Faery. Bruno Bettelheim says that fairy stories "take place on a very different level from everyday 'reality.'. . . The 'truth' of fairy stories is the truth of our imagination, not that of normal causality" (117). Tolkien puts it this way:

> The dragon had the trade-mark *Of Faërie* written plain upon him. In whatever world he had his being it was an Other-world. Fantasy, the making or glimpsing of Other-worlds, was the heart of the desire of Faërie. I desired dragons with a profound desire. . . . I was keenly alive to the beauty of "Real things," but it seemed to me quibbling to confuse this with the wonder of "Other things." I was eager to study Nature, actually more eager than I was to read most fairy-stories; but I did not want to be quibbled into Science and cheated out of Faërie by people who seemed to assume that by some kind of original sin I should prefer fairy-tales, but according to some kind of new religion I ought to be induced to like science. Nature is no doubt a life-study, or a study for eternity (for those so gifted); but there is a part of man which is not "Nature," and which therefore is not obligated to study it, and is, in fact, wholly unsatisfied by it. (41, 79 n.D)

In Coleridgean terms, tales of Faery are symbolic and, at the same time, provide an occasion of symbolic encounter for the reader. As the reader reads the tale, he or she experiences Faery. Dickens's sense of the import of fairy tales is similar. He regarded "the fairy tale and its correlatives—fantasy, enchantment, legends, signs and correspondences, indeed all the thronging manifestations of the invisible world—as potent instruments and incarnations of imaginative truth. The fairy tale was the most important of those incarnations" (Stone 4). The tale of Faery gives us a means of perceiving differently. This experience of an incarnation of imaginative truth—an experience that is, of course, one of the imagination—is most typically imaged either as walking through a door into another world or as a dream state.

In summarizing a discussion of fantasy works for children, including fairy tales, Jane Langton says: "You do not itemize and analyze a miracle either. . . . The secret of their deathless charm [is that] they are all dreams. They are waking dreams. They make up to us for the sense of loss we feel when we wake up and find our dreams shrinking out of memory. A literary fantasy gives us a dream back to keep. . . . It feeds a hunger we didn't know we had" (178–79). The world of Faery is the Other World, visited as in dreams, a place of passion and imagination that counterpoints the wakeful day world of analytic reasoning—in Coleridge's terms, the Understanding—and societal restrictions. "Subjected to the rational teachings of others, the child only buries his 'true knowledge' deeper in his soul and it remains untouched by rationality" (Bettelheim 46). "True knowledge" is kept alive in the Other World of Faery. C. G. Jung says: "Fairytales are only infantile forms of legends, myths, and superstitions taken from the 'night religion' of primitives. What I call 'night religion' is the magical form of religion, the meaning and purpose of which is intercourse with the dark powers, devils, witches, magicians and spirits" (10: 33). Entry into Faery is dangerous. "A fantasy is a journey," says Ursula K. Le Guin in her essay "From Elfland to Poughkeepsie." "It is a journey into the subconscious mind, just as psychoanalysis is. Like psychoanalysis, it can be dangerous; and *it will change you*" (207). Defining "Elfland," or Faery, Le Guin explains:

Elfland is what Lord Dunsany called the place. It is also known as Middle Earth, and Prydain, and the Forest of Broceliande, and Once Upon a Time; and by many other names. . . . A great many people want to go there, without really knowing what it is they're really looking for, driven by a vague hunger for something real. . . . The point about Elfland is that you are not at home there. It's not Poughkeepsie. It's different. . . . Its affinity is not with daydream, but with dream. It is a different approach to reality, an alternative technique for apprehending and coping with existence. It is not antirational, but pararational; not realistic, but surrealistic, superrealistic, a heightening of reality. In Freud's terminology, it employs primary, not secondary process thinking. It employs archetypes, which, as Jung warned us, are dangerous things. Dragons are more dangerous, and a good deal commoner, than bears. Fantasy is nearer to poetry, to mysticism, and to insanity than naturalistic fiction is. It is a real wilderness, and those who go there should not feel too safe. (195–96)

Fairy tales take us to the place of Faery and allow us to encounter the reality that has been buried. Maureen Duffy describes the encounter: "Feyrie or fayrie is another word for enchanted or enchantment. It is the whole world that is enchanted as if with a fifth dimension. The lays and romances describe men and women who seem real until suddenly, as if there were a gauze curtain hung before the whole scene which we hadn't noticed until that moment, time and space begin to tremble like a heat dance and we have walked through the border into another realm that is usually just below the threshold of consciousness" (48). When we walk "through the border into another realm," we move into another level of existence, different from ordinary waking consciousness but also real and existing always, simply waiting for us to notice it.

Once we do notice Faery, time and space and the limits of ordinary perception shift, move, expand. Fairy tales "open a door on Other Time, and if we pass through, though only for a moment, we stand outside our own time, outside Time itself, maybe" (Tolkien 32). In fairy tales, there is a "marvellous independence or true imaginative absence of all particular place & time—it is neither in the domains of History or Geography, is ignorant of all artificial boundary" (*CN* 3: 4501). While this Other World is not the world of our ordinary consciousness, it nevertheless is experienced by us as the "really real," the place where "what is," *is*. "When fantasy is the real thing, nothing, after all, is realer" (Le Guin 209). For Coleridge, what *is* is the I AM of Spirit, and tales of Faery allow the "I am" of the individual soul an opportunity for symbolic encounter. In a fallen world, not only has the Whole become divided, but the spirit's way of seeing has been perverted. In a fallen world, the only way to speak of Wholeness and Spirit is symbolically, through story. Within the conventions of the fairy tale, Coleridge finds a traditional mode, already in essence a metaphor for his speaking.

Elizabeth Cook, in *The Ordinary and the Fabulous*, would agree with Coleridge's solution: "There is another door that can be opened by reading legends and fairy tales, and for some children, at the present time, there may be no other key to it" (105–06). John Beer, discussing Coleridge's strong predilection for the genre of romance, comments: "In Coleridge's view the romance is not simply an aid to the transmission of moral truth; it conveys a truth of its own which cannot easily be transmitted in any other way." Romance, including its subgenres, "keeps the mind open to possibilities which a dominant rationalism might otherwise hide" ("Supernatural" 52). Faery tale can be the key, the right language for the "part of man" that is "wholly unsatisfied" by the study of what we have come to call Science. This is true because faery tale speaks metaphorically of the soul's existence with Spirit before the Fall. As the truths of mystery are enunciated, remarks Coleridge, "the soul of man awakes, and starts up, as an exile in a far distant land at the unexpected sounds of his native language, when after long years of absence, and almost of oblivion, he is suddenly addressed in his own mother-tongue" (*SM* 24).

Faery tale speaks the "mother-tongue," and what it speaks is true. "Fairy tales are unreal, but they are not untrue; they reflect essential developments and conditions of man's existence" (Luthi, *Once upon a Time* 70). The German romanticists, explains Robert Wernaer, were "rediscoverers of the fairy times of old, and re-discoverers of the spiritual realm somewhere in us—still left in us even to-day—whence the spirit of childhood comes. It seemed to them . . . the purest portion in man's spiritual makeup; yes, his true home, the place from which he came and to which he was going" (252). Further, comment Iona and Peter Opie, "the magic in the tales (if magic is what it is) lies in people and creatures being shown to be what they really are" (14)—a precise description of the soul's encounter with Spirit. In symbolic encounter, the soul comes to know itself for what it is. It intuits its existence as, and participation in, the reality of Spirit/Oneness/Wholeness. Faery, for Coleridge, is a symbol of Wholeness, and—along with nature, music, imagination, and androgyny—it becomes a part of his symbolic matrix.

The intuitive quality of Faery—or "high fantasy," to use a twentieth-century term—and its association with music and imagination and the rest of Coleridge's symbolic metaphors is commented on by numerous writers of the genre. Peter Beagle, in describing Tolkien's Middle-earth, says that "the book is full of singing. Ballads and poetry and rhymes of lore belong to the daily lives of the peoples of Middle-earth, and epic poetry is their history and their journalism. . . . And the music is never imposed from outside; it springs from the center of this world" (134). Susan Cooper is even more explicit. When we read fantasy or tales of Faery, she says,

> we're going out of time, out of space, into the unconscious, that dreamlike world which has in it all the images and emotions accumulated since the human race began. We aren't escaping out, we're escaping in, without any idea of what we may encounter. Fantasy is the metaphor through which we discover ourselves. So it is for the writer, too. Every book is a voyage of discovery. . . . When working on a book which turns out to be a fantasy novel, I exist in a state of continual astonishment. The work begins with a deep breath and a blindly trusting step into the unknown; I know where I'm going, and who's going with me, but I have no real idea of what I shall find on the way, or whom I'll meet. Each time, I am striking out into a strange land, listening for the music that will tell me which way to go. And I am always overcome by wonder, and a kind of unfocused gratitude, when I arrive; and I always think of Eliot:
>
> > We shall not cease from exploration
> > And the end of all our exploring
> > Will be to arrive where we started
> > And know the place for the first time. . . .

Cooper concludes that "true fantasy" casts "a spell so subtle and overwhelming that it has overpowered the reader's imagination, carried him outside all rules, before he has noticed what is happening." Her further supposition is that the writer is not really aware of what has happened either. Writing tales of Faery—whether fantasy or fairy tales—is a matter of writing down the music of Faery: "You can't write fantasy on purpose. It won't come when called. Like poetry, it is a kind of happy accident which overtakes certain writers before they are born" (282–83). George MacDonald relates the fairy tale to music and nature, arguing that their most important function is to awaken within the individual the inner awareness of incomprehensible things:

> A fairytale, a sonata, a gathering storm, a limitless night, seizes you and sweeps you away. . . . The greatest forces lie in the region of the uncomprehended. . . . The best thing you can do for your fellow, next to rousing his conscience, is—not to give him things to think about, but to wake things up that are in him; or say, to make him think things for himself. The best Nature does for us is to work in us such moods in which thoughts of high import arise. . . . She rouses the something deeper than the understanding—the power that underlies thoughts. Does she not set feeling, and so thinking at work? . . . Nature is mood-engendering, thought-provoking: such ought the sonata, such ought the fairytale to be. (18–19)

Nature, the sonata, and the fairy tale all rouse "the something deeper than the understanding." That "something," Coleridge would say, is the Reason or Spirit that constitutes the soul's existence. Coleridge and the early German Romantics Tieck and Novalis have in common an acute awareness of the reality of the mystery of Spirit. In addition, they all see the traditional folk fairy tale's potential as a vehicle for the exploration of the nature of this mystery. Tolkien says that fairy tales have three faces: "the Mystical towards the Supernatural; the Magical towards Nature; and the Mirror of scorn and pity towards Man. The essential face of Faerie is the middle one, the Magical. But the degree in which the others appear (if at all) is variable and may be decided by the individual story-teller. The Magical, the fairy-story, may be used as a *Mirour de l'Omme*; and it may (but not so easily) be made a vehicle of mystery" (26). Coleridge and Tieck and Novalis, in their

63

Kunstmärchen, achieve the more difficult variable: the fairy tale becomes the vehicle of mystery.

Speaking of the early German Romantics, James Trainer says: "The Romantic mind was dominated by the mystery of existence, and in its earliest phases at least its writing was concerned primarily with the penetration of such mystery. The view of the classical ideal as the quest for order, harmony, and beauty in a rational world, and the Romantic ideal as the transcending of this world to pursue those elements which point beyond the finite to something eternal, is one that finds substantiation in the concern of these writers with the deceptive appearances of reality and the darker regions of the human mind" (98–99). Coleridge, says his granddaughter, was a "traveller through the heavenly country" (Sara Coleridge 2: 30). And because "fairy tales are primarily a theory of existence" (Thalmann 4), the romantic fairy tale becomes an appropriate genre for writers concerned with the nature and mystery of existence. "In adding this dimension of metaphysical speculation, the Romantic *Märchen* lifts itself out of the sphere of children's literature to become a confrontation between man and the ultimate" (Trainer 100). Put another way, the marvelous world of Faery or magic or illusion presented to us in a work must be accepted by us as reality; at the same time, this Faery world must truly contain elements that we perceive as "objectively" real. "The analogy made is that of the dream, where cause and effect break down, empirical values mean nothing, yet the figures which inhabit this unfamiliar world seem recognizable to us" (Trainer 101). We come to know the familiar world because it is made strange; we are made to shift our perception; we encounter and recognize the world of wonder. The "real" world and the world of Faery are not separate but coexistent and interpenetrable.

The interrelationship—implied by all of the writers discussed—of the reality of Spirit, the human spirit, and the fallen world—can be put simply in a series of propositions: (1) the original meaning of the world has to do with Spirit and Unity and Wholeness and Love; (2) this original meaning has been lost or distorted, but it can be recovered; (3) the world of Spirit is available to us through self-knowledge; and (4) it is the tale of Faery that can most adequately present the world to be recovered and the process of recovery. The connection with Coleridge is clear. In his hands, the tale of Faery becomes a symbolic tale in which Faery represents the prelapsarian world, the world before the fall into division. Within the tale of Faery, the androgynous character, nature, music, and the creative imagination of the poet of genius function as metaphors for the state of Faery itself. And all are symbols of Spirit. Taken separately and together, the symbolic metaphors show forth the reality of the consubstantial world. Given form in faery tale, they present occasions of symbolic encounter for the reader, occasions of self-knowledge, occasions of Love.

> In order to possess what you do not possess
> > You must go by the way of dispossession.
> In order to arrive at what you are not
> > You must go through the way in which you are not.
> And what you do not know is the only thing you know
> And what you own is what you do not own
> And where you are is where you are not.   ("East Coker," 3)

CHAPTER TWO

On the Borders of Faery

C *rossing the border* into Faery, drawn by the music, lured by the garden, sensing the possibility for love, the spirit may find itself

> in a dark wood, in a bramble,
> On the edge of a grimpen, where is no secure foothold,
> And menaced by monsters, fancy lights,
> Risking enchantment. Do not let me hear
> Of the wisdom of old men, but rather of their folly,
> Their fear of fear and frenzy, their fear of possession,
> Of belonging to one another, or to others, or to God.
>
> ("East Coker," 2)

At night, the bright garden can become dark wood, soft songs of love modulate into wails of grief, vision shades into nightmare. The human spirit must encounter Love in a fallen world. Faery is real. Love may be manifested and known. But in a fallen world, Love may also be denied or betrayed. To risk enchantment is to risk participation, to risk being caught up in relationship with other human spirits and with God, to risk the intuitive knowledge of wholeness. *Not* to risk enchantment is extreme and ultimate folly.

Coleridge's tales of Faery take the reader across the border into Faery, simultaneously presenting the Reality of Spirit and Love and providing for the reader occasions of symbolic encounter. In effect, the tales of Faery encourage the reader to risk enchantment. The motto and fable that begin the first essay of *The Friend* make clear Coleridge's sense of obligation as a poet to foster the soul's intuitive knowledge of God, as well as his acute awareness of the difficulties present in retaining a sense of wholeness in a fallen world. Quoting Plutarch, Coleridge says:

> Believe me, it requires no little confidence, to promise Help to the Struggling, Counsel to the Doubtful, Light to the Blind, Hope to the Despondent, Refreshment to the Weary. These are indeed great things, if they be accomplished; trifles if they exist but in a promise. I however aim not so much to prescribe a Law for others, as to set forth the Law of my own Mind; which let the man, who shall have approved of it, abide by; and let him, to whom it shall appear not reasonable, reject it. It is my earnest wish, I confess, to employ my understanding and acquirements in that mode and direction, in which I may be enabled to benefit the largest number possible of my fellow-creatures. (*Friend* 1: 9)

One good description of the law within Coleridge's own mind is contained in his superscription for all the essays that *The Friend* comprises: "Seek thou the derivation of thy Soul . . . whence and from what rank having fallen into slavery to the Body, to that rank, from which thou wert precipitated, Thou mayest re-ascend, uniting thy energy with the Holy *Word*" (*Friend* 1: 2). The similarities between this and the motto for "The Rime of the Ancient Mariner" are evident. Spirit exists, and the soul, once united with the Holy Word, has fallen from knowledge and participation in that Word. The Soul's task, therefore, is to seek its own derivation so that it may once again experience wholeness. Teaching the awareness of symbolic existence is an integral part of Coleridge's tales of Faery.[1]

In each of these works, Coleridge talks the "language of Sight" (*Friend* 1: 70). He assumes that however varied, however now impaired, we all, at one time, had some possibility for inner sight. The teacher must speak to that possibility: "Either says the Sceptic, you are the Blind offering to lead the Blind, or you are talking the language of Sight to those who do not possess the sense of Seeing. If you mean to be read, try to entertain and do not pretend to instruct. To such objections it would be amply sufficient, on my system of faith, to answer, that we are not all blind, but all subject to distempers of the 'mental sight,' differing in kind and in degree; that though all men are in error, they are not all in the same error, nor at the same time; and that each therefore may possibly heal the other" (*Friend* 1: 10). Furthermore, if a listener can more easily be persuaded of the consubstantial nature of the world and of his or her own soul by hearing a work that entertains or "delights the imagination or affects the generous passions" (*Friend* 1: 10), it is the obligation of the teacher to use such a work. This, perhaps, is no small part of the reason why Coleridge takes the reader so often into the Land of Faery. People enjoy fairy tales. And fairy tales that are also symbolic tales of Faery teach a love of "the Whole": "For from my early reading of Faery Tales, & Genii &c &c—my mind has been habituated *to the Vast*—& I never regarded *my senses* in any way as the criteria of my belief. I regulated all my creeds by my conceptions not by my *sight*—even at that age. Should children be permitted to read Romances, & Relations of Giants & Magicians, & Genii?—I know all that has been said against it; but I have formed my faith in the affirmative.—I know no other way of giving the mind a love of 'the Great,' & 'the Whole'" (*CL* 1: 210). Stories and tales that lead to the truth of Wholeness become symbolic, as does the experience of the audience in reading the work.

Coleridge uses "The Fable of the Madning Rain" at the beginning of *The Friend* (1: 7–9) to show the position of the soul in the world before and after the Fall. Additionally, it can serve instructively as a kind of gloss for a number of poetic tales of Faery, for "Kubla Khan," "The Rime," and "Christabel" in particular. In "The Fable of the Madning Rain," the prelapsarian universe is explicitly juxtaposed with the fallen world so that we can see the difference clearly. Consubstantiality is always the reality, but the ability to perceive that reality is often diminished in a fallen world. The setting for the story is some "indefinite period, dateless as Eternity, a State rather than a Time." This is once-upon-a-time, the "mental space" that is Faery.[2] This state, says the narrator, which once existed as actual, now "presents itself to our imagina-tion . . . as a holy Tradition." The state of consubstantiality is knowable, but knowable symbolically through inner sight. The narrator continues:

> It was toward the close of this golden age (the memory of which the self-dissatisfied Race of Men have everywhere preserved and cher-ished) when Conscience acted in Man with the ease and uniformity of Instinct; when Labor was a sweet name for the activity of sane Minds in healthful Bodies, and all enjoyed in common the bounteous harvest produced, and gathered in, by common effort; when there existed in the Sexes, and in the Individuals of each Sex, just variety enough to permit and call forth the gentle restlessness and final union of chaste love and individual attachment, each seeking and finding the beloved *one* by the natural affinity of their Beings; when the dread Sovereign of the Universe was known only as the universal Parent, no Altar but the pure Heart, and Thanksgiving and grateful Love the sole Sacrifice.

The world, as described, is a world of wholeness in which each individual conscience instinctively, intuitively, acts at one with universal Spirit. It is a world in which body and mind are recon-ciled, a communal world characterized by harmony and fullness and joy. It is also an androgynous world in which the sexes are very like and yet individual enough to call forth the ongoing creative reconciliation which is the mark of unity. The loved ones are drawn together by "the natural affinity of their Beings," just as in a single individual, self-consciousness intuits wholeness.

This state of existence is called the "blest age of dignified Innocence," thereby differentiating it from the naive state of inno-cence we attribute to childhood and describing the mature inno-cence that preceded the Fall. This "blest age" becomes a story—a tale of Faery—that we tell ourselves and a state that we can now approach only with difficulty, using the language of Sight: "A condition of complete simplicity / (Costing not less than every-thing)" ("Little Gidding," 5).

In the fable, an honored elder relates how "in the warmth of the approaching midday as I was reposing in the vast cavern, out of which, from its northern portal, issues the river that winds through our vale, a voice powerful, yet not from its loudness, suddenly hailed me." Having been warned by the voice of a rain, soon to fall, which on contact would bring madness of spirit, the elder repeats the warning to the people and retires to the cavern to wait for the rain to be over. The people, however, losing their awe of the prophecy and not understanding what madness is, do not protect themselves. When the prophet emerges from the cave, he sees madness: lack of communal wholeness, the inability to distinguish between dreams and waking perceptions, and a distorted vision that calls all else madness.

> He stood gazing and motionless, when several of the race gathered around him, and enquired of each other, Who is this man? how strangely he looks! how wild!—a worthless idler! exclaims one: assuredly, a very dangerous madman! cries a second. In short, from words they proceeded to violence: till harrassed, endangered, solitary in a world of forms like his own, without sympathy, without object of love, he at length espied in some foss or furrow a quantity of the maddening water still unevaporated, and uttering the last words of reason, IT IS IN VAIN TO BE SANE IN A WORLD OF MADMEN, plunged and rolled himself in the liquid poison, and came out as mad and not more wretched than his neighbors and acquaintance.

The cavern, river, and warning voice of "The Fable of the Madning Rain" are very like the cavern, river, and ancestral voices of "Kubla Khan." The "ancestral voices prophesying war" in the poem precisely foretell the fallen world of the fable, a world which, maddened, has lost its healthy androgynous wholeness. The elder of the tale, in his solitary sanity, hears the others exclaim, "How strangely he looks! how wild! . . . assuredly, a very dangerous madman!" He is not unlike the Mariner who, on return from his voyage, is greeted as the devil by the crazed Pilot's boy and asked by the Hermit to say "what manner of man thou art." The elder, unable to endure being "without sympathy, without object of love," joins his friends and neighbors in madness, whereas the Mariner must pass "from land to land," only occasionally enjoying "a goodly company." Christabel, "o'er-mastered by the mighty spell," can neither retreat into madness nor tell her story.

She, like the elder and like the Mariner—who prays, "O let me be awake, my God! / Or let me sleep alway"—is perplexed about which is the dreaming and which the waking state. And in each instance, a central question emerges concerning what is madness and what sanity.

The "poems of mystery" are all poems of encounter with Spirit, an encounter made "mysterious," in the ordinary sense of the word, by the fact that it occurs within the context of the fallen world. In each case, the poet-narrator's own encounter—and that of characters within the narrative—is conveyed so as to allow an analogous encounter for the reader. There is an attempt to make secular words speak the Word of Love and Wholeness—to speak, in other words, the language of Sight—an attempt almost always finally and inevitably fragmentary or somehow inadequate because the words must be spoken in a fallen world. The poet's intimate involvement in the tale being told increases his awareness both of the reality of Spirit and the impossibility of ignoring the fact of the Fall. Still, underlying everything, the symbolic metaphors of the tales, which are the means of conveying Spirit and Love through symbolic story, affirm consubstantiality.

Symbolic metaphors, as well as references to a kind of fairy landscape, are present in a seemingly "unconscious" and almost inconsequential way in a number of Coleridge's early poems. In these, the "dark wood" of the mystery poems is as yet a lightsome fairy grove. Faery borders lie close to home, can be easily crossed and recrossed in the innocence of childhood and early adolescence:

> Quick, said the bird, find them, find them,
> Round the corner. Through the first gate,
> Into our first world, shall we follow
> The deception of the thrush? Into our first world.
> . . . .
> And the bird called, in response to
> The unheard music hidden in the shrubbery.
>
> ("Burnt Norton," 1)

Coleridge's "Songs of the Pixies" follows the bird and the "faery feet" of the pixies—"Fancy's children"—into the "elfin-haunted grove" (62, 3, 105) which is their home. An occasional poem written in 1793, "Songs of the Pixies" is an early poem that invites the reader-viewer to visit for a while the dwelling of beings who, because they are "invisibly small" (preface), are usually "veil'd from the grosser ken of mortal sight" (52). The preface to the poem, which appears in all editions, reads as follows:

> The Pixies, in the superstition of Devonshire, are a race of beings invisibly small, and harmless or friendly to man. At a small distance from a village in that country, half-way up a wood-covered hill, is an excavation called the Pixies' Parlour. The roots of old trees form its ceiling; and on its sides are innumerable cyphers, among which the author discovered his own cypher and those of his brothers, cut by the hand of their childhood. At the foot of the hill flows the river Otter.
>
> To this place the Author, during the summer months of the year 1793, conducted a party of young ladies; one of whom, of stature elegantly small, and of complexion colourless yet clear, was proclaimed the Faery Queen. On which occasion the following Irregular Ode was written.

The Pixies' Parlour is evidently a place of fascination for Coleridge. Part of the country tales of superstition and faery, the Parlour becomes the object of Coleridge's excursion with the young ladies, and at one level, of course, the excursion is simply a day's entertainment. At another level, however, the visit of mortals to the home of the pixies is an entry into—and an encounter with— Faery. That the poem is cast as an irregular ode should alert us to the fact that the intention of the poem may be more significant than the somewhat frivolous title would suggest, and the "slightness" of the poem should not veil from sight the almost offhand and intuitive presence of the later, more deliberately recurring, symbolic metaphors.

The pixies, whom Coleridge describes as "harmless or friendly to man," are androgynous inhabitants of the world of Faery who— as the collective "we" of the poem—sing their songs and "welcome" (4) the visitors to their cell. The cell of "Fancy's children" is a place of music and imagination, distinct and yet inseparable from the natural world itself:

> Here the wren of softest note
>   Builds its nest and warbles well;
> Here the blackbird strains his throat.   (5–7)

Music issues from the nests of birds hidden in the forest cell or cave,

> O'ercanopied by huge roots intertwin'd
> With wildest texture, blacken'd o'er with age:
> Round them their mantle green the ivies bind.   (27–29)

The place of Faery is a place of rich imaginative reconciliation. Its roof is a protective canopy of "huge roots," intertwined to form a "wildly" textured surface of intricate pattern. The roots are also textured with the innumerable cyphers—texts—of generation after generation of children and lovers who have intertwined their individual inscriptions into the living but ancient roots of text, the whole of which, though "blacken'd o'er with age," still reveals the wildest texture beneath the green ivy whose growth forms a mantle that at once protectively conceals and holds fast the inscriptions.

The place of Faery contains and fosters and makes manifest forms of creativity—music, words, poetry—and Coleridge the poet lays claim to his own welcomed visit to the cave or cell of Faery, "half-way up a wood-covered hill." When he was a child, Coleridge and his brothers had visited this place where Fancy's children live, cutting with "the hand of their childhood" their own cyphers among those other innumerable cyphers. Through the enduring cypher, something of the child remains forever in the Faery place, openly available to the adult Coleridge's sight and memory. The child is present, then, both in the adult visit of Coleridge with the young ladies and in the poem proper—just as the adult Coleridge is present in the poem as the pixies recall a visitor to their cell:

> Thither, while the murmuring throng
> Of wild-bees hum their drowsy song,
> By Indolence and Fancy brought,
> A youthful Bard, "unknown to Fame,"

> Wooes the Queen of Solemn Thought,
> And heaves the gentle misery of a sigh
>   Gazing with tearful eye,
>   As round our sandy grot appear
>   Many a rudely-sculptur'd name
>   To pensive Memory dear!   (33–42)

Surrounded by the hum and drowsy song of the "wild-bees," the young poet revisits the pixies' cell and returns in memory to his childhood visit. The place of Faery then becomes the source of imaginative activity as the pixies—agents of Faery—weave the tapestries of poetry and cover his soul with the "soothing witcheries" that give promise of the poet's future laurel:

> Weaving gay dreams of sunny-tinctur'd hue,
>   We glance before his view:
> O'er his hush'd soul our soothing witcheries shed
> And twine the future garland round his head.   (43–46)

The imaginative agency of Faery is further emphasized by the pixies' account of their activities. During the "blaze of day / When Noontide's fiery-tressed minion / Flashes the fervid ray" (22–24), the pixies retreat to their cave; but when evening comes, the "visionary hour" (53), the pixies—seeming to be merely part of the natural world—"tremble to the breeze" or guide the glances of lovers. The pixies admit that sometimes "we flash our faery feet in gamesome prank"; or play with the winds, "circling the Spirit of the Western Gale"; or play in the "quivering light" of the moon, "aye dancing to the cadence of the stream" (62, 64, 87–88).[3]

In this poem, Coleridge does not make the symbolic nature of imaginative play explicit, but the metaphors of Spirit are all present, interacting with and reinforcing one another. The poem itself, however, conveying as it does the songs of the pixies, is symbolic of the "future garland"; and as a symbolic poem, it becomes an occasion for the reader's encounter with Faery. The reader, along with the young ladies and the youthful Bard and his childhood self, is given an invitation of welcome to visit the Pixies' Parlour and hear the songs that are sung there.

Another poem written during the same time, "Lines: On an Autumnal Evening" (1793), and an earlier draft of it, "An Effusion at Evening" (August 1792), like "Songs of the Pixies," equates the activity of imagination with the province of Faery, while relating this activity to love. "Effusion" begins: "Imagination, Mistress of my Love! / Where shall mine Eye thy elfin haunt explore?" (1–2). The speaker, having conjectured that the "elfin haunts" are the "rich Cloud" or "other worlds" (3, 6), implores Imagination, "lovely Sorc'ress," to "aid the Poet's dream. / With faery wand O bid my Love arise" (14–15). The faery wand of Imagination then creates the image of the speaker's love for him. In the expanded "Lines," the "Spirits of Love" are asked to heed the "powerful spell" of her name and "hither wing your way, / Like far-off music, voyaging the breeze" (43–44). The Lover, then, if he had a "wizard's rod" (57), would build a "flower-entangled Arbor" (59) of myrtle trees, rather like the pixies' cell, which would shield his love from "Noontide's sultry beam" (60) and make a kind of natural paradise "where Love a crown of thornless Roses wears" (89). Again, in these poems, there is an almost unconscious metaphoric use of Faery and imagination, music and the breeze, to create Love.

Two years later, when Coleridge writes "The Eolian Harp" (1795), all the metaphors of Spirit are very consciously present as metaphors for one another and as symbolic metaphors of Spirit; the youthful Bard is beginning to wear the promised "future garland." Again, as in earlier poems, the faery time is evening, the time when "twilight Elfins . . . voyage on gentle gales from Fairy-Land" to make a "soft floating witchery of sound" (20–22). The cell of the pixies, "half-way up a wood-covered hill," is re-created in the poet's mind as he lies "on the midway slope / Of yonder hill" (34–35). The "rich snows" that "blossom on the Myrtle-trees" ("Lines" 40) to form a "flower-entangled Arbor" reappear in the "cot o'ergrown / With white-flower'd Jasmin, and the broad-leav'd Myrtle," but now they are explicitly "meet emblems . . . of Innocence and Love" (3–5).

The center of "The Eolian Harp"—structurally, thematically,

and imaginatively—is in lines 12–48. Here, the music created by the breeze playing across the lute is a metaphor for the imaginative play that dances behind the poet's "half-clos'd eye-lids" (35) and a metaphor for the creative polarity of Life itself:

O! the one Life within us and abroad,
Which meets all motion and becomes its soul,
A light in sound, a sound-like power in light.   (26–28)

But the music and the poet's imaginative creation—both the activity of imagination and the resulting poem—and the synesthetic light and sound of the one Life activated by the breeze are metaphors for Faery, too:

                                        And now, its strings
Boldlier swept, the long sequacious notes
Over delicious surges sink and rise,
Such a soft floating witchery of sound
As twilight Elfins make, when they at eve
Voyage on gentle gales from Fairy-Land,
Where Melodies round honey-dropping flowers,
Footless and wild, like birds of Paradise,
Nor pause, nor perch, hovering on untam'd wing!   (17–25)

The "desultory breeze" (14) that caresses the lute is also one of the "gentle gales from Fairy-land" which carry the twilight Elfins and the Melodies like birds of Paradise and, always hovering, are always in motion, causing a "soft floating witchery of sound" that is somehow in Fairy-land and in the music of the lute and in the music of the poem. The poem at this point becomes a symbolic tale of Faery, participating in and simultaneously showing forth (and allowing that same experience for the reader) the Reality of Spirit, the one Life. This tale of Faery is also, both metaphorically and symbolically, a tale of Love. At one level, the entire conversation poem is structured as a love story, told by the poet-lover to his wife, "my Love" (34), and their love is analogous to and symbolic of the Love that is God. Additionally, however, within the tale of Faery and existing at the center of the poem, there is a love story embedded as a simile for the breeze/lute/music/faery/imagination/one Life metaphor. The lute, lying "length-ways in the clasp-ing casement," is caressed by the breeze as the maid, lying in the clasp of her lover, is caressed by him. And as the "delicious surges" of the melodies borne from Fairy-land "sink and rise" and both instruments are "boldlier swept," the poet participates in the mu-sic of love always being created as the one Life: "Methinks, it should have been impossible / Not to love all things in a world so fill'd" (30–31). The imaginative summation of the symbolic en-counter provided by the tale of Faery is explicit:

> And what if all of animated nature
> Be but organic Harps diversely fram'd,
> That tremble into thought, as o'er them sweeps
> Plastic and vast, one intellectual breeze,
> At once the Soul of each, and God of all? (44–48)

The question, given the structure of the poem and the intuitive Reason of the symbolic encounter, should merely be a rhetorical one. Music and imagination and Faery and love are symbolic metaphors of Spirit/Love. It is the failure to complete the "logic" of self-knowledge and encounter which makes the actual concluding lines of "The Eolian Harp" disappointing and false.[4] The "Incom-prehensible" (59)—that is, Love—cannot be comprehended, but it *can* be encountered. And it *has* been encountered in the course of the poem, by the poet and by the reader.

"Hymn before Sunrise, in the Vale of Chamouni," first pub-lished 11 September 1802 in the *Morning Post*, has received critical attention primarily because of its unacknowledged indebtedness to sources other than the poet's imagination. A good portion of Coleridge's introductory note to the poem as well as some of the lines are direct or loose translations of a much shorter work by Friederica Brun, a Danish-German poet.[5] Leaving the details of the plagiarism and speculation about its import aside for the moment, I want to focus on several additions Coleridge makes to the intro-ductory note and the way in which he develops Brun's poem to show how the sight of Mont Blanc becomes an occasion of sym-bolic encounter for the poem's speaker. Coleridge's introductory note reads as follows:

Chamouni is one of the highest mountain valleys of the Barony of Faucigny in the Savoy Alps; and exhibits a kind of fairy world, in which the wildest appearances (I had almost said horrors) of Nature alternate with the softest and most beautiful. The chain of Mont Blanc is its boundary; and besides the Arve it is filled with sounds from the Arveiron, which rushes from the melted glaciers, like a giant, mad with joy, from a dungeon, and forms other torrents of snow-water, having their rise in the glaciers which slope down into the valley. The beautiful *Gentiana major*, or greater gentian, with blossoms of the brightest blue, grows in large companies a few steps from the never-melted ice of the glaciers. I thought it an affecting emblem of the boldness of human hope, venturing near, and, as it were, leaning over the brink of the grave. Indeed, the whole vale, its every light, its every sound, must needs impress every mind not utterly callous with the thought—Who *would* be, who *could* be an Atheist in this valley of wonders!

The parts of the note that belong entirely to Coleridge are the phrases "exhibits a kind of fairy world," "(I had almost said horrors)," and "like a giant, mad with joy, from a dungeon," and the final assertion that such a scene "needs must impress every mind not utterly callous with the thought—Who *would* be, who *could* be an Atheist in this valley of wonders!" Coleridge transforms Brun's description of Chamouni into an awe-inspiring "valley of wonders" in the Land of Faery, a "kind of fairy world" of reconciled opposites, filled with enormous companies of blue blossoms, blooming next to "never-melted ice," and rivers loud with melted glaciers and powerful as giants, "mad with joy," rushing from their dungeons. The mountain itself becomes a wild tale of Faery, reconciling the grave with hope, symbolic of God, and bringing about the speaker's encounter with the Invisible. The narrator describes how he gazed upon the mountain

> Till thou, still present to the bodily sense,
> Didst vanish from my thought: entranced in prayer
> I worshipped the Invisible alone.
>
> Yet, like some sweet beguiling melody,
> So sweet, we know not we are listening to it,
> Thou, the meanwhile, wast blending with my Thought,
> Yea, with my Life and Life's own secret joy:
> Till the dilating Soul, enrapt, transfused,

Into the mighty vision passing—there
As in her natural form, swelled vast to Heaven.　　　(14–23)

The music metaphorically blends the mountain with the poet's thought, his "Life and Life's own secret joy," till his Soul swells to Heaven. The poet's recognition of the metaphoric relation of symbols is explicit as he tells his heart to "awake" and join in the "voice of sweet song." The resulting poem is a hymn of praise to God for the glorious way in which the Chamouni itself sings the praises of God. Asking,

Who made you glorious as the Gates of Heaven
Beneath the keen full moon? Who bade the sun
Clothe you with rainbows? Who, with living flowers
Of loveliest blue, spread garlands at your feet?　　　(54–57)

the speaker answers with resounding affirmation:

GOD! let the torrents, like a shout of nations,
Answer! and let the ice-plains echo, GOD!
GOD! sing ye meadow-streams with gladsome voice!
Ye pine-groves, with your soft and soul-like sounds!
And they too have a voice, yon piles of snow,
And in their perilous fall shall thunder, GOD!　　　(58–63)

As the Mount "utter[s] forth God, and fill[s] the hills with praise" (69), the consubstantial universe is clearly articulated, and the Mount—and the poem—are seen to be "dread ambassador[s] from Earth to Heaven" (82).

The most articulate manifestation or symbol of the consubstantial Reality of Love—"the Great Invisible (by symbols only seen)"—is Christ, "Him whose life was Love" (*RM* 9–10, 29). Ambassador from Heaven to Earth, as well as "ambassador from Earth to Heaven," his life and his death were instances of Love. "Religious Musings," another of Coleridge's hymns to Love, was written on Christmas Eve, 1794. It begins with the poet joining in vision the heavenly multitude that sang at the birth of Christ. The Christmas story is a symbolic story, and as worked out in both "Religious Musings" and "Destiny of Nations: A Vision"—a closely related poem written a short time later, which Carl Woodring calls a "romantico-politico-religious patchwork" (*Politics* 169)—this symbolic story of Love serves two important theoretical functions. First, it provides the underpinning for Coleridge's view of the history of society and the history of the human soul. And second, along with the scriptural tradition of the parable as a teaching device, it eventuates in a theory of imaginative literature in which secular story is seen to function symbolically to initiate an understanding of sacred story. Taken together, "Religious Musings" and "Destiny of Nations" provide a rationale for Coleridge's symbolic use of tales of Faery.

Both poems, as works of political prophecy, are replete with scriptural reference and allusion, primarily to the book of Revelation, as might be expected. However, it is I Corinthians 13.9–13 that provides the context for Coleridge's explanatory story of the journey of the Soul and for the role that symbolic tales play in that journey. Symbolic stories, which are explicitly paralleled to tales of Faery in "Destiny of Nations," teach the Soul and become instances of symbolic encounter. The traditionally seminal I Corinthians passage is appropriate scripture for a poem concerned with the way in which the personhood of Christ is related to the individual mind and soul and to the state of society:

> For we know in part, and we prophesy in part. But when that which is perfect is come, then that which is in part shall be done away. When I was a child, I spake as a child, I understood as a child, I thought as a child: but when I became a man, I put away childish things. For now we see through a glass, darkly; but then face to face: now I know in part; but then shall I know even as also I am known. And now abideth faith, hope, charity, these three; but the greatest of these is charity.

Several parallel or analogous movements are set up in the biblical passage. First is the movement from childhood to maturity, a movement characterized by a change in perception in which partial perception yields to perception that encompasses the whole. To understand only partially, as the child inevitably does, is to understand imperfectly. That which is perfect is the personhood of Christ, and "when that which is perfect is come, then that which is in part shall be done away." When the individual perceives the wholeness of the perfect One, he or she puts away childish partiality. Using images of light and dark to denote degrees of perception and imperception, and the image of the glass which, though it can be seen through, still separates, the Corinthians passage then describes the analogous movement from this mortal life to the one of spirit. In the afterlife, instead of dark, partial understanding, we will have full and perfect knowledge, knowledge that is "face to face" and reciprocal: "Now I know in part; but then shall I know even as also I am known."

In describing the person of Christ and the process of the human soul's response to Christ, the first forty-five lines of "Religious Musings" reiterate the Corinthians passage. God, the "Great Invisible," is seen "by symbols only" (9–10): that is, through a glass. One of these symbols is nature:

> Fair the vernal mead,
> Fair the high grove, the sea, the sun, the stars;
> True impress each of their creating Sire!　　　　　(14–16)

Though the meads and groves and sun and stars of nature have the clear impress of the Creator, nothing has ever "imaged the supreme beauty . . . with such majesty of portraiture" as the "meek Saviour," Christ (20–22). Christ is Love; Christ is Light; Christ and the Father are One. "Diviner light" (26) filled the heavens at Christ's birth, asserts the poem, yet Christ was "more bright than all the Angel-blaze" (7). Coleridge concludes that though the Godhead is One, the lack of understanding and dark idolatry of the children of the human race and "thought-benighted Sceptic[s]" (30) have split the wholeness of the Godhead into parts so that now "we know in part." What is necessary, then, is a movement of Soul, a movement from childhood to maturity, from partiality to wholeness, from separation to an awareness of the individual's identity with the "perfect Love" (39) that is God. What is the process whereby this movement occurs?

The process, as Coleridge describes it in the poem, moves one through a progression of perceptive-intuitive-feeling states of being: that is, into progressive self-knowledge. Initially, the Soul is portrayed as "drowsy." It has been charmed into an unnatural, inactive state, although its nature is, and always has been, noble. The Soul must be awakened so that it will, through self-knowledge, remember what it is. Fear, asserts Coleridge, serves as the awakener:

> And first by Fear uncharmed the drowséd Soul.
> Till of its nobler nature it 'gan feel
> Dim recollections; and thence soared to Hope,
> Strong to believe whate'er of mystic good
> The Eternal dooms for His immortal sons.   (34–38)

Fear soars to Hope. Then the Soul, "From Hope and firmer Faith to perfect Love / [is] Attracted and absorbed" (39–40). There is a progression from Fear to Hope to Faith to the perfect Love that is God. Dim and partial recollection yields to total absorption in the light of God. Separation gives way to Identity, as the Soul completes its journey:

>   and centered there
> God only to behold, and know, and feel,
> Till by exclusive consciousness of God
> All self-annihilated it shall make
> God its Identity: God all in all!
> We and our Father one!   (40–45)

At the end of the journey, the Soul, consubstantial with God, is aware only of its oneness with the Father.

The next section of the poem repeats the progression from Fear to Hope to Faith to "strong . . . love" (57) as Coleridge explains that the "elect of Heaven" (46)

>   patiently ascend
> Treading beneath their feet all visible things
> As steps, that upward to their Father's throne
> Lead gradual.   (50–53)

Fear, "sure-refug'd" in Hope, "hears his hot pursuing fiends / Yell at vain distance" (70–71). "The Elect [Soul], regenerate through faith" (88), sees Love "face to face" and is one with it:

There is one Mind, one omnipresent Mind,
Omnific. His most holy name is Love.
Truth of subliming import! with the which
Who feeds and saturates his constant soul,
He from his small particular orbit flies
With blest outstarting! From himself he flies,
Stands in the sun, and with no partial gaze
Views all creation; and he loves it all,
And blesses it, and calls it very good!
This is indeed to dwell with the Most High!   (105–14)

The Elect Soul views creation "with no partial gaze," and "he loves it all." Because it is one with God, the Soul also can pronounce the blessing of the Creator on the creation and thus "calls it very good."

The journey completed, the Soul dwells with the Most High: "And now abideth faith, hope, and charity, these three; but the greatest of these is charity." Those who abide with Love know themselves to be "parts and proportions of the wondrous whole" (128). This awareness of wholeness also makes the individual conscious of being at one with other human souls, since God, "diffused through all . . . doth make all one whole" (131). Having risked enchantment, there is no longer any "fear of possession, / Of belonging to one another, or to others, or to God" ("East Coker," 2). In contrast, the person who still speaks and understands and thinks as a child is "toy-bewitched" (146) and "disherited of soul" (147):

A sordid solitary thing,
Mid countless brethren with a lonely heart
Through courts and cities the smooth savage roams
Feeling himself, his own low self the whole;
When he by sacred sympathy might make
The whole one Self! Self, that no alien knows!
Self, far diffused as Fancy's wing can travel!
Self, spreading still! Oblivious of its own,
Yet all of all possessing!   (149–57)

The Soul that sees "in part" feels isolated, cut off from other souls and from God, even in the midst of "countless brethren." This unhappy, "sordid solitary thing" is always roaming, wandering the earth, never at home, since the true home of the Soul is in the dwelling of the Most High.

"The Destiny of Nations: A Vision" takes up the same theme of the progression of the human Soul. The narrator of "Religious Musings" explains that the savage, in the childhood of the race, is lonely and alien. Gradually, however, Imagination nurses the Soul "to forms of beauty, and by sensual wants / Unsensualize[s] the mind," until eventually the activity of imagination becomes more pleasurable than the "grossness of the end" (209–11), and the Soul breathes the "empyreal air / of Love, omnific, omnipresent Love" (414–15). Thus, the secular eventuates in the sacred. But "The Destiny of Nations," more explicitly than "Religious Musings," delineates the role of Imagination and the products of that Imagination—such as legends and stories—in the progress of the Soul. In "Destiny," the glass through which we can see only darkly as we see in part becomes a veil between us and the Sun of Reality and Infinite Love. "Man's free and stirring spirit" is once again seen to lie "entranced," in need of a "soliciting spell" (DN 11–12) that will free it

> to view
> Through meaner powers and secondary things
> Effulgent, as through clouds that veil his blaze.
> For all that meets the bodily sense I deem
> Symbolical, one mighty alphabet
> For infant minds; and we in this low world
> Placed with our backs to bright Reality,
> That we may learn with young unwounded ken
> The substance from its shadow. Infinite Love,
> Whose latence is the plenitude of All,
> Thou with retracted beams, and self-eclipse
> Veiling, revealest thine eternal Sun.   (15–26)

The soul in the fallen world is under a false enchantment so that it "lies entranced," mistakenly thinking itself most free when it has chained "down the wingéd thought" (29). The music in praise of Spirit frees the "stirring spirit" so that it has "unfettered

85

use / Of all the powers which God for use had given." The song of praise, which is actually the entire poem itself, will free the human spirit to use its freedom to view God "through meaner powers and secondary things / Effulgent"—that is, symbolically. That which veils also reveals symbolically, and Coleridge gives examples of the kinds of "soliciting spells" that bring to life the ability of people living in darkness to see the Reality of the Light of Love behind the veil, "spells" that are actually instances of encounter with Faery/Spirit.

For his examples, Coleridge uses the Laplander who, literally, lives in "stern and solitary Night" (67). However, as Coleridge tells the tale, the Laplander watching the lights of the Aurora Borealis imagines that he "himself those happy spirits shall join / Who there in floating robes of rosy light / Dance sportively" (78–80). The Laplander's imagination peoples the light with spirits who dance in the light; then, in imagination, his spirit joins theirs. The human spirit no longer need be asleep or alone; instead, it can image itself—put itself into the story—as a being who is active and joyous and at one with invisible spirits which, nonetheless, it still holds in fearful awe:

> For Fancy is the power
> That first unsensualises the dark mind,
> Giving it new delights; and bids it swell
> With wild activity; and peopling air,
> By obscure fears of Beings invisible,
> Emancipates it from the grosser thrall
> Of the present impulse, teaching Self-control,
> Till Superstition with unconscious hand
> Seat Reason on her throne.   (80–88)

Because the dark mind, through the power of Fancy, can imagine itself participating in a sportive dance with spirits robed in rosy light, it can begin the movement from fearful Superstition to Reason.

Coleridge then describes a "polar ancient," a storyteller who "thrills his uncouth throng" with "legends terrible" (90–91). These are frightening, terrifying stories of "pitying Spirits that make their moan / O'er slaughtered infants" or stories of a "Giant Bird"

> of whose rushing wings the noise
> Is Tempest, when the unutterable Shape
> Speeds from the mother of Death, and utters once
> That shriek, which never murderer heard, and lived.   (94–97)

These terrible, terrifying legends do not frighten for the Soul's abasement, however; rather, the legends are "impressed" with "permitted power" (89); that is, they serve to help the Soul begin the journey toward God. The story of the Giant Bird, which contains many of the elements of the Ancient Mariner's story, is a good example. Like the giant Albatross and the tyrannous and strong STORM-BLAST, who strikes with "his o'ertaking wings" and chases the ship with "yell and blow" (Rime 43, 46) for the ultimate purpose of the Mariner's encounter with Spirit, this Giant Bird, an "unutterable Shape," is a form of the dove of God which the Souls of the primitive Laplanders can comprehend and hear—though the hearing is frightening even unto death for those who are bringers-of-death rather than life to the world. As the ancient storyteller recounts this tale of Faery, the listeners hear for themselves the shriek of the Giant Bird of unutterable Shape and, like the Wedding-Guest, increase in self-knowledge.

Finally, there is the story of the Greenland Wizard (98–121), whose spirit "in strange trance" leaves his body surrounded in his "dark tent within a cow'ring group" of Laplanders to journey the floor of the ocean to the "uttermost cave" of the "Fury Form" that controls the Elements of Nature. "Arm'd with Torngarsuck's power, the Spirit of Good," the Wizard's spirit forces the Fury Form to release the fish that provide food for the Laplanders. That accomplished, the Wizard's spirit returns "thence thro' the realm of Souls, / Where live the Innocent." This, even more explicitly than the other tales, is the story of the Soul's encounter with Spirit, and, once again, the experience and language of the "Rime" are already present as the Wizard's spirit "returns with far-heard pant, hotly pursued / By the fierce Warders of the Sea . . . to repossess / His fleshly mansion." Having been "cast into a trance; for the angelic power causeth the vessel to drive northward faster than human life could endure," the Mariner awakens

> Like one, that on a lonesome road
> Doth walk in fear and dread,
> And having once turned round walks on,
> And turns no more his head;
> Because he knows, a frightful fiend
> Doth close behind him tread. (Rime 446–51)

The Soul's journey can be frightening—as tales of Faery sometimes are—but the journey of encounter with Spirit and the symbolic story of that journey is of ultimate significance, both for the individual and for humankind as a whole. Because symbolic stories have the power to call forth the imaginative participation of the listener, these fearful tales can bring the children of the world out of darkness. Coleridge calls these stories of the imagination:

> Wild phantasies! yet wise,
> On the victorious goodness of high God
> Teaching reliance, and medicinal hope,
> Till from Bethabra northward, heavenly Truth
> With gradual steps, winning her difficult way,
> Transfer their rude Faith perfected and pure. (DN 121–26)

The awe with which the fearful Soul hears "wild phantasies" teaches Hope, which is next transferred to a Faith in the heavenly Truth of Love.

Thus, secular stories, "wild phantasies," teach sacred story. This is essentially what Coleridge says in his 1798 letter to Poole (quoted earlier): "Should children be permitted to read Romances, & Relations of Giants & Magicians, & Genii?—I know all that has been said against it; but I have formed my faith in the affirmative.—I know no other way of giving the mind a love of 'the Great,' & 'the Whole.'—Those who have been led to the same truths step by step thro' the constant testimony of their senses, seem to me to want a sense which I possess—They contemplate nothing but *parts*—and all *parts* are necessarily little—and the Universe to them is but a mass of *little things*" (CL 1: 210). But the

Universe is not a "mass of *little things*"; it is, rather, vast and whole, at One in God. The value of imaginative stories, "wild phantasies" of giants and magicians and Giant Birds, is that they teach children the essential Unity and Wholeness of the Universe; they teach children, of whatever age, not to see "in part."

Coleridge's view of story as a way to teach "children" the Reality of Spirit or Love is similar to his opinion about miracles: "The Bible, concerned originally with the childhood of the race, spoke the language of the senses, and hence miracles play a prominent part in its furtherance of the spiritual education of mankind" (*SM* 10 n.3).[6] Additionally, the function of secular story as a means of teaching sacred story is validated by the scriptural tradition of parables:

> The same day went Jesus out of the house, and sat by the sea side. And great multitudes were gathered together unto him, so that he went into a ship, and sat; and the whole multitude stood on the shore. And he spake many things unto them in parables. . . . And the disciples came, and said unto him, why speakest thou unto them in parables? He answered and said unto them, Because it is given unto you to know the mysteries of the kingdom of heaven, but to them it is not given. . . . Therefore speak I to them in parables: because they seeing see not; and hearing they hear not, neither do they understand. (Matthew 13.1–3, 10–11, 13)

Parables—secular stories—teach the "mysteries of the kingdom of heaven" to those who cannot yet see or hear, to those who are still children in their understanding. Parables and tales of faery are clearly different kinds of secular stories; nonetheless, through appealing and seemingly uncomplicated narratives, both provide easy access to profound truths. Anya Taylor's commentary is apt: "The language of the Bible—in parables, for example—fuses the individual in the universal, the sense in the spirit and works to heal the dissociations of contemporary thinking. Without a language that incorporates spiritual realities, ways of thinking also gape apart. . . . Mere understanding is not enough; nor is the spiritual life, without a personal and individual enactment of it" (*Defense* 190). Secular stories of the imagination teach the truth of sacred story; they free the entranced and drowsy Soul to know that

God is Love and that we are one with God in Christ. There is no separation; there is nothing merely partial: "When that which is perfect is come, then that which is in part shall be done away."

The story of the "warrior-maid of France" (138), which completes "Destiny of Nations," is the story of one who is already free in soul, one who grows up "urged by the indwelling angel-guide" (186) to free the spirits of others. The primary symbol of Freedom in this poem—the Maid who goes forth—is an androgynous character, combining in both appearance and action stalwart "masculinity" and gentle "femininity":

> The Virgin's form,
> Active and tall, nor Sloth nor Luxury
> Had shrunk or paled. Her front sublime and broad,
> Her flexile eye-brows wildly haired and low,
> And her full eye, now bright, now unillumed,
> Spake more than Woman's thought; and all her face
> Was moulded to such features as declared
> That Pity there had oft and strongly worked,
> And sometimes Indignation. Bold her mien,
> And like a haughty huntress of the woods
> She moved: yet sure she was a gentle maid!
> And in each motion her most innocent soul
> Beamed forth so brightly, that who saw would say
> Guilt was a thing impossible in her!   (162–75)

She is tall, strong and muscular, active and able, yet still a virginal "gentle maid" whom the "pollutions of the Dead" (178) have not touched. This androgynous, innocent maid, her unfettered spirit shining with the Sun's own light, symbolizes Freedom, and her actions and her story occasion freedom for others. Both her androgynous description and the poem's "annunciation" scene single her out as a character in a symbolic story:

> Thus as she toiled in troublous ecstacy,
> A horror of great darkness wrapt her round,
> And a voice uttered forth unearthly tones,
> Calming her soul,—"O Thou of the Most High
> Chosen, whom all the perfected in Heaven
> Behold expectant—"   (272–77)

As she calls out to the "Spirits of God," "instantly faint melody /
Melts on her ear" (326, 328–29), and she hears the music heard in
the "holy dream[s]" of Hermits which "fortell and solace death"
(331–32). As a symbol of Love—"Maiden beloved, and Delegate of
Heaven" (451)—her death will be "lovely" in the same way that
"lovely was the death / Of Him whose life was Love" (RM
28–29).

In "Kubla Khan," the faery bower of imagination—briefly
described in "Song of the Pixies" and "The Night-Scene" and "The
Three Graves"—is enlarged to Xanadu, and its detailed description is the ostensible subject matter of more than half the poem.
The world of Xanadu is the world of Faery, its creation by Kubla
symbolic of the creation of nature by the I AM. "Kubla Khan" in its
entirety has been taken to be a representation of the creative
imagination itself, and thus the various creators and creations
that make up the poem have been discussed extensively, as has its
multiple "reconciliation of opposites."[7] "Kubla Khan"—whatever
else one may want to say about it—is a symbolic instance of
symbolic encounter. The music of the poetry reinforces and is
reinforced by the natural description of "sinuous rills" and the
"mazy motion" of the river and the "mingled measure" (KK 8, 25,
33) heard beneath the pleasure dome. The poem is built to music. I
want to focus here on Coleridge's use of the symbolic metaphors of
androgyny and faery—interwoven with those of nature, music,
and imagination—to present incipient tales of Faery that simultaneously validate the consubstantial nature of the world and acknowledge the world's present fallenness. I also want to explore
the relationship of the poet to this symbolic encounter and the
analogous relationship of the reader.

At one level, "Kubla Khan" can be seen as promising a series of
stories that never get told. The promises remain to haunt the
mind, but the stories are actually told only in the reader's imagination. Even without *Purchas's Pilgrimage*, we would expect an
oriental tale from a man who, with a mixture of fear and delight,
read and reread *The Arabian Nights* in his childhood. And "Kubla
Khan" begins as an introduction to just such a tale:

On the Borders of Faery

> In Xanadu did Kubla Khan
> A stately pleasure-dome decree:
> Where Alph, the sacred river, ran
> Through caverns measureless to man
> Down to a sunless sea.   (1–5)

All the ingredients for a tale of enchantment, a tale of Faery, are present: a faraway place, a faraway time, a powerful ruler who creates a pleasure-dome, a sacred river, and caverns so extensive as to be measureless. Stories of the imagination must surely lie hidden in these underground caverns, waiting only the word of the storyteller to emerge and, in their turn, enchant.

But they are stories only hinted at and never told. Instead, the narrator moves to a description of the area surrounding the pleasure-dome and then, as though choosing one part of that larger description for magnification, he shows us the "deep romantic chasm" (12) out of which the "mighty fountain" (19), the source of the river, is forced. In the midst of this description of the creative impulse, a second story possibility is created:

> A savage place! as holy and enchanted
> As e'er beneath a waning moon was haunted
> By woman wailing for her demon-lover!   (14–16)

This time, the story is lost in a simile, tied to the poem only by thin threads of grammar and evocations of feeling. The woman stands in waning moonlight, waiting and abandoned, haunting—through her presence and her wail of grief—the place where she waits. By grammatical extension, the romantic chasm is seen to be as savage, holy, and enchanted—as imbued with the desire for fulfillment— as the woman wailing for her demon-lover. Who is she? What sort of love can there be between the woman and the demon? Why has he left? Again, the elements of a tale of Faery are present, but the story exists "off the text" and in the reader's imagination. The demon-lover will not return in the poem, and the woman will always yearn for love's completion, her situation reminiscent of that of the Dark Ladié, though even more desolate.

The completion that does exist in the poem occurs with the

birth of the river. That birth completes the descriptive journey as the narrator's description of the path of the sacred river returns the poem and the reader to the caverns and pleasure-dome, to Kubla Khan—and to the promise of another story: "And 'mid this tumult Kubla heard from far / Ancestral voices prophesying war!" (29–30). Whose are these ancestral voices? Whence in the past comes knowledge of the future? Who will wage the war and for what purpose? Will Xanadu be destroyed? Are the voices, heard in the tumult in the midst of the Khan's creation, another creation of his own imagination? The story is told only by inference.

The narrator's description of Xanadu, then, embeds at least three distinct stories left untold. But just as surely, these stories also bind together the natural description and are analogous in several ways to the "story" of the river. The river moves from birth through a present to death; Kubla's caverns are source and endpoint; the wailing woman waits forever. Beginning and ending go on forever. There are three sets of "characters" in the stories: Kubla, the woman and her demon-lover, and the ancestral voices. All are characters of fairy tale. Taken both separately and together, they form a triad of creative wholeness. As a creator, a "maker," Kubla Khan necessarily takes on aspects of both the feminine and the masculine. The woman and her lover form a female-male pair, one that crosses ordinary bounds, since the lover is also demon and since the woman has moved outside human boundaries in her love and now haunts the source of the mighty fountain as surely as the demon still haunts her. The ancestral voices are neither male nor female, yet both. Like Kubla, the woman and the ancestral voices create, and each uses words in the making. Kubla "decrees" a pleasure-dome and the rest of Xanadu, a perfect paradise of the imagination. The ancestral voices "prophesy," speak the words that make a prophecy. The wail of the woman is more formless, made up not of orderly words but of a keening that nonetheless carries its own emotional message in sound.

Speaking the language of Sight, Kubla decrees an earthly paradise that is symbolic of—manifests and participates in—the

Wholeness of Spirit. Xanadu is an analogue of the prelapsarian Garden. But the ancestral voices, in their prophecy of loss of wholeness, echo the Fall that has already occurred. Thus, from the tumult of the sacred waters of creation issues the inevitability of destruction. The wailing woman, present and not present in the poem, embodies the loss of wholeness. Once there had been a union of masculine and feminine, human and nonhuman—a savage, holy, enchanted union—existent, no doubt, in the very place the woman now haunts, her wail anticipating the wails of those in the aftermath of the war prophesied by the ancestral voices: the articulate language of Sight and creation blurred into inarticulate keening fall.

Out of the savage, holy, and enchanted romantic chasm, is born the river:

> And from this chasm, with ceaseless turmoil seething,
> As if this earth in fast thick pants were breathing,
> A mighty fountain momently was forced:
> Amid whose swift half-intermitted burst
> Huge fragments vaulted like rebounding hail,
> Or chaffy grain beneath the thresher's flail:
> And 'mid these dancing rocks at once and ever
> It flung up momently the sacred river.   (17–24)

The creation of the river is symbolic of the creative energy of God, and it is analogous to Kubla's own creation. However, whereas Kubla creates in a fallen world, the fountain within the chasm always and eternally speaks forth God the Creator. Though the chasm itself is like the place haunted by the wailing woman, its savagery is eternally reconciled with holiness, an enchanted place indeed. Similarly, the fragments of rock, thrown up like "rebounding hail" or "chaffy grain" in the turmoil of the fountain, are reconciled into dance, as though to a music heard only by symbolic nature or the inner ear of the poet: the "sacred river" is "flung up," "at once and ever," " 'mid these dancing rocks." Kubla hears ancestral voices in the "tumult" as the river sinks into the caverns; but the river itself, in cycle after unending cycle, will be reborn from the chasm, "with ceaseless turmoil seething."

This ongoing creative energy, symbolic of Spirit, is presented in the androgynous metaphors appropriate to that Spirit. In the description of the birth of the fountain, feminine and masculine images of engendering and procreation are so intertwined that each—while individually recognizable—is inextricably unified with the other. The feminine womb of earth pants in childbirth, successfully forcing the sacred fountain/child into the world. But the "fast thick pants" are also those of sexual climax as the masculine (fountain) ejaculates in "swift half-intermitted burst." Masculine and feminine, the seed sown and the river born—creation accomplished in ceaseless, seething turmoil: symbolic nature. This "story," unlike the fragmentary hints of the tales embedded in it, is complete.

> At the still point of the turning world. Neither flesh nor
>   fleshless;
> Neither from nor towards; at the still point, there the dance is,
> But neither arrest nor movement. And do not call it fixity,
> Where past and future are gathered. Neither movement from
>   nor towards,
> Neither ascent nor decline. Except for the point, the still point
> There would be no dance, and there is only the dance.
>
>   ("Burnt Norton," 2)

And where is the poet in relation to creative symbolic nature or to Kubla's paradise, his pleasure-dome filled with music like the music nature dances to? Whichever critical attitude one chooses to assume toward the Preface to "Kubla Khan," still it remains as Coleridge's commentary on the creation of the poem and may serve, like others among his prefaces, as part of the entire composition. Reading the story of Kubla Khan in *Purchas's Pilgrimage*, Coleridge falls asleep and dreams: "The Author continued for about three hours in a profound sleep, at least of the external senses, during which time he has the most vivid confidence, that he could not have composed less than from two to three hundred lines; if that indeed can be called composition in which all the images rose up before him as *things*, with a parallel production of the correspondent expressions, without any sensation or consciousness of effort." In the dream, the poet encounters the images of Purchas's account as "*things*"; that is, they assume concrete reality and integrity. The description of Xanadu which existed as words in a book are now seen as images that are real things in Coleridge's dream, images that coalesce symbolically.

Further, there is a fusion of the thing itself with the words for the thing. The expressions are "correspondent" with each other, and they rise up in the mind of the poet as though coming out of his own "cavern" of imagination. Purchas's description of Xanadu functions as a symbolic text for the poet's encounter with it in dream. Small wonder he calls it a vision. The vision-encounter having been interrupted, or fragmented, by the "person on business from Porlock," Coleridge attempts to write the vision: "On his return to his room, [he] found, to his no small surprise and mortification, that though he still retained some vague and dim recollection of the general purport of the vision, yet, with the exception of some eight or ten scattered lines and images, all the rest had passed away like the images on the surface of a stream into which a stone has been cast, but, alas! without the after restoration of the latter! . . . Yet from the still surviving recollections in his mind, the Author has frequently purposed to finish for himself what had been originally, as it were, given to him." The sense of the vision as having been "given" to him is very strong, as is the inadequacy of words to convey the language of Sight. The sacred Word is whole, available, given, in encounter or vision, but only "seen in part" in the fallen world outside the vision.[8]

"Kubla Khan" is not fragmentary in its structure, as it exists on the page; rather, it is a fragment of the poet's vision, of his self-knowledge, of his intuitive oneness with Wholeness. The desire is to remake the encounter of the symbolic imagination into symbolic poem. The first thirty-six lines are an attempt to do just that, and we as readers encounter "Kubla Khan" as symbolic poem in much the same way that Coleridge encountered Purchas's account of Kubla's Xanadu. Our vision does not occur within a dream, but the effect of the music of "Kubla Khan" is to put us for the moment into some "Other World" in which we see and hear and know intensely, an Other World in which image and word are one and known intuitively. Coleridge "gives" us a tale of Faery. The tale exists in the imaginative space of our own creation, set in motion by the encounter with Coleridge's symbolic poem. In this first section, Coleridge speaks to us simply as a speaking voice, not intruding on our encounter, though we sense a simultaneous sharing of the symbolic encounter: that is, Coleridge's own participation as audience, both in the indrawn breath of "But oh!" (12) and in the emotional intensity that pervades the lines.

The first-person narrator of the last section of the poem comes as something of a surprise, then. In effect, the speaker is reclaiming the experience for himself, and in lines 37–45 the first-person pronouns "I" and "me" are used five times. The speaker-Coleridge emerges because of his awareness that the preceding poem *is* but a fragment. It is symbolic, and it is the occasion for symbolic encounter—for the reader and the poet—but the poem, like Kubla Khan's creation, is timebound. Through it, we enter for a while the Other World of unity and creation and Spirit and Love, but the wailing woman and the ancestral voices are inevitably present for us, though not for the fountain and river and caverns. The problem implicit in "Kubla Khan" is that of the appropriate response of the individual self-conscious spirit to the fallen world. The "at-homeness" of the human spirit is with Spirit. Left alone in a disordered world with those crazed by the maddening rain, the elder chooses companionship in madness. In contrast, the speaker in "Kubla Khan" reaffirms his vision, choosing participation in Spirit, even though he may be alone in his choice. The attempt of the last section of the poem is to rise above the fallen world, to proceed as though the fallen world were not fact.

To do this, the poet remakes his vision, trying in the process to spiritualize and dematerialize it. Thus, Kubla Khan decreeing Xanadu is transposed into a "damsel with a dulcimer." The change does several things. The "creator" is now a woman and an innocent, "an Abyssinian maid" (37, 39) rather than an experienced, despotic ruler. It is she, the speaker now says, whom "in a vision once I saw" (38). And her creation is "symphony and song" (43). It

97

is the music of the vision brought about by reading Purchas that is now imaged, not the earthly Kubla Khan and his paradise; the damsel and her music give form to the harmonious music of vision itself.[9] Thus, if the speaker can revive that music within himself, he will be joined in androgynous union with the damsel and with the harmonious Oneness and Love she symbolizes. The "deep delight" the poet anticipates, with its erotic overtones of love, is analogous to the "dancing rocks" that accompany the fountain's birth. Once united with her in her song, he will then be able to build the "sunny dome" and "caves of ice" (46) in air, safe from the prophecies of ancestral voices.

The poet's desire to symbolize and dematerialize at the same time causes him to use images that are tied to Kubla Khan's Xanadu by evocative association but removed to a level of reference even further from the ordinary—and closer to images of immaterial Spirit—than the exotic, faraway Xanadu description can provide. Kubla Khan and Xanadu and Abyssinia are associationally related, but Mount Abora is even more distant and mythical. Yet the song of Mount Abora is the one the poet has heard the damsel sing in a vision.[10] And he too, could he but see and hear "wholly," not in fragment, would find himself caught up in a Dionysion delight inside the magic fairy ring, fed only with the food of the Paradise of Spirit as he, in building his song in air, would become one with the harmonious music of Oneness. And wondrously, as he sings his poem, the poet does for that moment— and, eternally, each time that moment is re-created in a listener's imagination—exist within the faery circle.

The last section of "Kubla Khan" succeeds as symbolic poem, becoming in the process a tale of Faery in which both the poet and his audience participate, for the reader is once again included as the "all" who act as viewers and hearers of the song and dome and caves. In its entirety, "Kubla Khan" is as intensely sustained a symbolic encounter as a poet could hope to create. Still, for all the poet's success, the reality of the fallen world is present. The tale of Faery the poet tells is real and symbolic and true; it is also transient and hypothetical. The poet says he saw a damsel with a dulcimer once, in a vision; what he creates in lines 45–54 is another vision, a vision anticipated as a state of being but existent now in mental space. The verbs are "could" and " 'twould" and "would" and "should" (42–49). Within the conditional, the poet's audience speaks a warning in the present imperative:

And all should cry, Beware! Beware!
His flashing eyes, his floating hair!
Weave a circle round him thrice,
And close your eyes with holy dread.   (49–52)

Weave a circle (closing in and closing out), close your eyes, and beware. At the same time that the poet places himself within the circle, he is also—because of the conditional and because he is a participant in the symbolic experience of his making—outside the circle. Thus, he reestablishes community while existing separated from it. The poet, so enchanted that he is not of this world but truly of the Other World, is a figure of awe, a figure to fill one—even if one is the poet—with "holy dread." Who would dare enter the circle entirely? Still, in "Kubla Khan," the poet risks enchantment and, through his poem, provides the occasion—if we as audience are willing to suspend our disbelief—for our risk also.

If "The Rime of the Ancient Mariner" seems more overtly a tale of Faery than "Kubla Khan," the likely cause is its ballad narrative, composed of a story within several other frame stories and making use of the sparse, concrete details and direct, sensory images of ballads and fairy tales.[11] As in "Kubla Khan," there are stories only hinted at: for example, the story of the Bride and Groom whose wedding the Wedding-Guest is so eager to attend; the story of the albatross and the Polar Spirit; the story of the Mariner and his brother, whose son sails on the Mariner's ship; the story of the hermit. But there is also a core story told in full: the juxtaposition of the fallen world of the land with the Spirit Other World of the sea. The moral voices of the Understanding spoken by the gloss comment on and draw conclusions about the events of imagination and encounter with Spirit in which the Mariner is engaged, but they do not usurp imaginative authenticity.[12] Because "The Rime" functions directly as a teaching story, a symbolic tale of Faery that teaches the reality of consubstantiality, the Mariner first moves into the realm of Spirit/Faery and then returns to relate his experience. "The Rime" establishes three primary teacher-pupil relationships: the Spirit world teaches the Mariner; the Mariner, in turn, teaches the Wedding-Guest (as he has already taught the speaker-poet and the hermit); and finally and most broadly, the speaker-poet teaches the reader. The teaching has nothing to do with the classroom or the church or the conventions of society within which the Understanding operates. Rather, the Reason teaches itself by providing an experience of symbolic participation in Spirit. What is taught in each case is the mystery of the oneness of Love. Coleridge's concern in "The Rime" is not (as it is in "Kubla Khan") somehow to leave the fallen world behind altogether but instead to make others aware that the fallen world is itself consubstantial, that as essential as the knowledge provided by the Understanding may be, it is not adequate for the truths of the Spirit. He intends, whatever psychological or metaphysical difficulties may accompany the attempt, "to set forth the Law of [his] own Mind" in the "earnest wish" to "benefit the largest number possible of [his] fellow-creatures," while recognizing that we are all "subject to distempers of 'the mental sight'" (*Friend* 1: 9–10).

The Mariner's encounter with Spirit functions not only as the most overtly symbolic of the three teaching situations but also as the most immediate, the most "naked," and the least protected. Indeed, the only real protection or respite there seems to be for the Mariner occurs in his being allowed to fall asleep twice in Part V. A world filled with beings named STORM-BLAST, DEATH, Night-mare LIFE-IN-DEATH, and Polar Spirit—while it displays an emotional and psychological reality that we recognize immediately and intuitively—clearly does not describe the ordinary, everyday world in which we live. And yet this Other World contains the natural world, too. The sun and moon that rise and set above the Mariner's ship, the sea on which DEATH and Night-mare LIFE-IN-DEATH sail, and the drought and the slimy water-snakes that follow the dice

game are quite familiar and quite real. The very "this-ness" of the
Other World in "The Rime" emphasizes the consubstantial nature
of the universe; the natural world, and all the creatures in it, are
consubstantial with Spirit. It seems an "other world" because
human perception is a fallen one. Symbolic encounter enables the
Mariner—and by extension, us as readers—to see without distortion, to "set right" our mental sight.

Love, harmony, reconciliation, and ongoing creative inter-
relationship define the nature of Spirit. In "The Rime," Spirit
manifests itself—teaches that and what it is—symbolically
through animate and inanimate nature. Once the STORM-BLAST
has brought the Mariner's ship to the place of encounter in the
land of mist and snow, the Other World sends its messenger, the
Albatross: "At length did cross an Albatross, / Thorough the fog it
came" (63–64). The Albatross is "given" to the mariners; it comes
unbidden and unlooked for—a gift of grace. At a simple level,
beyond all the other complex associations it calls forth, the Albatross remains a bird that establishes community with human
companions, sharing food, play, work, and worship. Its presence
reconciles the human and animal worlds; it shows love. We later
learn that the Polar Spirit "loved the bird that loved the man"
(404), so that the Albatross's love constitutes a continuation, or
passing on, of love that it has experienced between itself and the
Polar Spirit—that is, between the animal world and a spirit of the
inanimate one—thus linking the universe in love. The Mariner,
however, returns death for love, separation for unity. A fallen
man, he reenacts the Fall and refuses the gifts of Love.

Appropriately, then, the Mariner's suffering must serve to
teach him his communal relationship with nature. Separating
himself from the Spirit and Love extended to him through the
Albatross, the Mariner finds himself separated from all love and all
community:

> I looked upon the rotting sea,
> And drew my eyes away;
> I looked upon the rotting deck,
> And there the dead men lay.

I looked to heaven, and tried to pray;
But or ever a prayer had gusht,
A wicked whisper came, and made
My heart as dry as dust.

I closed my lids, and kept them close,
And the balls like pulses beat;
For the sky and the sea, and the sea and the sky
Lay like a load on my weary eye,
And the dead were at my feet.   (240–51)

The Mariner surveys his world, but there is no place to rest his eyes. Decay and death surround him. Sight brings no lifegiving sense of connection. "A wicked wisper"—coming from his own unloving heart—dries up any possible prayer. The Mariner's entire being assumes the weight of the state of separation.

Reconciliation comes as a result of seeing differently, a curing of the distemper of the "inner sight." Having destroyed the beautiful and loving Albatross, the Mariner is left with only the water-snakes, creatures of a much lower order than the Albatross, to the Mariner's mind—so low, in fact, that his sense of unity with nature must begin with them. The water-snakes mirror the Mariner's own inner state—"And a thousand thousand slimy things / Lived on; and so did I" (238–39)—and the water-snakes become the symbolic metaphor for the Mariner. Loss of an awareness of Love includes the loss of an ability to love oneself, and so, ironically, the Mariner must learn the lesson of Love from the water-snakes. Since one knows Love through self-knowledge and since even the water-snakes are part of unified Love, when the Mariner perceives them in the light of love, he simultaneously intuits the love that is the reality of his own spirit and symbolic of Love/Spirit. Originally, he watches the rotting deep as

slimy things did crawl with legs
Upon the slimy sea.

About, about, in reel and rout
The death-fires danced at night;
The water, like a witch's oils,
Burnt green, and blue and white.   (125–30)

Later, as his perception shifts, he watches the water-snakes again:

> They moved in tracks of shining white,
> And when they reared, the elfish light
> Fell off in hoary flakes.
>
> Within the shadow of the ship
> I watched their rich attire:
> Blue, glossy green, and velvet black,
> They coiled and swam; and every track
> Was a flash of golden fire. (274–81)

These are the same snakes, but the changes are obvious and signifi-cant: The water that burns green and blue and white becomes the "rich attire" of "blue, *glossy* green, and *velvet* black" (my em-phasis); the "death-fires" of "witch's oils" become "elfish light" and "golden fire"; the witch's "reel and rout" changes to coiling and swimming in "tracks of shining white." The deadly witch's reel has become a richly textured and beautiful dance of Faery. The Mariner's response to the beauty of life, in whatever form, is analogous to the coming of the Albatross to the ship:

> O happy living things! no tongue
> Their beauty might declare:
> A spring of love gushed from my heart,
> And I blessed them unaware. (282–85)

The "spring of love" comes unbidden. "Given" from within and extended to the water-snakes in blessing, his blessing serves to bless the Mariner as well.

It is interesting to note that this "spring of love" comes in the context of light and shadow, a context that is part of a larger inter-action of Sun and Moon in the poem, an interaction that forms an androgynous reconciliation.[13] The light under which Spirit teaches the Mariner provides, therefore, another symbolic manifestation of that Spirit. For androgynous reconciliation to occur, each part of the duality must retain its own integrity, while appearing as "two forces of one power. . . . In Life . . . the two component counter-powers actually interpenetrate each other, and generate a higher Third, including both the former" (*TL* 393, 399). The Sun and Moon in "The Rime" are the two sources of light or "two forces of one power." Their equal and complete integrity is made very clear. At the same time, certain passages of the poem show their "interpenetration," their mingling, or reconciliation. For this purpose, a dual cluster of associations operates. The Sun is associated with daylight, with masculine light and imagery, the color red, and bright, active firelight. The Moon's night light is feminine, shining or glimmering white, associated with calm starlight. These clusters occur separately and distinctly and also commingled.

The poem insists on the constant presence of the masculine Sun and feminine Moon. The second stanza of the Mariner's story begins, "The Sun came up upon the left"; the next to last stanza of Part I ends, "Whiles all the night, through fogsmoke white, / Glimmered the white Moon-shine" (25, 77–78). Moon and Sun are the same but different; though one by night and one by day, together they give the earth its light. In "The Rime," Sun and Moon almost become "characters," heightening the sense of androgynous reconciliation. Not only do they follow each other in endless cycles, but they are seen to have equal duration and dominance. The presence of one gives over to the presence of the other in the time it takes to let out one breath and draw in another: "The Sun's rim dips; the stars rush out: / At one stride comes the dark" (199–200). Punishment and blessing occur equally under the Sun and Moon. As the punishment begins and the sails drop down,

> All in a hot and copper sky,
> The bloody Sun, at noon,
> Right up above the mast did stand,
> No bigger than the Moon.   (111–14)

The "bloody Sun" burns by day, but it is no bigger than the Moon beneath which the "witch's oils / Burnt green, and blue and white." DEATH and Night-mare LIFE-IN-DEATH come when "the western wave was all a-flame. / The day was well nigh done!" (171–72), but the crew drops dead, "one after one, by the star-dogged Moon" (212). "Seven days, seven nights" (261), by Sun and

Moon light, the Mariner sees the curse in dead men's eyes. Equally, however, reconciliation and blessing take place in Sunlight and Moonlight. The blessing of the water-snakes occurs as "the moving Moon went up the sky" (263), and the gloss at this point beautifully tells the story of the return of the stars to their "native country,"[14] paralleling the section in *The Statesman's Manual* in which Coleridge explains that as the truths of mystery are enunciated, "the soul of man awakes, and starts up, as an exile in a far distant land at the unexpected sounds of his native language, when after long years of absence, and almost of oblivion, he is suddenly addressed in his own mother-tongue" (*SM* 24). The gloss reads: "In his loneliness and fixedness he yearneth towards the journeying Moon, and the stars that still sojourn, yet still move onward; and every where the blue sky belongs to them, and is their appointed rest, and their native country and their own natural homes, which they enter unannounced, as lords that are certainly expected and yet there is a silent joy at their arrival." The gloss narrator's voice in this section assumes for a moment the highly poetic quality of the poet-narrator and thus abandons the categorical specificity and moralizing thrust it usually has. It is as though the gloss narrator, identifying with the Mariner's yearning for rest and comfort and wholeness, risks moving into Faery and thus is able to speak in the voice of imagination and Reason. As the Mariner yearns toward the Moon and stars, the scene is one of peace and fulfillment and joy; and at this point, "by the light of the Moon [the Mariner] beholdeth God's creatures of the great calm" (gloss) and sees their beauty.

In both the blessing of the water-snakes scene and the baptismal rain scene that follows, the masculine and feminine lights and shadows of both Sun and Moon are present. The Moonlight of the blessing "bemocks the sultry main" (267). Conversely but additionally, "within the shadow of the ship," the charmed water burnt alway / A still and awful red"; that is, there is Sunlight in the ship's shadow, light that comes to parallel Moonlight in the two parallel stanzas:

Beyond the shadow of the ship,
I watched the water-snakes:
They moved in tracks of shining white,
And when they reared, the elfish light
Fell off in hoary flakes.

Within the shadow of the ship
I watched their rich attire:
Blue, glossy green, and velvet black,
They coiled and swam; and every track
Was a flash of golden fire.   (272–81)

The water-snakes swim in and out of shadow, yet wherever they swim, they are made beautiful by the light, whether it be the "shining white," "elfish light" of the Moon or the flashing "golden fire" of residual Sunlight on "charmed water." Rearing and swimming and coiling, moving in both lights, the water-snakes effect reconciliation. Similarly, when in Moonlight it begins to rain,

The upper air burst into life!
And a hundred fire-flags sheen,
To and fro they were hurried about!
And to and fro, and in and out,
The wan stars danced between.   (313–17)

The brilliant "fire-flags," associated with the Sun, dance with the stars under Moonlight in a "stitching together" kind of pattern that fills the heavens with the light of life. Then, while "the Moon was at its edge" (321),

The thick black cloud was cleft, and still
The Moon was at its side:
Like waters shot from some high crag,
The lightning fell with never a jag,
A river steep and wide.   (322–26)

Out of the "one black cloud" (320), the lightning, again associated with the bright light of the Sun, falls like a "flash of golden fire," like a river. The lightning is a river, "shot . . . with never a jag," like the "spring of love" that gushes from the heart of the Mariner—the symbolic universe evident in the individual and in the whole.

Under Moonlight the baptism of rain falls, but in Sunlight "sweet sounds" rise from the mouths of the "inspirited" bodies on the deck:

> Around, around, flew each sweet sound,
> Then darted to the Sun;
> Slowly the sounds came back again,
> Now mixed, now one by one.
>
> Sometimes a-dropping from the sky
> I heard the sky-lark sing;
> Sometimes all little birds that are,
> How they seemed to fill the sea and air
> With their sweet jargoning!
>
> And now 'twas like all instruments,
> Now like a lonely flute;
> And now it is an angel's song,
> That makes the heavens be mute.   (354–66)

The music that comes from the mouths of the dead crew, transformed into an angel troop, is a perfect example of the reconciliation of the many with the One, of the androgynous wholeness of the natural world and the Creator. The path of the sweet sounds forms two circles: the first horizontal as the sounds fly "around and around" above the surface of the sea; the second vertical as the sounds fly to the Sun and then drop back to the surface, filling both "sea and air" with music. As the sounds return, they are mixed yet individual: the single sky-lark sings alone and in chorus with all other birds; the music of a lonely flute also plays with a symphony of instruments; an angel's song can be heard singled out from the music of the spheres. The reality of Spirit and the consubstantiality of the human spirit with it are made evident in the scene.

The Mariner's experience leaves him with a sense of "holy dread" strong enough to make him want to join in the warning of "Beware! Beware!"

> Like one, that on a lonesome road
> Doth walk in fear and dread,
> And having once turned round walks on,
> And turns no more his head;

Because he knows, a frightful fiend
Doth close behind him tread.   (446–51)

The "frightful fiend" treading close behind is reminiscent of the STORM-BLAST, striking "with his o'ertaking wings" so that the one "pursued with yell and blow / Still treads the shadow of his foe" (43, 46–47). But the Mariner *must* turn round, again and again—in story:

> Forthwith this frame of mine was wrenched
> With a woful agony,
> Which forced me to begin my tale:
> And then it left me free.
>
> Since then, at an uncertain hour,
> That agony returns:
> And till my ghastly tale is told,
> This heart within me burns.
>
> I pass, like night, from land to land;
> I have strange power of speech;
> That moment that his face I see,
> I know the man that must hear me:
> To him my tale I teach.   (578–90)

Just as it was necessary for Spirit to "teach" the Mariner, the Mariner is now compelled to teach others. The imperative operates in both the telling and the hearing, though the tale is not for everyone. Most, in fact, cannot—are unable to—listen to the tale. Of the Hermit, Pilot, and Pilot's Boy, the tale is only for the Hermit; similarly, the Mariner stops only one of a group of three wedding guests. He stops the one who "must hear" and teaches him. The Wedding-Guest, for his part, "cannot choose but hear" (18, 38). The story is necessary for those who can hear it: "Who hath ears to hear, let him hear" (Matthew 13.43).

The Mariner's tale is quite unabashedly, then, a teaching story. Once the Mariner "holds him with his glittering eye," the Wedding-Guest "listens like a three years' child" (15). And it is the listening "three years' child" who receives the Mariner's reassurances and the simplified form of the moral at the end. The "true moral" is the encounter itself, an encounter filled with strangeness and mystery. The meaning of the encounter cannot be put satisfactorily into words; the words will always sound reductive and moralizing. The knowledge gained is intuitive self-knowledge, an imaginative perception peculiar to each person. The extent of even the Mariner's perception remains unclear. At various points in the story, the Wedding-Guest (much like the child Coleridge himself, reading the *Arabian Nights*, or Sara Coleridge, frightened by the tales the grownups tell her) becomes frightened and interrupts:

> "I fear thee, ancient Mariner!
> I fear thy skinny hand!
> And thou art long, and lank, and brown,
> As is the ribbed sea-sand.
>
> I fear thee and thy glittering eye,
> And thy skinny hand, so brown."—
> Fear not, fear not, thou Wedding-Guest!
> This body dropt not down. (224–31)

And again: "'I fear thee, ancient Mariner!' / Be calm, thou Wedding-Guest!" (445–46). The Mariner's "Fear not" echoes the angel's reassurance to the shepherds: "Fear not: for, behold, I bring you good tidings of great joy" (Luke 2.8); and Christ's own later words to his disciples: "Let not your heart be troubled: Ye believe in God, believe also in me" (John 14.1). Or, "He saith unto them, It is I; be not afraid" (John 6.20). Mystery is awesome, glorious but also a "holy dread." The Wedding-Guest, encountering mystery through symbolic story, does not want to find himself trapped in the woven circle. The Mariner (like the father Coleridge giving Sara the lighted candle) reassures him that it is only a human spirit who is relating the tale.

The moral is true and true to the tale the Mariner tells, but the language reflects the level of the Mariner's perception, the difficulty of conveying symbolic encounter in words, and the words that are most appropriate for the listener of the tale:

> He prayeth well, who loveth well
> Both man and bird and beast.

> He prayeth best, who loveth best
> All things both great and small;
> For the dear God who loveth us,
> He made and loveth all.   (612–17)

The Wedding-Guest, though he rises "a sadder and a wiser man" (624) the following morning, has only begun his understanding of Spirit.

But the moral is for the readers of "The Rime of the Ancient Mariner" as well—since we also are presumably in need of teaching—so Coleridge addresses the reader in the simplest terms possible, much as one would speak to a three years' child, wanting to reach everyone in the audience and assuming perhaps that anyone older in self-knowledge and in understanding the ways of Spirit will see immediately the complexity implied in the simple moral. For the simple is also the essential. Further, Coleridge, supposing that we will be as fearful as the Wedding-Guest of being held by the Mariner's glittering eye, ultimately provides even more reassurance for the reader than the Mariner does for the Wedding-Guest. "The Rime" is "merely" a story, but it is a symbolic story that provides an occasion for symbolic encounter. Coleridge must at the same time verify its authenticity and reassure the reader that there will be a return from the voyage. The third-person narrator-poet who begins and ends the poem and oversees the rest of it—and who exists both in and outside of the Mariner's experience—serves both purposes; he himself has been on the journey with the Mariner. The speaker of the prose gloss, by providing an unsuccessful interpretation of the Mariner's tale, turns the reader toward symbolic participation. The Argument (at least in the 1798 version), while giving the route before the ship leaves the harbor and assuring the reader of the Mariner's— and his or her—return, also piques the imagination to wonder about the "strange things" that will befall. The epigraph lends authority, as well as explanation. Still, for all of this, the purpose of this story is symbolic encounter; and as the reader goes this journey, he or she must be

Alone, alone, all, all alone,
Alone on a wide wide sea!   (232–33)

There is no "secure foothold" ("East Coker," 2) on the "wide wide sea" any more than in the "dark wood" or "on the edge of a grimpen." Nonetheless, "The Rime" encourages us, like the Mariner, to risk enchantment.

CHAPTER THREE

Romantic Faery Tales of Love

*A*s we have seen, Coleridgean tales of Faery may be brief moments of symbolic encounter or expanded journeys of spirit, whether in works which, at least ostensibly, have other than metaphysical purposes or in works concerned in a primary way with mystery and imagination—works ranging from "Songs of the Pixies" to "Kubla Khan." Occasionally, however, still using the same symbolic metaphors, Coleridge writes tales of Faery that deliberately and overtly use the narrative structures and techniques of the two closely related traditional genres of fairy tale and ballad. These two genres, both in their similarities and differences, suit Coleridge's explorative purposes and provide narrative forms for his symbolic stories.

In addition to the similarities of narrative stance, character presentation, and emphasis on stark, significant action and detail in traditional ballads and fairy tales, Faery and the rich potential for Faery exist in both genres. The progress of love is essential to the narratives of both. However, a primary difference occurs in the resolution of the narrative. The vast majority of fairy tales end happily for the central characters who, growing and maturing, find love and live happily ever after. Ballads, on the other hand, are fraught with tragedy. Love is unrequited, betrayed, or acknowledged too late. Fairy tales, despite the horrific things that can and do occur in them, are finally tales of the triumph of love. Ballads, despite the potential for love they exhibit, prove unable to sustain it. Fairy tales are *eucatastrophic*; ballads *dycatastrophic*. In symbolic terms, then, fairy tales affirm consubstantiality; ballads show that consubstantiality exists within a fallen world. One implication would seem to be that in our world, Faery can triumph only if it is somehow separate from "real life," self-contained as "story." Once a writer like Coleridge begins to use the fairy tale genre to write tales of Faery that are concerned in a primary way with the psychology of human nature and, simultaneously and inextricably, the soul's metaphysical context and import, the genre of fairy tale becomes more and more difficult to sustain. The reality of the fallen world asserts itself, and what begins as fairy tale ends as ballad.

This chapter looks at a group of five poems, all of which are romantic faery tales: "Love," "The Dark Ladié," "The Night-Scene," "Alice du Clos," and "The Three Graves." Each of these is a narrative, comprising in its focus and in its entirety a tale of Faery. All are love stories; all, except for "The Night-Scene," are cast as ballads.[1] In each poem, elements of ballad and elements of fairy tale or romance are merged—or, perhaps more accurately, thrown into tension with each other, especially as regards the ending of the tales. These poems are Coleridge's *Kunstmärchen*, in which characters and situation and endings are not always clearly defined, not always "black and white" as in traditional tales, but often ambiguous and gray. This ambiguity, in turn, reflects the metaphysical import of the tales. Coleridge's romantic faery tales are symbolic. They present the possibility of human love that is symbolic of the harmony of Love in a world that is fallen. In these poems, the metaphors of Spirit are present, but because the world is a fallen one, the ending of the tale may be the tragic one of ballad love stories rather than the happy one of romance and fairy tale. Again, and in keeping with the romantic fairy tale genre, the subjective is brought to the fore more directly than in either traditional ballads or fairy tales. Accordingly, emotional/psychological states assume prominence, and the narrator's relationship to the tale being told is emphasized. Finally, since the stories are symbolic, the significance of the story to the reader/listener is also a function of the tale: that is, Coleridge's romantic faery tales become occasions of symbolic encounter.

The poem most entirely satisfactory, both in the completeness of its conception and the symbolic affirmation of its structure and ending, is—appropriately enough—"Love." First published as "Introduction to the Tale of the Dark Ladié" in the *Morning Post*, 21 December 1799, "Love" has never been viewed as a poem of major significance in Coleridge's canon, although it has been awarded a place of affectionate indulgence as a poem about romantic love and, as such, the "first of many poems Coleridge was to write to or about Sara [Hutchinson]" (Whalley 38). Tolerance for the poem, however, can easily shade into acerbity, as when Patricia Adair comments that "the poem has little reality, transcendental or otherwise. . . . The ending . . . spreads a tone of rather sickly sentiment over the whole" (184–85).[2] Nonetheless, "Love" is demonstrably a more ambitious and significant poem than it has previously been seen to be. Max Schulz's commentary is suggestive: "When we turn from 'Christabel' to 'The Ballad of the Dark Ladié,' 'Love,' 'Alice du Clos,' and 'Baron Guelph of Adelstan,' we see that Coleridge accepts as had Collins and Chatterton the view of the century that the ballad is a tale of knights and ladies cavorting sometimes tragically but always romantically in forest glades" (*Poetic Voices* 67). And, he might have added, cavorting with the fairies who live in those forest glades. Within "Love," Coleridge melds romance, ballad, and fairy tale, manipulating the narrative conventions of these closely related genres to write a love story that functions in several analogous retellings as a metaphysically symbolic story of the Reality of Love.

That this purpose is uppermost in Coleridge's mind when he writes "Love" is evidenced by his statements in the *Biographia* concerning the occasion and origins of *Lyrical Ballads*: "With this view I wrote the 'Ancient Mariner,' and was preparing among other poems, the 'Dark Ladié,' and the 'Christabel,' in which I should have more nearly realized my ideal, than I had done in my first attempt" (*BL* 2: 7). The ideal that these poems would realize is contained in the purpose of the series of poems Coleridge agreed to write, in which

> the incidents and agents were to be, in part at least, supernatural; and the excellence aimed at was to consist in the interesting of the affections by the dramatic truth of such emotions, as would naturally accompany such situations, supposing them real. And real in *this* sense they have been to every human being who, from whatever source of delusion, has at any time believed himself under supernatural agency. . . . It was agreed, that my endeavors should be directed to persons and characters supernatural, or at least romantic; yet so as to transfer from our inward nature a human interest and a semblance of truth sufficient to procure for these shadows of imagination that willing suspension of disbelief for the moment, which constitutes poetic faith. (*BL* 2: 6)

Specifically, then, it was Coleridge's intention that the presentation of the emotions of a character in these romantic fairy tale ballads elicit from the reader a corresponding interest or emotion, arising from our inward nature. This process is possible because we feel the emotion elicited to be a truth powerful enough to allow us momentarily to suspend our disbelief and participate in the created character's experience. "Love" is a prime example of the imaginative process that Coleridge intends.

It is easy to see why Coleridge chooses the blended genres of fairy tale, ballad, and romance to fulfill his purposes, since these are precisely the kinds of stories which—because they have strong emotional appeal and because they call into reality the supernatural world of Spirit—can function symbolically, both as symbolic tale and as an occasion of symbolic encounter for the audience. Coleridge's romantic fairy tale ballads are symbolic stories that participate in the Eternal and, by representing that Unity, make it intelligible to the audience. The poem "Love" contains several overt and implied love stories, ranging from the love of the

Knight for the Lady of the Land to the narrator's love for Genevieve to Coleridge's love for Sara. Ultimately, all these love stories are symbolic analogues of the audience's relationship with Eternal Love.

At the same time that Coleridge is making use of the blended imaginative genres of fairy tale, ballad, and romance to tell a symbolic tale, he remains cognizant of the oral roots of these genres and his literary remaking of the genres for his own purposes. This simultaneous presentation of the oral tradition and literary use of that tradition is most evident in the variety of narrator-audience relationships in the poem. These relationships are distinct but interconnected: a number of love stories are being told, but all the stories are finally symbolic of the One story of Love.

"Love" is a ballad about a ballad about love. At the initial level of form, Coleridge acknowledges his debt to the traditional oral ballad by making such a ballad the center of the poem and by casting his poem as a ballad. At this same initial level, however, he announces his intention to use the traditional genre for his own purpose by varying the traditional ballad stanza: he keeps the *a b c b* rhyme; but instead of the standard 4-3-4-3 alternating beat, he uses a 4-4-4-3 pattern. The center of "Love" is "a soft and doleful air," "an old and moving story— / An old rude song" (21–23) about a Knight's unsuccessful ten-year wooing of the Lady of the Land. The Lady scorns his love, a "cruel scorn / That crazed that bold and lovely Knight" (41–42), leaving him a restless wanderer, with neither a home nor the companionship of love:

> That sometimes from the savage den,
> And sometimes from the darksome shade,
> And sometimes starting up at once
>   In green and sunny glade,—
>
> There came and looked him in the face
> An angel beautiful and bright;
> And that he knew it was a Fiend,
>   This miserable Knight!   (45–52)

The "angel beautiful and bright," who represents the Knight's love for the Lady and should, therefore, be his companion, becomes instead a "Fiend" in his perception, reminding him of the scorn with which the Lady has returned his love. The broken and thwarted unity and wholeness of love are mirrored in the disharmony and discord of the lover's mind. The turningpoint in the Lady's feelings for the Knight occurs when he acts instinctively to save her from "a murderous band" and an "outrage worse than death" (54–55). Rejecting the true love of the Knight has left the Lady vulnerable. The threat of rape by the murderous band as a "crazed" replacement for physical union in wedded love parallels, in relation to the Lady, the beautiful angel that appears to the Knight as a Fiend. Even in his crazed state, the Knight acts instinctively to save the Lady, causing her scorn to melt into tears and love. At last his madness goes away, but he is left dying on the "yellow forest-leaves" (63).

The story of the Knight and the Lady is the traditional ballad story of the Lady who scorns her lover, rejecting him only to discover—too late—her love for him. The story, in its various versions and particulars, is well known, an oral tale that assumes a communal audience and an anonymous singer. In "Love" the narrator, having been part of that communal audience, now takes on the role of singer. Though he is known, of course, to Genevieve, he still retains a degree of anonymity, since we never learn his name. Genevieve is a particular young girl, but she is also a fairy tale and romance figure; and by symbolic extension, she is a communal audience. In this love story, the oral and literary narrator-audience relationships are present simultaneously. In the poem, the narrator-lover very deliberately sings the doleful ballad of the Knight and the Lady of the Land as a way to woo Genevieve:

I told her how he pined: and ah!
The deep, the low, the pleading tone
With which I sang another's love,
    Interpreted my own.   (33–36)

Thus, Genevieve—who must surely possess golden hair and be the fairest of the fair—becomes a romance heroine, both by analogy with the Lady and independently within her own romance. As such, she has power to control her own story and, additionally, to change the ending of the ballad. The ballad, because it is sung and not written down, is transitory and available for revision. The narrator-singer has almost reached the end of the story:

> And that she nursed him in a cave;
> And how his madness went away,
> When on the yellow forest-leaves
>   A dying man he lay;—
>
> His dying words—   (61–65)

But Genevieve interrupts him. The traditional ballad ending would leave the Knight dead and the Lady lying beside him, dying of a broken heart. Genevieve, however, shifts the ballad to romance and fairy tale: rather than being the scornful Lady—and suffering the consequences—she unites with her lover, calling out his name, enclosing him within her embrace, and becoming his bride.

For Genevieve, the ballad becomes an occasion of symbolic encounter. The encounter can occur because the ballad story is the sort that evokes an emotional response that suspends Genevieve's disbelief and places her within the story, which is the intent of her lover-singer in the first place. Because she is symbolically the Lady, Genevieve partakes of and experiences the reality of broken love and the possibility of its opposite, the harmonious unity of fulfilled love. Further, the symbolic participation can occur because the emotional response the ballad calls forth effects an imaginative participation in an experience Genevieve has not actually yet had. She is described in the beginning of the poem as extremely innocent, a young girl who has "few sorrows . . . of her own" (17). If she cannot participate imaginatively, symbolically, in the Lady's story, she may be doomed to the traditional ballad ending. But because, as the narrator says, "She loves me best, whene'er I sing / The songs that make her grieve" (19–20), the narrator-lover's confidence in the imaginative ability of the ballad to effect Genevieve's participation is not misplaced. In fact, when he reaches the "tenderest strain of all the ditty," his "faultering voice and pausing harp / Disturbed her soul with pity!"

All impulses of soul and sense
Had thrilled my guileless Genevieve;
The music and the doleful tale,
    The rich and balmy eve;

And hopes, and fears that kindle hope,
And undistinguishable throng,
And gentle wishes long subdued,
    Subdued and cherished long!

She wept with pity and delight,
She blushed with love, and virgin-shame;
And like the murmur of a dream,
    I heard her breathe my name.   (66–80)

The "guileless Genevieve" is touched and moved to imaginative participation by the "music and the doleful tale"; the pity she feels for the Knight and Lady is transferred by imagination to her own romance, bringing about an awareness of her love and desire, both of which have long been present within her, waiting to be awakened. The doleful tale is reinforced by the scene of the ruined tower and the "statue of the arméd knight" against which Genevieve leans to listen to the ballad in the "lingering light" of "moon-shine" (14, 16, 9), but the story and the natural setting are able to affect her because the requisite emotions are already latent within her, ready to be brought into active play by symbolic identification with the Lady.

    The first two audiences—the communal audience of the oral tale and Genevieve—listen to the tale as it is sung, and the power of the sung ballad is such that in its oral form it becomes a symbolic story, shifting its narrative ending from the tragedy of the ballad to the happy marriage of the fairy tale and romance. But within the poem proper, the narrator is not actually singing the ballad to Genevieve. Instead, he is telling another—again particular yet communal—audience the story of his having sung the ballad to her. Although we can imagine the narrator speaking the story to an individual standing next to him, we, as readers of his story, also become the audience; so the community at this level is a literate one. The narrator begins in the present tense, explaining that in his memory, he often retells to himself the story of his wooing of Genevieve:

> Oft in my waking dreams do I
> Live o'er again that happy hour,
> When midway on the mount I lay,
> Beside the ruined tower. (5–8)

As he repeats to his present audience the story that he often repeats to himself—much as a singer would repeat a ballad—he moves into past tense, to emerge again in the present only in the last line of the poem. Not only is there an immediate audience within the poem and a literate audience outside the poem proper, but the narrator-singer's repeated tellings of the story also allow him to become his own audience and to experience his own story as symbolic tale. This relationship, in turn, anticipates the next analogous love story in the poem and the next narrator-audience relationship.

Kelvin Everest calls "Love" a "transparently veiled account of [Coleridge's] covert 'courtship' of Sara Hutchinson" (67), and Adair notes that the ten years of the Knight's wooing is "an unconscious prophecy of the duration of Coleridge's own love" (184). If this is so, then when Coleridge writes his romantic literary ballad, he particpates symbolically in the tales of the wooing Knight and narrator-singer; and Sara, as audience, is given the option of having as symbolic analogue the Lady of the Land or the guileless Genevieve. In this love story, Coleridge will die for love of Sara, crazed by her scorn, unless she interrupts the tragic ending and responds to his love. As ultimate narrator of the stories, Coleridge is in the same position as his narrator-singer:

> I told her how he pined: and ah!
> The deep, the low, the pleading tone
> With which I sang another's love,
> Interpreted my own. (33–36)

And he hopes that Sara will respond as Genevieve did:

> She listened with a flitting blush,
> With downcast eyes, and modest grace;

And she forgave me, that I gazed
    Too fondly on her face!   (37–40)

The irony of the Coleridge and Sara love story is that although Sara does choose Genevieve's fairy tale romance ending, the happy ending that should result becomes, instead, the tragic ballad ending. Because Coleridge is already married to one Sara, the second Sara cannot be his "bright and beauteous Bride" (96).

But the irony takes yet another turn, a turn that points ultimately toward the last love story of the poem and the last narrator-audience relationship. Although Sara Hutchinson is never Coleridge's actual bride, his model of sacramental wedded love is based on their love for each other. Wedded love, in Coleridge's view, is the highest form of friendship; it is intensely emotional; it rightly desires physical expression; and it is symbolic of the Supreme Love that is God. Coleridge is very specific about this, as one of his many notebook entries makes clear: "Real + symbolical.— Motion + Rest at the Goal. Love—and the grandeur of loving the Supreme in her—the real & symbolical united" (*CN* 2: 2530). Coleridge's love for Sara unites human love and its symbolic import. In their love, the two become one. Together, they are complete, united, whole—and thus their love is a symbol of the Deity. In an 1810 entry, Coleridge again describes the significance of his love for Sara: "My love . . . is not so much in my Soul, as my Soul in it. It is my whole Being wrapt up into one Desire, all the Hopes & Fears, Joys & Sorrows, all the Powers, Vigor & Faculties of my Spirit abridged into <one> perpetual Inclination. To bid me not love you were to bid me annihilate myself—for to love you is all I know of my Life, as far as my Life is an object of my Consciousness or my free Will. God is our Being, but thro' his works alone doth he reveal himself" (*CN* 3: 3996). God reveals himself through his works, and one of those "works," asserts Coleridge, is the love that he and Sara feel for each other. Therefore, their love story is also symbolic and analogous to the ones explicitly part of the ballads of the poem.

The last love story of "Love" is the story on which the significance of all the others rests: that is, the story of the Love that is

God. In other words, love of God ultimately gives all love its meaning. "Implicit in all Coleridge's discussion of love," says J. Robert Barth, "is what we might call an 'analogy of love.' For Coleridge, all love—like all being—is 'consubstantial,' that is, it shares in the same reality, as the Father is consubstantial with the Son, one yet distinctly other. He makes it clear . . . that all love is ultimately one, so that love begets love, one form of love nourishing and strengthening another. Thus any form of love is 'analogous' to any other, different yet deeply the same." This love that gives meaning to all other love is Coleridge's "prime analogate": "that being in which the perfection in question—being, truth, goodness, love—is contained in its fulness. There must be a 'resting-place' for the mind as it considers the meaning of such perfections" ("Ideal of Love" 138). The Knight in the original ballad— because the Lady scorns him—is left without the love that could give meaning to his life and make clear the consubstantial relationship between his love for the Lady and the Love that is God. Thus denied a "resting place," his mind is crazed, and he "nor rested day nor night" (44). This same situation, and the need for a resting place, recurs in the later poem "To Two Sisters" (1807):

> To know, to esteem, to love,—and then to part—
> Makes up life's tale to many a feeling heart;
> Alas for some abiding-place of love,
> O'er which my spirit, like the mother dove,
> Might brood with warming wings!
> > O fair! O kind!   (1–5)

The need for love to provide a resting place, an "abiding-place," is one of Coleridge's constant refrains. This "abiding-place" may be simply a warm, stable human love relationship and thus different from the "resting place" for the mind as it contemplates the perfection of the "prime analogate," but the one can serve to nourish the other. "All harmony is founded on a relation to rest—on relative rest" (*TT*, 10 Apr. 1832), Coleridge comments late in life in a statement that refers at several levels to music and love and Love.

Speaking in his own voice, Coleridge begins "Love" with an explicit assertion of the "prime analogate":

All thoughts, all passions, all delights,
Whatever stirs this mortal frame,
All are but ministers of Love,
    And feed his sacred flame.   (1–4)

For this final love story, Coleridge is the singer, and his ballad is his song. At the same time, as Coleridge the poet speaks the words of Truth, he speaks symbolically, manifesting the Word who is the narrator of Love. The sacred flame of Cupid becomes a symbolic metaphor for the flame of the Spirit. Both the traditional folk ballad and the literary romantic fairy tale ballad that the song comprises tell the story of thoughts, passions, and delights that are capable of stirring the mortal frame and thus become ministers of Love. As ministers of Love, the tales function as witnesses to that Love at the same time that they serve—because they do participate in and symbolize Love—to increase the flame. The audience that Coleridge has in mind for this symbolic story is both individual and communal. Each reader of the poem becomes an individual hearer of the song of Love. But every reader's symbolic encounter with Love through the poem is analogous to every other reader's encounter, so that finally a community is formed in which the "thoughts," "passions," and "delights" of each join together so that "all are but ministers of Love / And feed his sacred flame." In this ending, the fairy tale lives happily ever after.

In two other romantic faery tales, "The Ballad of the Dark Ladié" and "The Night-Scene," though the possibility for a fairy tale ending is left open, that ending fails to be achieved. Instead, the fragmentary form of both poems is indicative of the lack of resolution and lack of wholeness. These poems and their characters exist in a fallen world, a world in which symbolic love and encounter with Love is possible but not always present. There is no "resting place" for the characters or for the reader in these fragments.

"The Dark Ladié," written in the spring or early summer of 1798, somewhat earlier than "Love," in some ways reverses the situation of "Love."[3] Here, the Dark Ladié is the one who waits in anticipation for the lover's arrival. Long past the "flitting blush," the "downcast eyes and modest grace" of Genevieve, the Dark Ladié has given her love to her Knight, and now she waits "in silent pain; / The heavy tear is in her eye, / And drops and swells again" (6–8). The situation of the poem retells the ballad story of the "wronged maiden," and we and the narrator—and the Dark Ladié herself—await the Knight to see whether the ending will be tragic or resolve into fairy tale and romance.

The poem focuses on the love of the Dark Ladié for the Knight, a love that has existed outside the castle walls, outside the bounds of society, in Faery. She says to the Knight:

> My Henry, I have given thee much,
> I gave what I can ne'er recall,
> I gave my heart, I gave my peace,
>   O Heaven! I gave thee all.   (29–32)

She has given him everything: her body, her heart, her peace of mind. They no longer belong to her, and without him, therefore, she has no "resting place." Indeed, she has no place inside the walls of society at all. Cast out by her friends with words of scorn—"My friends with rude ungentle words / They scoff and bid me fly to thee!" (25–26)—she waits on the mossy rocks of a brook beneath a "birch with silver bark, / And boughs so pendulous and fair" (1–2), a Faery arbor. At home now only in the natural world, she must send her page as messenger to the castle and wait meanwhile for the Knight.

The Lady's isolated position is further accentuated by her name: the Dark Ladié. In an undated manuscript list, Coleridge calls the poem "The Black Ladie," meaning, perhaps to suggest a skin color or nationality that would set her apart from most of those around her and make her alien. At the least, the adjective "dark" denotes the dark shame of her implied pregnancy, as well as the pain and sorrow and despair that describe her state. Her acts of love have been "out-of-bounds"; and as she waits, "counting moments, dreaming fears" (15), her imagination mingles both love's past pleasures and the uncertainty of the future, the "thousand hopes and fears" with which, sobbing, she greets her Knight, Lord

Falkland, once he arrives.[4] She is also appropriately the "Dark Lady," becoming one with the night, since "the sun was sloping down the sky, / And she had linger'd there all day" (13–14) awaiting the Knight, who comes at dusk. Long past modesty and anxious in the extreme, "she springs, she clasps him round the neck" (21), pouring out her hopes and fears: "Her kisses glowing on his cheeks / She quenches with her tears" (23–24). The merging conjunction of hope and fear, light and dark, pleasure and pain, fairy tale and ballad is evidenced in her simultaneous kisses and tears.

Ballad and fairy tale oscillate in the encounter between the Lady and the Knight. The difficulty in coming to an appropriate and desired ending arises from the fact that the Faery world of love must somehow be brought into the everyday daylight world. What is at issue is the manner in which this is to occur. If the two cannot agree, the ballad ending will prevail. The need for a resting place is apparent as the Dark Ladié pleads, "O give me shelter in thy breast! / O shield and shelter me" (27–28). And we, as audience, are relieved and pleased when the Knight responds, "while to his heart he held her hand":

> Nine castles hath my noble sire,
>> None statelier in the land.
>
> The fairest one shall be my love's,
> The fairest castle of the nine! (35–38)

The Knight loves the Lady. Sheltering her hand at his breast, in an image Coleridge uses elsewhere for the union of lovers, the Knight promises to shelter his love in the fairest castle in the land—the happy reconciliation of Faery. But immediately, this ending is obviated by the next words of the Knight, words anticipated by his waiting till dusk to come to the Lady:

> Wait only till the stars peep out,
> The fairest shall be thine:
>
> Wait only till the hand of eve
> Hath wholly closed yon western bars,
> And through the dark we two will steal
>> Beneath the twinkling stars! (39–44)

The Knight, while not denying in any way the love of Faery, wants to keep the love in darkness, in a place separate—and, perhaps, even safe—from the ordinary fallen world, the world that scoffs at love with "ungentle words." He wants to move the Lady and their love by stealth and starlight into the "fairest castle of the nine." The love will thus be safe—and even brought within the castle— but still be hidden. The Lady is appalled.

Although she is the Dark Ladié, the lovers' "sacred vow" was pledged in bright daylight:

> The dark? the dark? No! not the dark?
> The twinkling stars? How, Henry? How?
> O God! 'twas in the eye of noon
>   He pledged his sacred vow!   (44–47)

The import of her dismay is that their love *belongs* in the light of day. The Knight's "sacred vow"—a wedding vow, sacred whether taken in a church or in the natural world—was made "in the eye of noon." Their vows of love, uniting them in the wholeness of love, are symbolic of God's Love and therefore rightfully repeated in the church's—and society's—symbolic marriage vows.

The ending of "The Dark Ladié" moves back to fairy tale as the Lady imaginatively creates the wedding day:

> And in the eye of noon my love
> Shall lead me from my mother's door,
> Sweet boys and girls all clothed in white
>   Strewing flowers before:
>
> But first the nodding minstrels go
> With music meet for lordly bowers,
> The children next in snow-white vests,
>   Strewing buds and flowers!
>
> And then my love and I shall pace,
> My jet black hair in pearly braids,
> Between our comely bachelors
>   And blushing bridal maids.   (49–60)

The Lady becomes a storyteller as she connects the "eye of noon" of the "sacred vow" with the "eye of noon" of the wedding. Through a tale of Faery, she effectively brings Faery—at least for the moment of the telling of the tale—into the castle world and illustrates the consubstantiality of the two. The innocent "boys and girls all clothed in white," the "children in snow-white vests"—precursors of the "comely bachelors / And blushing bridal maids" that encircle the Knight and Lady—strew buds and flowers in procession with the minstrels playing "music meet for lordly bowers." The previously unreconciled kisses and tears, light and dark, are intertwined in the bride's "jet black hair in pearly braids." The noontime celebratory ceremony of Love is one of harmonious Faery.

It may be argued that the fragmentary poem is still a fragment and that we do not have the Knight's reply or the actual ending, only the Lady's story. At the very least, however, the fragment serves as a moment of symbolic encounter; it asserts as its final statement the Reality of Spirit in a consubstantial world; and it draws the narrator and the reader into participating in affirmation and self-knowledge. The poem begins with the narrator as an outside observer who sees the Lady waiting. By the fourth stanza, however, the narrator is beginning to identify with her, so that the line "Oh wherefore can he stay?" (16) could be uttered by either of them. At that point, the Knight appears, and the narrator overhears his conversation with the Lady for us, intruding only once again to tell us that the Knight has taken the Lady's hand to his heart. Hereafter, the narrator—and we, as audience—are absorbed into the faery tale so that the concluding words of the narrator are those of the Dark Ladié's affirmative symbolic story.

The narrative frame of "The Night-Scene" provides similar, but even more ambiguous, commentary on the difficulty of maintaining the wholeness of love in this world, despite the experiences of the lovers within the Faery bower. The fragment's dramatic (rather than ballad) form itself insists on the presence and reality of this world, a world of uncertainty, skepticism, illusion, and betrayal. Structurally, "The Night-Scene" counterpoints the voice of love, Earl Henry, with the voice of skepticism, Sandoval, in alternating statements. The scene can be divided into four movements: (1) lines 1–15, in which Henry speaks longer than

Sandoval, though both describe a world of uncertainty; (2) lines 16–35 and (3) lines 36–55, in which Henry tells the tale of the Faery arbor, his story interrupted abruptly and framed by Sandoval's notes of sarcasm; and (4) lines 56–83, in which the Faery world is invaded by the fallen world. Although the center of the poem is devoted to Faery, encroachment is a constant danger; and Sandoval both opens and closes the scene. The dramatic fragment clearly implies that perhaps the Faery world of love and life can exist only in the still night, sheltered and hidden from the "scanning eye" (73) of outsiders.

The first section of "The Night-Scene" begins with a confusing series of questions, indirections, and inversions to arrive finally at the fact that Henry loves Oropeza:

> *Sandoval.*   You loved the daughter of Don Manrique?
> *Earl Henry.*   Loved?
> *Sandoval.*   Did you not say you wooed her?
> *Earl Henry.*   Once I loved
> Her whom I dared not woo!
> *Sandoval.*   And wooed, perchance,
> One whom you loved not!
> *Earl Henry.*   Oh! I were most base,
> Not loving Oropeza.   (1–5)

With the repetition of "loved" in line 1, the reader is even uncertain whether it is the tense of the verb or the content of the word that is in question. Nor is the matter much clarified in the next exchange. Even the declaration of love carries with it the information that Henry had at first wooed Oropeza, "hoping to heal a deeper wound" (6), rather than out of love. Then, the "impassioned pride" (7) with which she meets his less-than-impassioned wooing acts to kindle a true love within him, to which she then responds in kind. Fairy tale and romance heroes can expect to have to overcome more than one obstacle, however, so the reader is not surprised by the next impediment: parental objection. Oropeza's father, hoping to be king, rejects Henry's suit "with insult" (11), using the pretext of "ancient feuds" to pour curses on Henry and thus surround the love with ancient hatred. For the second time, however, Oropeza provides the means whereby the love can be sustained: "Her blessings overtook and baffled" her father's curses (13). Love is stronger than hate. The first section would thus end in affirmation of love except that Henry notices Sandoval's disbelief: "But thou art stern, and with unkindly countenance / Art inly reasoning whilst thou listenest to me" (14–15).

Sandoval's response opens section two with doubt: "Anxiously, Henry! reasoning anxiously. / But Oropeza—" which Henry interrupts with "Blessings gather round her!" (16–17) to begin his tale of Faery. Once again Oropeza is the initiator, providing the means for love to find fulfillment as she leads Henry through the dark and silent night to a secret garden:

> Within this wood there winds a secret passage,
> Beneath the walls, which opens out at length
> Into the gloomiest covert of the garden.—
> The night ere my departure to the army,
> She, nothing trembling, led me through that gloom,
> And to that covert by a silent stream,
> Which, with one star reflected near its marge,
> Was the sole object visible around me.
> No leaflet stired; the air was almost sultry;
> So deep, so dark, so close, the umbrage o'er us!
> No leaflet stirred;—yet pleasure hung upon
> The gloom and stillness of the balmy night-air.
> A little further on an arbour stood,
> Fragrant with flowering trees—I well remember
> What an uncertain glimmer in the darkness
> Their snow-white blossoms made—thither she led me,
> To that sweet bower! Then Oropeza trembled—
> I heard her heart beat—if 'twere not my own. (18–35)

Sexual imagery and sexual tension underlie the description in what amounts to Oropeza's seduction of Henry. Sure of herself, knowing the path, Oropeza leads Henry down a winding "secret passage" within the wood which opens out into the "gloomiest covert of the garden." A "silent stream," in which a single star is reflected, runs through the covert, where everything is quiet and still. The place is utterly without confusion, a perfect, hidden resting place that is yet fully alive with intensity: "So deep, so dark, so close, the umbrage o'er us!" Pleasure hangs upon the night-air like the fragrance of the flowering trees, the Faery arbor which is the lover's destination. The "stillness of the balmy night-air" is "the mute still air" of "The Eolian Harp" (33), "music slumbering on her instrument." The "rich snows" that blossom in the flower-entangled arbors and canopied foliage of the pixies' cell and in the lover's imagination in "Lines" fill the night-scene with sensuous, erotic, imaginative fragrance, and the "snow-white blossoms" cause "an uncertain glimmer in the darkness." It is to this "sweet bower," the bower of bliss and Faery, that Oropeza leads Earl Henry for the consummation of their love: "Then Oropeza trembled— / I heard her heart beat—if 'twere not my own." In the moment of union, the lovers are individual and yet one, their participation in Faery an encounter with Spirit.

Sandoval destroys Henry's re-creation of the moment in faery tale with his uncomprehending skepticism: "A rude and scaring note, my friend!" (36). Sandoval's intrusion is similar in its effect to that of the Wedding-Guest in "The Rime"; but, much like the Mariner, Henry continues his tale, making explicit for those who have ears to hear the signficance of the tale of Faery he has just related:

> Oh! no!
> I have small memory of aught but pleasure.
> The inquietudes of fear, like lesser streams
> Still flowing, still were lost in those of love:
> So love grew mightier from the fear, and Nature,
> Fleeing from Pain, sheltered herself in Joy.
> The stars above our heads were dim and steady,
> Like eyes suffused with rapture. Life was in us:
> We were all life, each atom of our frames
> A living soul—I vowed to die for her:
> With the faint voice of one who, having spoken,
> Relapses into blessedness, I vowed it:
> That solemn vow, a whisper scarcely heard,
> A murmur breathed against a lady's ear.
> Oh! there is joy above the name of pleasure,
> Deep self-possession, an intense repose. (36–51)

The movement from fear to love and wholeness which "Religious Musings" and "Destiny of Nations" delineate is present here also, as the "lesser streams" of fear are "lost in those of love" so that emotional pleasure predominates. The spiritual import of the physical union—and the participation of nature—is made explicit in the stars "like eyes suffused with rapture." The physical union of the lovers is a moment of symbolic encounter and self-knowledge, and Henry unhesitatingly explains the connection: "Life was in us: / We were all life, each atom of our frames / A living soul."[5]

The world of Faery is the realization of consubstantiality; the unity of love is symbolic of Life and Love and Spirit. Existing in "blessedness," Henry—like Henry Falkland, the Dark Ladié's Knight—vows a "solemn vow," a whisper in the silence of love; and in the context of his symbolic knowledge, Henry can confidently assert: "Oh! There is a joy above the name of pleasure, / Deep self-possession, an intense repose." The joy is the joy of mystery and reconciliation; the silence, the silence of mystery. This section of "The Night-Scene" recalls Coleridge's notebook entry describing the lovers' union that reveals God:

> The two sweet Silences—first, in the purpling Dawn of Love-troth, when the Heart of each ripens in the other's looks within the unburst calix—& fear becomes so sweet; it seems but a fear of losing Hope in Certainty—the second, when the Sun is setting in the calm Even of confident Love, and in mute recollection enjoy each other—"I fear to speak, I fear to hear you speak"—So deeply do I now enjoy your presence, so totally possess you in myself, myself in you—The very sound would break the union, and separate *you-me* into you and me. We both, and this sweet Room, are its books, its pictures & the Shadows on the Wall Slumbering with the low quiet Fire are all *our* Thought, one dear a harmonious Imagery of Forms distinct on the still substance of one deep Feeling, Love & Joy—A Lake—or if a stream, yet flowing so softly, so unwrinkled, that its flow is *Life* not Change—/—That state, in which all the individuous nature, the distinction without Division, of a vivid Thought is united with the sense and substance of intensest Reality. (*CN* 3: 3705)

The movement from fear to confident love, the silence that speaks more than words, the androgynous intermingling of selves that is self-possession and Love and Joy, the state of "distinction without

Division" that is intensest life—all are present in Henry's description as well. The lovers *are* the resting place; they *are* the joy of "intense repose." They are "at the still point of the turning world" in the rose-garden of the "first world" ("Burnt Norton," 1).

And once again the repose, the moment out of time, is shattered by Sandoval, who says "with a sarcastic smile":

> No other than as eastern sages paint,
> The God, who floats upon a Lotos leaf,
> Dreams for a thousand ages; then awaking,
> Creates a world, and smiling at the bubble,
> Relapses into bliss. (52–56)

Sandoval's condescension and disbelief are palpable: Henry's tale is an illusion; a bubble waiting to be popped; pretty, perhaps, but silly; not real. Sandoval is the Apollonius of Keats's "Lamia"; the two who, "habituated to the petty things of daily life" (Rime, Epigraph), are not stopped by the Mariner; the man of Understanding rather than Reason; the man whose consciousness is a "fearful desert" (*BL* 1: 244).

Henry, taking up Sandoval's last words, begins the final section of the fragment by putting his finger directly on the problem: "Oh! was that bliss / Feared as an alien, and too vast for man?" (57–58). Human beings are afraid of bliss, says Henry. It seems "too vast" and therefore alien. A previously quoted *Biographia* passage provides an apt gloss:

> The first range of hills, that encircles the scanty vale of human life, is the horizon for the majority of its inhabitants. On *its* ridges the common sun is born and departs. From *them* the stars rise, and touching *them* they vanish. By the many, even this range, the natural limit and bulwark of the vale, is but imperfectly known. Its higher ascents are too often hidden by mists and clouds from uncultivated swamps, which few have courage or curiosity to penetrate. To the multitude below these vapors appear, now as the dark haunts of terrific agents, on which none may intrude with impunity; and now all *a-glow*, with colors not their own, they are gazed at, as the splendid palaces of happiness and power. But in all ages there have been a few, who measuring and sounding the rivers of the vale at the feet of their furthest inaccessible falls have learned, that the sources

must be far higher and far inward; a few, who even in the level streams have detected elements, which neither the vale itself or the surrounding mountains contained or could supply. (*BL* 1: 237–39)

Even those few who are aware of the source of power and mystery, those who have experienced symbolic encounter, sometimes falter: "For suddenly, impatient of its [bliss's] silence," Oropeza, in a "hollow voice," cries, "Oh! what if all betray me? what if thou?" (58, 62). If Henry were to betray her, she would be in the same situation as the Dark Ladié. But Henry, restating his vow to Oropeza in Sandoval's presence, leaves to join her:

> by that winding passage, to that bower
> I now will go—all objects there will teach me
> Unwavering love, and singleness of heart. (67–69)

If Life is in the lovers when they are united, then death—loss of wholeness—is their lot if they separate themselves from each other. Henry ends his speech by affirming the reality of repose and Love and Faery. There are two interpretations of his last lines: "Nay, leave me, friend! I cannot bear the torment / And keen inquiry of that scanning eye" (72–73). Either Sandoval's "keen inquiry" makes Earl Henry nervous about his position, or the lack of belief in the mystery of joy and bliss is painful to him, a "torment." In either case, he does not want Sandoval to accompany him to the hidden bower. The existence of mystery must be kept safe.

Sandoval's final comments reiterate his feeling that Earl Henry is living in an illusion:

> O Henry! always striv'st thou to be great
> By thine own act—yet art thou never great
> But by the inspiration of great passion.
> The whirl-blast comes, the desert-sands rise up
> And shape themselves; from Earth to Heaven they stand,
> As though they were the pillars of a temple,
> Built by Omnipotence in its own honour!
> But the blast pauses, and their shaping spirit
> Is fled: the mighty columns were but sand,
> And lazy snakes trail o'er the level ruins! (74–83)

The scene of Sandoval's commentary is the desert of the man without self-knowledge. He believes inspiration to be a desert whirlwind which builds the pillars of a temple that seems to connect earth and heaven. But when the wind dies down, "their shaping spirit" flees, the columns become level sand once more, and "lazy snakes trail o'er the level ruins!" Imagination inevitably betrays, Sandoval says, since it builds a false construct. Sandoval tells a tale, but it is not a tale of Faery. Instead of the Faery bower of Love and Life, he gives the reader a tale of the desert. Because the bower generates Life, it continues to exist; the desert, on the other hand, cannot sustain its temple, and the snakes slither over the ruins. The reader is left to choose which tale he or she will listen to.

In "Alice du Clos," written late in Coleridge's career, the world of Faery is betrayed by the false tongue of jealousy—disordered love. The garden bower, while still a place of Faery, exists as a place within the fallen world, not safely hidden away. Since this is so, words—texts—are capable of dual meaning; truth can be distorted into falseness, and it is the task of interpretation to distinguish truth from lie. "The Forked Tongue" serves as the subtitle for "Alice du Clos"; the epigraph for the ballad reads: " 'One word with two meanings is the traitor's shield and shaft: and a slit tongue be his blazon!' (Caucasian Proverb)." Sir Hugh has the forked tongue, but Lord Julian fails to discern the lie within Hugh's falsely accurate words. As a result, Lord Julian himself kills Alice, his love. He is a hunter after the wrong prey.

The poem opens in the light before sunrise, while it is still faery time, and ends a few moments after sunrise. Unlike Earl Henry in "The Night-Scene," who goes to Oropeza's hidden bower alone, rejecting the company of the skeptical Sandoval, Lord Julian has sent a message to Alice by his "vassal knight" (15), Sir Hugh. Thus, the opening lines of the ballad belong to Sir Hugh:

The Sun is not yet risen,
But the dawn lies red on the dew:
Lord Julian has stolen from the hunters away,
Is seeking, Lady! for you.
Put on your dress of green,

> Your buskins and your quiver;
> Lord Julian is a hasty man,
>   Long waiting brook'd he never.
> I dare not doubt him, that he means
>   To wed you on a day,
> Your lord and master for to be,
>   And you his lady gay.
> O Lady! throw your book aside!
> I would not that my Lord should chide.   (1–14)

Sir Hugh's words are always utterly accurate and proper. It is his tone and the interpretation that tone conveys that are false. Here, the reader learns several things: Lord Julian wants to be with Alice; he is a hunter, as is Alice, and both have hunted for each other; Lord Julian intends to wed Alice, a fact that Sir Hugh "dare[s] not doubt," implying both the truth of Julian's intention and Hugh's dislike for the marriage. We also learn that Lord Julian is a "hasty," impatient man, used to having his own way, who in marriage will be Alice's "lord and master" and before marriage will not stint to chide her tardiness in obeying his wishes. Julian's need to dominate bodes ill for a union embodying wholeness. Sir Hugh implies that Alice du Clos would do well to begin being obedient if she wants to marry Lord Julian. At the same time, his seeming concern over Lord Julian's chiding of Alice functions, in fact, as a veiled threat. Alice du Clos, an accurate interpreter of texts, can separate truth from lie; she hears the jealousy in Sir Hugh's words, calls him "traitor friend," and—without looking up from her book—says:

> Off, traitor friend! how dar'st thou fix
>   Thy wanton gaze on me?
> And why, against my earnest suit,
>   Does Julian send by thee?   (44–47)

Sir Hugh wants Alice du Clos for himself. She knows this and has asked Lord Julian to protect her from Hugh by keeping him away from her. Instead, Julian has sent the forked-tongue snake into the garden, and the snake's poison begins its work: "The vassal's speech, his taunting vein, / It thrill'd like venom thro' her brain"

(39–40), even though she tells him to be off. Sir Hugh is a deceitful traitor, but it is Lord Julian who, in his carelessness and pride, gives Sir Hugh license to act.

Alice du Clos lives in the bower of imagination and Love, and she herself is a symbol of Love. A "studious maid" (26), Alice has gone, before the dawn, to her "garden bower" to read "Dan Ovid's mazy tale of loves, / And gods, and beasts, and men" (36–37). She herself, dressed in "maiden white" (22), is still an innocent virgin, but she imaginatively participates in sensual love through Ovid's stories. Alice illustrates the androgynous feminine; she is a "spotless fair" (17) beauty who, in addition to being well-read, is active in a sport usually associated with men:

> The huntress is in her dress of green,—
> And forth they go; she with her bow,
> > Her buskins and her quiver!—
>
> . . . .
> See! see! that face of hope and joy,
> > That regal front! those cheeks aglow!
> Thou needed'st but the crescent sheen,
> A quiver'd Dian to have been,
> > Thou lovely child of old Du Clos!   (85–87, 182–86)

The comparison with the huntress goddess Diana reinforces Alice's androgynous nature, since Diana, the twin sister of Apollo, is the chaste moon goddess, the female counterpart of the archer sun god. Alice's association with Diana makes Julian's jealous questioning of her chastity all the more inappropriate. Up before dawn, Alice is

> As spotless fair, as airy light
> > As that moon-shiney doe,
> The gold star on its brow, her sire's ancestral crest!   (17–19)

Alice, bearing the ancestral crest of the gold star, is watched over by the "morning star [which] shone opposite / The lattice of her bower" (29–30). Alice is as beautiful and innocent as "a snow-drop on a tuft of snow" (24). The natural comparisons emphasize Alice's association with the world of imagination through the mythological allusions. These allusions are also intertwined with the metaphoric relationship between the natural world of the elements, the bower, and Alice, as each shows imaginative reconciliation. Alice is the "earliest-open'd flower," "a snow-drop" growing in the garden bower. In that bower

> There stands the flow'ring may-thorn tree!
> From thro' the veiling mist you see
>   The black and shadowy stem;—
> Smit by the sun the mist in glee
> Dissolves to lightsome jewelry—
>   Each blossom hath its gem!   (65–70)

The "flow'ring may-thorn tree" of this garden recalls other flower-entangled faery arbors of imagination as the sun and mist together gleefully bestow jewels on the blossoms of the may-thorn tree. And Alice, the flower, is also the imaginatively reconciled light and mist:

> With tear-drop glittering to a smile,
> The gay maid on the garden-stile
>   Mimics the hunter's shout.
> "Hip! Florian, hip! To horse, to horse!
>   Go, bring the palfrey out.
>
>   "My Julian's out with all his clan,
>   And, bonny boy, you wis,
> Lord Julian is a hasty man,
>   Who comes late, comes amiss."   (71–79)

Her "tear-drop glittering to a smile" parallels mist dissolved "to lightsome jewelry"; the glee and light gemlike tone of nature is reflected in her "gay" mimicking of the hunter's shout and also in her playful mockery of Sir Hugh's words.

In many ways, Alice du Clos is an innocent fairy tale heroine, abandoned without protection. She has no mother. Her father, "old Du Clos," gives no help. Of the two retainers who should act in her behalf, one is actively malevolent and the other even more innocent and closer to childhood than she. Florian tries to be helpful, and he clearly has an adolescent crush on Alice, but the

poem insists on his youth. He is a "stripling squire," a "gallant boy
. . . no younger e'er was seen," who "blush'd to hold . . . his Lady's
. . . train" (80–81, 84, 88)—hardly a protector from the likes of Sir
Hugh. In the end, Florian's inexpert horsemanship—"A youth,
that ill his steed can guide" (175)—provides the occasion for
Alice's death. Though Alice herself is an appropriate heroine for a
symbolic tale of Faery, her story is told in a fallen world. True to
her words that "slow is sure" (48) and true to her nature as symbolic character, Alice

stay'd the race,

And stopp'd to see, a moment's space,
   The whole great globe of light
Give the last parting kiss-like touch
To the eastern ridge.   (91–95)

Ironically, this delay gives Sir Hugh the opportunity to represent
Alice falsely to Lord Julian as "with stifled tones the knight re-
plied, / And look'd askance on either side" (135–36) in response to
Julian's query as to Alice's whereabouts.

Sir Hugh's low voice, shifty eyes, and seeming reluctance to
convey his story all imply the interpretation that Lord Julian does
indeed give to the words. But it is Julian's own inability to perceive
the truth of Alice's love that makes him susceptible to the falseness
of deceiving partiality. Lord Julian is given the opportunity for
wholeness. He waits for Alice du Clos in the forest in a place which
is potentially an extension of the faery bower:

Straight from the forest's skirt the trees
   O'er-branching, made an aisle,
Where hermit old might pace and chaunt
   As in a minster's pile.

From underneath its leafy screen,
   And from the twilight shade,
You pass at once into a green,
   A green and lightsome glade.   (113–20)

The "o'er-branching" trees form a natural cathedral, a holy place
of worship. The "leafy screen" provides a faery "twilight" which

leads into a "green and lightsome glade." But Lord Julian is any-thing but serene and worshipful; rather, he is a man "with an anger'd mind" (102):

> Betroth'd not wedded to his bride,
>> In vain he sought, 'twixt shame and pride,
>> Excuse to stay behind.
> He bit his lip, he wrung his glove,
> He look'd around, he look'd above,
>> And pretext none could find or frame.
> Alas! alas! and well-a-day!
> It grieves me sore to think, to say,
> That names so seldom meet with Love,
> Yet Love wants courage without a name!   (103–12)

Angry because Alice delays in obeying him before his kinsmen but wanting to wait for her anyway, Lord Julian is pulled in two directions. Biting his lip and wringing his glove, he casts this way and that for an excuse to stay. He needs a "pretext" because his masculine pride will not allow him to appear "weak" by saying the truth—that he wants to wait for Alice because he loves her. Lack-ing the courage of Love, unable to be at rest in Alice's love for him, he is divided, torn. He projects his own uncertainty and lack of trust onto Alice, thus becoming vulnerable to the misinterpreta-tion that Sir Hugh's forked tongue presents for text.

Sir Hugh tells the surface truth. He did come "unlook'd for" at an "unwelcome hour." He did find "the daughter of Du Clos / Within the lattic'd bower" (145–48). It was true that only Alice and "one more" (144) were as yet up. Even the most crucial part of Sir Hugh's account is literally true:

> " 'Go! (said she) tell him,—slow is sure;
>> Fair speed his shafts to-day!
> I follow here a stronger lure,
>> And chase a gentler prey.'
>
> "The game, pardie, was full in sight,
> That then did, if I saw aright,
>> The fair dame's eyes engage;
> For turning, as I took my ways,
> I saw them fix'd with steadfast gaze
>> Full on her wanton page."   (160–69)

Once Lord Julian, "o'ermaster'd by the sudden smart" (154) of jealousy, interprets the "wanton page" of Ovid's book to be page Florian—as Sir Hugh had of course intended—Hugh's "feigning wrath, sharp, blunt, rude," part of his "subtle shift" (155), becomes true wrath in Lord Julian's heart. Divisive hate and jealousy replace the wholeness of love entirely. Intending to kill Florian, Julian instead shoots Alice. Lack of wholeness causes the death of love, and the fallen world triumphs.

"The Three Graves," written in collaboration with Wordsworth, is the darkest of Coleridge's shorter romantic faery tale ballads—and the most terrifying. The "[Racedown] manuscripts prove conclusively that the second part, and therefore presumably the first, as well as the original of the poem are Wordsworth's. . . . [Coleridge] was probably led to undertake it, after Wordsworth had thrown it aside, partly . . . because of its obvious psychological possibilities" (De Selincourt 30).[6] Bosteller comments: "The superiority of Coleridge's portion of the poem to Wordsworth's is marked; and the difference in conception and development is notable, too. Here we can watch the emergence of the distinctive characteristics that come so quickly to perfection in 'The Rime.' Obviously, Coleridge's imagination was set afire by the religious and sexual ambiguities in the poem. The power of evil in a universe of good preoccupies him here as in later poems" (*Ventriloquists* 107). Although Coleridge first published Parts 3 and 4 in *The Friend* (No. 6, 21 September 1809), the actual composition was concurrent with that of "The Rime" and the first part of "Christabel," as the thematic concerns and the narrative techniques of the poems attest.[7] The narrative structure of "The Three Graves" is a variation on that of "The Rime," with the structure of both poems ultimately necessitated by the intensity of the experience being related. In all three poems, the focus is on the psychological and on imaginative response. All three are tales of Faery.

In his Preface to "The Three Graves," Coleridge describes the poem as a "common Ballad-tale" whose "merits, if any, are exclusively psychological." In brief, the story is about Edward, a young farmer, who meets Mary at her friend Ellen's house; they fall in love and wish to marry. Mary's mother, a widow, agrees at first, but gradually she herself falls in love with Edward and declares herself to him, denouncing her daughter and promising her lands and fortune to Edward if he will marry her instead. Edward, startled and appalled, laughs and says she must be mad or drunk, whereupon the mother curses the daughter. The rest of the story deals with the effect of this curse and a later curse on Ellen. Coleridge explains:

> I was not led to choose this story from any partiality to tragic, much less to monstrous events (though at the time that I composed the verses, somewhat more than twelve years ago, I was less averse to such subjects than at present), but from finding in it a striking proof of the possible effect on the imagination, from an idea violently and suddenly impressed on it. I had been reading Bryan Edwards's account of the effects of the *Oby* witchcraft on the Negroes in the West Indies, and Hearne's deeply interesting anecdotes of similar workings on the imagination of the Copper Indians (those of my readers who have it in their power will be well repaid for the trouble of referring to those works for the passages alluded to); and I conceived the design of shewing that instances of this kind are not peculiar to savage or barbarous tribes, and of illustrating the mode in which the mind is affected in these cases, and the progress and symptoms of the morbid action on the fancy from the beginning. (*Complete Poetical Works* 269)

The story is indeed concerned with the progress of the effects on the imagination of "an idea violently and suddenly impressed on it." But what, exactly, is the sudden idea that calls forth responses as extreme as those portrayed in the poem? Is it the mother's jealous statement, Edward's disbelieving and shaming laughter, Mary's overhearing of the exchange—or all of these? A mother's falling in love with her daughter's fiancé is not usual, but the significance and consequences seem more intense than even a penetrating psychological analysis of such an event can account for, though the psychological perception displayed in the poem is quite acute.

The horror in the poem and in the reader comes, finally, not just from the suddenness of the idea but, rather, from the fact that the idea symbolizes a violation of innocence. The idea is a stark and sudden realization of the fallen world as it manifests itself in the human psyche, and the gathering horror comes from the further realization of the extreme difficulty, if not impossibility, of escaping the fallen world in one's own person. The violation of innocence is equivalent to the violation of Love.[8] In a "world of sin" (C 673), the mother's curse is inescapable. The central question of the poem is, what, then, are the available responses?

The stark, inevitable ballad form universalizes this tragic love story, while also giving some much-needed distance. Just as the Mariner's story of the violation of love is framed by third-person narration, the story of the three graves is told to a traveler by a sexton who has known all the participants. He has had the story from Edward and from Mary's sister, and he, like the third-person narrator of "The Rime," gives us a voice we can trust. The objectifying function of the prose epigraph in "The Rime" is fulfilled in "The Three Graves" by Coleridge's Preface, in which he assures us: "The outlines of the tale are positive facts, and of no very distant date, though the author has purposely altered the names and scene of action, as well as invented the characters of the parties and the detail of the incidents." The story is true, not dismissable as fabrication. This true story becomes, in Coleridge's hands and imagination, a ballad tale of Faery. Just as the ballad form universalizes and yet gives emotional distance, so also do the fairy tale elements in the poem. In addition, the strong presence of both genres emphasizes the difficulty of the "happy ending" in a fallen world.

The primary relationship in "The Three Graves" is the relationship of mother and daughter, and its closest fairy tale analogue is "Snow White,"[9] of which Bruno Bettelheim says:

"Snow White" tells how a parent—the queen—gets destroyed by jealousy of her child who, in growing up, surpasses her. . . . The queen's fear that Snow White will excel her is the theme of the fairy tale. . . . We do not know why the queen in "Snow White" cannot age gracefully and gain satisfaction from vicariously enjoying her daughter's blooming into a lovely girl, but something must have happened in her past to make her vulnerable so that she hates the child she should love. How the sequence of the generations can account for a parent's fear of his child is illustrated in the cycle of myths of which the story of Oedipus is the central part. . . . When a parent cannot accept his child as such and be satisfied that he will have to be replaced by him eventually, deepest tragedy results. (195, 198)

As in "Snow White," the motivating emotion in "The Three Graves" is maternal jealousy of a growing, maturing young girl, and the result, once again, is tragedy. The two stories parallel each other in several ways, beginning with the older women's pride in their physical beauty. Since the Queen-stepmother depends on her magic mirror's assurance that she is fairest in the land, the mirror's statement that Snow White is fairer precipitates the action of the tale; until then the Queen seems to be a perfectly agreeable step-mother. Only when Snow White surpasses the Queen in beauty does the jealousy emerge. Coleridge's Preface to "The Three Graves" emphasizes the physical attractiveness of the mother: "A widow-woman bordering on her fortieth year, and from constant health, the possession of a competent property, and from having had no other children but Mary and another daughter (the father died in their infancy), retaining for the greater part her personal attractions and comeliness of appearance." Both the Queen and the mother have avoided the things that make older women phys-ically unattractive: bad health, poverty, and too many children. Both are without husbands (and consequently, the daughters—in usual fairy-tale fashion—are without father-protectors); but both, perhaps even more so because they are husbandless, are very sex-ually aware.

The mother, unlike the Queen, at first seems happy to help her daughter achieve a satisfying, mature sexual love: when Edward asks for Mary's hand, she says: "In truth you are a comely man; / You shall my daughter wed" (40–41). Gradually, however, her own emotional needs change her love and good wishes for her daughter into disordered and disordering jealousy:

The mother, more than mothers use,
    Rejoiced when they were by;
And all the "course of wooing" passed
    Beneath the mother's eye.

And here within the flowering thorn
How deep they drank of joy:
The mother fed upon the sight. (50–56)

The mother's rejoicing, protective watchfulness becomes more than is natural. Within the faery "flowering thorn" bower of love, Mary and Edward appropriately drink deep of joy, but the mother inappropriately feeds upon their love, attempting to satiate her own longing vicariously. The Queen in "Snow White" demands that the hunter take Snow White into the forest, kill her, and bring the Queen the girl's heart to eat. In like fashion, Mary's mother can feed her hunger only if Mary is destroyed and she herself can take her daughter's place with Edward in the bridal bed. As Edward and the mother sit together in the bower listening to Mary prepare the bridal bed, the mother leaves the bower and meets Mary at the door:

She stood, her back against the door,
And when her child drew near—
"Away! away!" the mother cried,
"Ye shall not enter here.

"Would ye come here, ye maiden vile,
And rob me of my mate?"
And on her child the mother scowled
A deadly leer of hate. (74–81)

Fairy tales commonly deal with a child's sexual jealousy of the same-sex parent and competition for the other-sex parent so that these emotions can gradually be resolved as part of the child's developmental process. In "The Three Graves," however, in an emotional reversal, the mother's outburst sounds disturbingly like an externalized expression of a child's feelings of emotional frustration and violence. Everything is disordered. The mother becomes the child; a child's natural sexual jealousy becomes a parent's "unnatural" jealousy of a child. The result is destruction and tragedy. As the mother denounces Mary to Edward, she abandons her role of mother-nurturer-protector and instead becomes a figure of destruction. She displaces her own feelings and distorted nature

onto Mary, calling her "fierce," "proud," "envious," and "giddy"—
a "wily hypocrite" (102–05). The mother then offers herself in
Mary's stead: "Sweet Edward, for one kiss of yours / I'd give my
house and land" (124–29). When the startled Edward laughs at
her, what should be a mother's blessing becomes instead a mother's
curse:

> Thou daughter now above my head,
>> Whom in my womb I bore,
> May every drop of thy heart's blood
>> Be curst for ever more.
>
> And curséd be the hour when first
>> I heard thee wawl and cry;
> And in the Church-yard curséd be
>> The grave where thou shalt lie!   (138–45)

Traditional fairy tales split the mother into two figures: the
good mother who is an "all-giving protector" and a stepmother or
witch who is cruel and evil. Snow White's real mother dies, leaving
Snow White with a stepmother who eventually desires Snow
White's death. "The typical fairy-tale splitting of the mother into a
good (usually dead) mother and an evil stepmother serves the child
well. Not only does it preserve an internal all-good mother when
the real mother is not all-good, but it also permits anger at this bad
'stepmother' without endangering the goodwill of the true mother,
who is viewed as a different person" (Bettelheim 69). In traditional
tales, the evil stepmother is always defeated. In "The Three
Graves," the convenient split does not occur. Instead, the poem
insists that the good mother *is* the bad mother; they are one and the
same. The battle is not between two contrasted and opposed characters; rather, the human dual nature exists in one character.
Because the world of Coleridge's tale is a fallen one, the mothers
must exist together; nor can the bad mother be denied or entirely
defeated. The Hunter in "Snow White" does not follow the Queen's
orders; instead, he turns Snow White loose so that ultimately she
can be rescued from her deathlike state by the Prince. In "The Three
Graves," Edward rescues Mary by carrying her out of her mother's
house and marrying her. But the mother's curse remains; not even

she can escape it. The most terrifying scene in the poem occurs as
Edward and Mary leave the mother's house:

> The mother still was in the bower,
>   And with a greedy heart
> She *drank perdition* on her knees,
>   Which never may depart.
>
> But when their steps were heard below
>   On God she did not call;
> She did forget the God of Heaven,
>   For they were in the hall.
>
> She started up—the servant maid
>   Did see her when she rose;
> And she has oft declared to me
>   The blood within her froze.
>
> As Edward led his bride away
>   And hurried to the door,
> The ruthless mother springing forth
>   Stopped midway on the floor.
>
> What did she mean? What did she mean?
>   For with a smile she cried:
> "Unblest ye shall not pass my door,
>   The bride-groom and his bride.
>
> Be blithe as lambs in April are,
>   As flies when fruits are red;
> May God forbid that thought of me
>   Should haunt your marriage-bed.
>
> "And let the night be given to bliss,
>   The day be given to glee:
> I am a woman weak and old,
>   Why turn a thought on me?
>
> "What can an aged mother do,
>   And what have ye to dread?
> A curse is wind, it hath no shape
>   To haunt your marriage-bed."
>
> When they were gone and out of sight
>   She rent her hoary hair,
> And foamed like any Dog of June
>   When sultry sun-beams glare.   (164–99)

147

As the mother had once fed upon the love of Edward and Mary, she must now drink perdition with a "greedy heart." Caught in the horror of emotional extremes, eternally lost and alone, she cannot save herself.

It would be a simple matter to dismiss the mother's words to Edward and Mary as ironic, but that interpretation leaves the narrator's "What did she mean? What did she mean?" as well as the psychological complexity operating here and the bad mother–good mother tension all unaccounted for. The lines are much more interesting and truer to the nature of the poem if read as emotion-charged but non-ironic. Read in this way, the mother can be seen to be making an extraordinary effort to become the good mother once more. As the lovers leave the house, she tries to bless them, making a wish for nighttime "bliss" and days filled with "glee." She is even willing to describe herself as "weak and old," "aged," as she attempts to dismiss the power of the curse: "A curse is wind, it hath no shape / To haunt your marriage-bed." When they have gone, she tears her hair in a gesture of contrition and sorrow, but immediately madness falls upon her. She is lost. Her curse is the curse of death, the curse of the fallen world, and she has no power to revoke it. She cannot be the wholly good mother, and so she becomes the evil stepmother, crazed by the division she has caused and her inability to rectify it or keep from causing harm.

The mother's failure to escape her fallen nature—which distorts, disorders, and destroys love—is emphasized by her second curse. On Ash Wednesday, as Mary's friend Ellen goes to church to pray, the mother enters the church and approaches her. Ellen welcomes her, thinking, "What if her heart should melt, / And all be reconciled!" (300–301). But the dark clouds and stormy wind and rain of the day are an analogue of the lack of harmony in the mother: she curses Ellen for her role in bringing Edward and Mary together.

"The Three Graves" does not end with the mother's curse. Instead, Coleridge steadfastly carries out the effects and implications of the curse in the mother-daughter relationship. If—as is most assuredly the case—the good mother and the stepmother are really one, whether split into two characters or trapped in one, then it is also true that in a very real sense the mother and daughter are one. Daughters "mirror" their mothers; each sees her own reflection in the other. The good mother is inevitably also the stepmother, and the innocent Snow White, once married, will continue the cycle. She will become the good mother and—eventually—the stepmother to her own daughter. Bettelheim notes: "The readiness with which Snow White repeatedly permits herself to be tempted by the stepmother, despite the warnings of the dwarfs, suggests how close the stepmother's temptations are to Snow White's inner desires" (211). Gilbert and Gubar extend the observation:

> Indeed, it suggests that . . . the Queen and Snow White are in some sense one: while the Queen struggles to free herself from the passive Snow White in herself, Snow White must struggle to repress the assertive Queen in herself. That both women eat from the same deadly apple in the third temptation episode merely clarifies and dramatizes this point. The Queen's lonely art has enabled her to contrive a two-faced fruit—one white and one red "cheek"—that represents her ambiguous relationship to this angelic girl who is both her daughter and her enemy, her self and her opposite. Her intention is that the girl will die of the apple's poisoned red half—red with her sexual energy, her assertive desire for deeds of blood and triumph— while she herself will be unharmed by the passivity of the white half. (41)

Coleridge's awareness of the implications of mother-daughter relationships is evident in "The Three Graves"—as it is also in "Christabel"—and his poem almost eerily foreshadows contemporary feminist critical analysis of "Snow White." Gilbert and Gubar set up the dichotomy represented by the Queen and Snow White: "The central action of the tale—indeed, its only real action— arises from the relationship between these two women: the one fair, young, pale, the other just as fair, but older, fiercer; the one a daughter, the other a mother; the one sweet, ignorant, passive, the other both artful and active; the one a sort of angel, the other an undeniable witch." This dichotomy exists, however, because the women exist within a patriarchal society, subject to the King's rules: "Having assimilated the meaning of her own sexuality (and having, thus, become the second Queen) [the Queen-Stepmother] has internalized the King's rules: his voice resides now in her own mirror, her own mind" (38). Coleridge would agree that the patriarchal world of "Snow White" is a dichotomous world, a world divided and without wholeness, a fallen world. The wicked Queen's hatred of Snow White grows out of disordered love, portrayed as sexual jealousy; but it also represents an ambivalence existing within the Queen herself as both innocent and experienced, passive and active, daughter and mother. The Queen, as Gilbert and Gubar put it, is

> a plotter, a plot-maker, a schemer, a witch, an artist, an impersonator, a woman of almost infinite creative energy, witty, wily, and self-absorbed as all artists traditionally are. On the other hand, in her absolute chastity, her frozen innocence, her sweet nullity, Snow White represents precisely the ideal of "contemplative purity" we have already discussed, an ideal that could quite literally kill the Queen. An angel in the house of myth, Snow White is not only a child but (as female angels always are) childlike, docile, submissive, the heroine of a life that *has no story*. But the Queen, adult and demonic, plainly wants a life of "significant action," by definition an "unfeminine" life of stories and story-telling. And therefore, to the extent that Snow White, as her daughter, is a part of herself, she wants to kill the Snow White *in herself*, the angel who would keep deeds and dramas out of her own house. (38–39)

In his own Snow White tale, Coleridge sees that the mother is the angry artist, the story teller, and he sees that the story that needs to be told is being frustrated. He also sees that the traditional ending of "Snow White" is not satisfactory. Gilbert and Gubar comment:

> If Snow White escaped her first glass coffin by her goodness, her passivity and docility, her only escape from her second glass coffin, the imprisoning mirror, must evidently be through "badness," through plots and stories, duplicitous schemes, wild dreams, fierce fictions, mad impersonations. The cycle of her fate seems inexorable. Renouncing "contemplative purity," she must now embark on that life of "significant action" which, for a woman, is defined as a witch's life because it is so monstrous, so unnatural. Grotesque as Errour, Duessa, Lucifera, she will practice false arts in her secret, lonely room. Suicidal as Lilith and Medea, she will become a murderess bent

on the self-slaughter implicit in her murderous attempts against the life of her own child. Finally, in fiery shoes that parody the costumes of femininity as surely as the comb and stays she herself contrived, she will do a silent terrible death-dance out of the story, the looking glass, the transparent coffin of her own image. Her only deed, this death will imply, can be a deed of death, her only action the pernicious action of self-destruction. (42)

Death and self-destruction are the actions carried out by the mother in "The Three Graves," and Coleridge's reading of Snow White's future is precisely that which Gilbert and Gubar delineate. His Preface not only insists on the mother's physical appeal; it also insists that this appeal has come because as a widow she has inherited the independent action that wealth and lands—usually reserved for men—bestow, as well as the freedom from many children. She has the "room of her own" necessary to the artist. Through her declaration to Edward, she attempts to make a story for herself. Gilbert and Gubar's reading of "Snow White," through Virginia Woolf, argues that the Queen must kill the passive, innocent angel in the house within—that is, Snow White—before she can create in a patriarchal world. Seeing the Queen-mother/ "Three Graves" mother as frustrated in her storytelling by a disordered world—a world of division, separation, nonwholeness— Coleridge makes the frustrated storyteller non-androgynous. The mother is an attractive, independent woman, but she is also cut off from love, and the Preface claims that she is a woman of "low education and violent temper." Lacking the wholeness of love, her story will never be the story of imaginative genius; instead, it will always be self-destructive.

Coleridge's solution, with his own self-interest as an artist at stake, is to retell the story of Snow White, hypothesizing other endings, looking for an ending that will not perpetuate the cycle of self-destruction; an ending in which the daughter's innocence does not have to be destroyed for the survival of the mother but can instead be reconciled into wholeness; an ending, therefore, that can allow Faery to exist in a fallen world. For this reason, Coleridge modifies the fairy tale convention of splitting a single char-

acter into two. While his mother embodies good mother and stepmother in one character, he multiplies the daughter into three.
Two are the mother's "own," Mary and Mary's sister; one—Ellen—
is like a sister to Mary, a kind of "stepsister" and therefore a
stepdaughter to the mother. A manuscript stanza reads:

> [In Mary's joy fair Eleanor
>   Did bear a sister's part;
> For why, though not akin in blood,
>   They sisters were in heart.]   (42–45)

Later, Ellen is said to be "more dear than any sister" (282). Rather
than splitting the mother as the traditional tales do, Coleridge
assumes the duality of fallen human nature and splits the character of the daughter into three. Doing so allows him to explore
various possible responses to the inevitable continuity of a destructive mother-daughter identity and, through this, to explore
alternatives for wholeness of spirit within a fallen world.

   "The Three Graves" makes a strong case for the one-in-three
identity of Mary, Ellen, and Mary's sister, as well as setting up the
ultimate identity of the daughters with their mother. Ellen and
Mary are similar from the beginning, and there is never any question that they "did love each other dear."

> Fair Ellen was of serious mind,
>   Her temper mild and even,
> And Mary, graceful as the fir
>   That points the spire to heaven.   (26–29)

Before the wedding, Mary, "though she was not gay, / Seemed
cheerful and content" (234–35). There is a change, however, as
the maiden becomes the "married maiden" (249):

> But when they to the church-yard came,
>   I've heard poor Mary say,
> As soon as she stepped into the sun,
>   Her heart it died away.

> And when the Vicar join'd their hands,
>   Her limbs did creep and freeze:
> But when they prayed, she thought she saw
>   Her mother on her knees.   (236–43)

The mother and daughter are joined in the praying figure; and as the wedding bells ring, a "chill like death" comes over Mary and seems "to stop her breath" (253, 255):

> Beneath the foulest mother's curse
> > No child could ever thrive:
> A mother is a mother still,
> > The holiest thing alive. (256–59)

Though the daughters must of necessity "deny" the mother, guilt and unease follow—as is shown by Ellen's hope for reconciliation—even when the "blame," if one can call it that, belongs to the mother. Further, of course, denying the mother is a form of self-denial for a daughter. Mary, though a "fond wife" (263), becomes "dull and sad" (269), and Ellen comes every day to help cheer Edward and Mary. When the mother curses Ellen—Mary's arms "round Ellen's neck she threw; / 'O Ellen, Ellen, she cursed me, / And now she hath cursed you!'" (352–55)—Ellen at first tries to ignore the curse: "She smiled, and smiled, and passed it off" (336). But the curse is real, of course, and the strain of trying to remain her old innocent, cheerful self—a psychologically and emotionally exhausting task—begins to show. Her "heart was not at ease" (340); she now has "a hurry in her looks" (344); her mirth, in Edward's eyes, "becomes fearful":

> When by herself, she to herself
> > Must sing some merry rhyme;
> She could not now be glad for hours,
> > Yet silent all the time. (422–25)

Ellen's inability to be at rest recalls the emotional intensity of the mother earlier when she declares herself to Edward and then tears her hair and foams like a mad dog; neither has the "resting place" of wholeness. Though in different ways, both Ellen and Mary bear the effects of the mother's curse.

The identity between Mary and Ellen is also shown in Edward's love for them both:

> Now Ellen was a darling love
> > In all his joys and cares:
> And Ellen's name and Mary's name

Fast-linked they both together came,
  Whene'er he said his prayers.

And in the moment of his prayers
  He loved them both alike:
Yea, both sweet names with one sweet joy
  Upon his heart did strike!   (368–76)

The three of them spend almost all their time together and are a comfort to one another. Once, however, as the three embrace and Mary and Edward weep,

Dear Ellen did not weep at all,
  But closelier did she cling,
And turned her face and looked as if
  She saw some frightful thing.   (385–88)

The "frightful thing" Ellen sees is that Mary, despite her sad, gentle innocence, is becoming more like the mother. One way not to become the mother is never to marry, and Ellen's situation exemplifies this alternative, an unfulfilling and frustrating one at best. But Mary has married, so she inevitably moves closer and closer to the state of motherhood.

These two alternatives to the mother's curse and their accompanying psychological states are shown in a set of four stanzas:

And oft she said, I'm not grown thin!
  And then her wrist she spanned;
And once when Mary was down-cast,
  She took her by the hand,
And gazed upon her, and at first
  She gently pressed her hand;

Then harder, till her grasp at length
  Did gripe like a convulsion!
"Alas!" said she, "we ne'er can be
  Made happy by compulsion!"

And once her both arms suddenly
  Round Mary's neck she flung,
And her heart panted, and she felt
  The words upon her tongue.

She felt them coming, but no power
    Had she the words to smother;
And with a kind of shriek she cried,
    "O Christ! you're like your mother!"   (430–47)

The spanning of the wrist, the tight grip "like a convulsion," the encircling of Ellen's arms around Mary's neck, and the long-smothered words all show an inability to break free of becoming the mother and a kind of claustrophobic terror that there may be no happy resolution possible. Is there, then, no escape?

To answer the question, it is important to keep in mind exactly what the curse represents and what escape from the curse means. The curse is the curse of the fallen world. It is love divided and therefore disordered, love that does not symbolize wholeness and Love. Rather than finding the love that becomes self-knowledge and an encounter with Love, the cursed human spirit wars with itself in darkness and passes the curse from generation to generation. Paradoxically, the only escape is through encounter and self-knowledge and wholeness: that is, through Love. Once aware of the curse, Mary and Ellen and Edward live out the Wedding-Guest's "curse": to rise the "morrow morn" (Rime 624) sadder and wiser. The three are subdued—Mary mournfully trying to smile, Ellen gentle but unable to bring cheer, Edward grieving with love. But they also live surrounding each other with love and with extreme gentleness. None of the three blames either of the others. Mary and Ellen are so close they become one; Edward loves them both; and there is no jealousy. When he cries, "Her heart is broke! O God! my grief, / It is too great to bear!" (466–67) he means Ellen equally with Mary. They live—heartbroken as they are—in wholeness of love.

This wholeness, as in the other Coleridgean faery tale ballads, is represented by the faery arbor where the last scene of the poem takes place. One Sunday morning, with the church bells ringing in the distance, the "three friends" (490) enter "a close, round arbor" (486) that stands next to a brook. In this poem, however, the arbor is filled not with fragrant white thorn blossoms but with the "scarlet berries" (489) of a cluster of "lone" (483) holly trees.

Edward, exhausted and unwell, falls asleep. Mary and Ellen sit beside him and whisper together playfully:

> The Sun peeps through the close thick leaves,
>   See, dearest Ellen! see!
> 'Tis in the leaves, a little sun,
>   No bigger than your ee;
>
> A tiny sun, and it has got
>   A perfect glory too;
> Ten thousand threads and hairs of light,
> Make up a glory gay and bright
>   Round that small orb, so blue."
>
> And then they argued of those rays,
>   What colour they might be;
> Says this, "They're mostly green"; says that,
>   "They're amber-like to me."   (505–17)

The sun, shining through the holly leaves, looks tiny but is surrounded by a "perfect glory." The women are at ease, at rest, safe in the arbor. Their conversation is full of imaginative play, the play of light through leaves which, with its "thousand threads and hairs of light," makes up a single perfect glory.

But the curse, foreshadowed by the scarlet holly berries, enters even the faery arbor of imagination. In his restless, troubled sleep, Edward speaks:

> "A mother too!" these self-same words
>   Did Edward mutter plain;
> His face was drawn back on itself,
>   With horror and huge pain.
>
> Both groaned at once, for both knew well
>   What thoughts were in his mind;
> When he waked up, and stared like one
>   That hath been just struck blind.
>
> He sat upright; and ere the dream
>   Had had time to depart,
> "O God, forgive me!" (he exclaimed)
>   "I have torn out her heart."   (522–33)

It is impossible to distinguish the referents for "mother" and "her heart"; the identity between the mother and Mary/Ellen is too strong. All are "mothers." All have had their hearts torn out.

> Then Ellen shrieked, and forthwith burst
>> Into ungentle laughter;
> And Mary shivered, where she sat,
>> And never she smiled after.   (534–37)

The end is madness and melancholy—the wholeness of joy never-more, for mothers or daughters. Tearing out the heart does end the curse: the mother dies; Mary is a "barren wife"; Ellen a "maid forlorn" (20–21). There are three graves. Snow White's mirror has shattered.

Even with all this, Coleridge leaves two hopeful possibilities, both related to symbolic story. There *are* three graves, but there are *only* three graves. Edward and Mary's sister live. Edward, through his "dream" action, has in some sense been the agent for the breaking of the heart-mirror-curse. Two of the daughter-alternatives, exemplified by Mary and Ellen, have been shown to be unsatisfactory alternatives; they, along with the mother, lie in the churchyard. The third daughter has stayed with the mother, neither of necessity denying her nor becoming the object of the stepmother's jealousy. There remains at least a possibility that the mother-daughter heritage for one of the daughters is the "good mother," that she has seen the fallen stepmother's face without being cursed.[10] Significantly, the Sexton has heard the story both from Mary's sister and from Edward. They tell him the story separately, but the story is the same. Though only by implication, Coleridge leaves open the possibility of a fairy tale ending for Edward and the third daughter. That ending would be outside the ballad but made possible by "The Three Graves" itself—made possible, that is, not only by the narrative action of the story but also by the very telling of the story. As the third daughter recounts the tale to the Sexton and the Sexton to the Traveller and the

Traveller to us, the story becomes universal and symbolic. The curse of the fallen world is not forgotten, but it is contained, placed within limits, by the story. And the possibility for a tale of Faery is left open. The poem thus becomes a true moral tale, teaching the desirability of wholeness and Love.

CHAPTER FOUR

"Christabel": "In a World of Sin"

*T**he fallen world* has no end:

> There is no end of it, the voiceless wailing,
> No end to the withering of withered flowers,
> To the movement of pain that is painless and motionless,
> To the drift of the sea and the drifting wreckage,
> The bone's prayer to Death its God. Only the hardly,
>   barely prayable
> Prayer of the one Annunciation.   ("The Dry Salvages," 2)

The fallen word has no end: there is no end to the "soundless wailing" and the withering of flowers. Still, and always, the "prayer of the one Annunciation" remains. And so, says Eliot's narrator, "Fare forward, travellers!" ("The Dry Salvages," 3). In Coleridge's poetry, the voyage into mystery and the accompanying sense of aloneness are at their most perilous in "Christabel." From this voyage, neither Christabel nor Coleridge nor we do, or can, return. The inherent necessity of the inability to return grows out of the very conditions Coleridge places on this particular journey.

More perplexing even than the other "mystery poems," "Christabel" is the true fragment of the three. Most overtly a fairy tale among all Coleridge's poems—called so by the poet himself and recognized as such by early critics—"Christabel" becomes Coleridge's most daring symbolic story.[1] The seeds of both its incompleteness and its sharply divided critical reception can be seen in the early response to the poem as well as in the questions the poem asks.

Most likely assuming the poem to be, as Coleridge asserts it is, a fairy tale, the Wordsworth household seems to have found "Christabel" fit for the ears of children. "On 1 May [1809] we catch a glimpse of Sara [Hutchinson] reading *Christabel* to little Johnny Wordsworth." Johnny "was excessively interested especially with the first part, but he asked 'why she [Christabel] could not say her prayers in her own room,' and it was his opinion that she ought to have gone 'directly to her Father's Room to tell him that she had met with the Lady under the old oak tree and all about it'" (Wordsworth, *Letters* 2: 324, qtd. in Whalley 78). The immediate critical reception of the poem, however, did not find it fit for much of anything. Most of the negative response centered on its supernatural character and characters, particularly the "witch" Geraldine, although most of the reviewers liked neither the poem nor the witch. The "little limber elf" of the Conclusion to Part II was seen as "absolutely incomprehensible."[2] An unsigned review in the *Anti-Jacobin*, July 1816 (qtd. in Jackson 217–21) sarcastically concludes that "Christabel is bewitched!" and that "in truth, a more senseless, absurd, and stupid, composition, has scarcely, of late years, issued from the press." William Roberts, writing in the *British Review* for August 1916, calls the poem "wild and singular," and though he admits that "there is a land of dreams with which poets hold an unrestricted commerce, and where they may load their imaginations with whatever strange products they find in the country," he argues that "there must be something to connect these visionary forms with the realities of existence." Further:

> It is only under the shelter of these properties and correspondencies that witchcraft has a fair and legitimate introduction into poetical composition. A witch is no heroine, nor can we read a tale of magic

for its own sake. Poetry itself must show some modesty, nor be quite unforbearing in its exactions. What we allow it the use of as an accessory it must not convert into a principal, and what is granted to it as a part of its proper machinery it must not impose upon us as the main or only subject of interest. But Mr. Coleridge is one of those poets who if we give him an inch will be sure to take an ell: if we consent to swallow an elf or fairy, we are soon expected not to strain at a witch; and if we open our throats to this imposition upon our good-nature, we must gulp down broomstick and all. (Qtd. in Jackson, 221–26)

Roberts concludes: "We really must make a stand somewhere for the rights of common sense"—clearly, here is a man who grew up with Mrs. Barbauld and Crew!

These reviewers fail to understand the most important thing about fairy tales: that they *are* concerned, in a very fundamental way, with "the realities of existence"; elves and fairies and witches are merely a way of talking about these realities. A review published in the *London Times* on 20 May 1816—five days before John Murray released *Christabel; Kubla Khan, a Vision; The Pains of Sleep*—makes a beginning in this understanding. While discussing the spell the "witchlike Geraldine" utters and extolling the realistic details that are characteristic of fairy tales, the reviewer also seems to answer in advance some of the future criticism by emphasizing: "The scene, the personages, are those of old, romantic superstition; but we feel intimate with them, as if they were of our own day, and of our own neighborhood." Even more significantly, the reviewer continues:

What we have principally to remark, with respect to the tale, is, that wild, and romantic, and visionary as it is, it has a truth of its own, which seizes on and masters the imagination, from the beginning to the end. In this respect we know of nothing so like it, in modern composition, as Burns's *Tom* [sic] *o'Shanter*. In both instances, the preternatural occurrences are not merely surprising—they possess a peculiar interest, as befalling individuals, for whom our affections have, from other causes, been kindled. (Qtd. in Schwartz 116–17)[3]

The reviewer's praise actually amounts to a confirmation that Coleridge has accomplished in "Christabel" what he asserts in the

Biographia Literaria was the purpose behind the writing of the poem. "Christabel" was originally to have been published in the *Lyrical Ballads* of 1798, and Coleridge associates the poem with the occasion and origins of that volume (*BL* 2: 5–7). The reviewer, in saying that "the preternatural occurrences are not merely surprising—they possess a peculiar interest, as befalling individuals, for whom our affections have, from other causes, been kindled," and that "it is impossible not to suppose that we have known 'Sweet Christabel' from the time when she was 'a fairy thing, with red round cheeks'" (qtd. in Schwartz 116), is echoing Coleridge: "The excellence aimed at was to consist in the interesting of the affections by the dramatic truth of such emotions, as would naturally accompany such situations, supposing them real." Coleridge's "persons and characters supernatural, or at least romantic," which yet "transfer from our inward nature a human interest and a semblance of truth sufficient to procure for these shadows of imagination that willing suspension of disbelief for the moment, which constitutes poetic faith," becomes in the review a tale which, "wild, and romantic, and visionary as it is, has a truth of its own, which seizes on and masters the imagination." What the fairy tale "Christabel" would do, then, through the presentation of the emotions of a character, is elicit from the reader a corresponding interest or emotion, arising from our inward nature. This process is possible because we feel the emotion elicited to be a truth powerful enough to allow us momentarily to suspend our disbelief and participate in the created character's experience. Further, the incidents and agents that call forth this imaginative sympathy will be of a supernatural character.

Submerged in these statements is Coleridge's belief in the consubstantial relationship between our inward nature and the realm of Spirit, and in this relationship lies the truth that will allow our imaginative suspension of disbelief. We, along with Christabel—if we allow for the time our spirits' suspension of disbelief—find ourselves in the realm of Faery: Coleridge's symbolic universe. Thus, the author of an unsigned essay in *Critical Review*, May 1816—one of the few favorable notices—is entirely correct when he admonishes: "The reader, before he opens the poem, must be prepared to allow for the superstitions of necromancy and sorcery, and to expect something of the glorious and unbounded range which the belief in those mysteries permits; the absurd trammels of mere physical possibility are here thrown aside, like the absurd swaddling clothes of infants, which formerly obstructed the growth of the fair symmetry of nature" (qtd. in Jackson (199–205).[4] In a fallen world, Spirit is often known "through a glass, darkly" as superstition and sorcery, or sideways, as it were, in fairy tale. The belief in the "mysteries," which is the underlying assumption of the genre, permits entry into the "glorious and unbounded range" of the infinite creative possibilities of Spirit. Rigidity of mind, brought about by regarding "*the senses*" as the "criteria of belief," is loosened and thrown aside like the swaddling clothes of an infant so that the inquiring soul can journey, imaginatively untrammeled for a space, into the mysteries without and within, reconciling all things in Spirit.

Coleridge himself says he has no doubt about the plan of "Christabel." Writing to Byron in 1815, he asserts, "I should say, that the plan of the whole poem was formed and the first Book and half of the second were finished—and it was not till after my return from Germany in the year 1800 that I resumed it—and finished the second and a part of the third Book" (*CL* 4: 601). Although the "part of the third" appears to be hyperbole, Coleridge never wavers in his statement that he knew what he wanted to do in the poem. Thomas Allsop records him as saying, "I had the whole of the two cantos in my mind before I began it; certainly the first canto is more perfect, has more of the true wild weird spirit, than the last" (94). And emphatically, in 1833, Coleridge asserts: "The reason of my not finishing Christabel is not that I don't know how to do it—for I have, as I always had, the whole plan entire from the beginning to end in my mind; but I fear I could not carry on with equal success the execution of the idea, an extremely subtle and difficult one" (*TT*, 6 July 1833). The "subtle and difficult" idea, I think, is to show the soul's existence in the fallen world subsequent to its encounter with Spirit.

Although "The Rime" is also about the soul's symbolic experience with mystery, "Christabel" does "over-go" it. The Mariner's voyage is a movement from land to sea to land—from the known and safe, epitomized by the physical objects of lighthouse, hill, and kirk, to the unknown and perilous, epitomized by the silent sea and the emerald green cliffs, and back again—from safe harbor to safe harbor. The journey out into mystery is bounded on each side by the familiar fallen world; the geographical movements of the Mariner's ship limit the duration and extent of his journey. He goes through the door to the Other World and returns safely. On reentering the harbor, the Mariner's relief is palpable:

> Oh! dream of joy! is this indeed
> The light-house top I see?
> Is this the hill? is this the kirk?
> Is this mine own countree?

> We drifted o'er the harbour-bar,
> And I with sobs did pray—
> O let me be awake, my God!
> Or let me sleep alway.   (Rime 464–71)

Nor would the Mariner willingly turn his head toward the "lonesome road" again "because he knows, a frightful fiend / Doth close behind him tread" (450–51). The Mariner's experience is an encounter with Spirit, but it is not one he cares to repeat. There is, of course, a sense in which the experience is repeated with each telling, but the repetitions occur in story and only after the Mariner reaches the safety of the land. Coleridge, on the other hand, turns his head to look down the road once again to see what else might be there and, in so doing, writes "Christabel." This time, however, the questions are harder, and the conditions of the poem are more perilous, since the journey is entirely in the mind and imagination.

In "The Rime," we know we are going on a voyage of exploration, that we have left the safe harbor and are moving into strange and unknown waters; even so, the unknown is not the strange land of dream vision. We see the sun come up and go down. The details of sight and sound are precise. The poem's superficial structures of ordinariness make us forget our defenses against mystery as the Mariner's glittering eye holds us. The voyage is stranger and more mysterious than we had anticipated, and the noisy creaking and growling of the ice serves to intensify the silence of the soul we begin to experience. Somehow we know the Mariner was really there, and our own involvement in his story is so complete that we are startled—jarred—by the Wedding-Guest's outbursts. Driven by the STORM-BLAST, we, like the Wedding-Guest, do not think to maintain our distance, and so we also go a symbolic voyage with the Mariner—except that we do not participate fully in the Mariner's terror lest he be compelled to remain outside the harbor. We have been assured from the beginning that we will return, and on the journey we have been guided by the knowing voice of the narrator and the even surer, if moralistic, voice of the gloss.

But what if we had no such assurance? What if we were unable to return to the safe harbor? And what if one of the reasons we could not return was that there had been no grounding like that provided by a geographical journey? After all, if you get on a ship, sail out, and see kirk, hill, and lighthouse disappear over the horizon, then you can reasonably expect—even though your journey is on unfamiliar waters that are at their most significant level spiritually rather than empirically experienced—that a return appearance of lighthouse, hill, and kirk will signal a return to the familiar. But what if you do not leave the known geographical location for your voyage? What if you do not journey to a "strange place" but, instead, the place you are in is transformed? What if, since the journey in that case becomes more insistently one of intuitive symbolic knowledge, it is your perception of the place in which you exist that has shifted, so that there is no "place" to return to? What if, in other words, you are stranded? And finally, what if you could not even tell anyone what had happened? These, I think, are the hypothetical questions that result in "Christabel."

In "Christabel," there is no safe harbor, no movement from the familiar to the unknown and back again. In effect, the poem begins in the middle. The only physical journey Christabel makes—her

165

exit from the castle to pray for her lover "a furlong from the castle gate" (C 26) and her return to the castle with Geraldine—is already half over as the poem begins. We, with Christabel, are placed immediately within an awareness of the consubstantial world fully manifested to the eye of imagination. The "ordinary" world is assumed to be, and seen to be, consubstantial. The symbolic, consubstantial world exists as a "given" in the poem, a "risky" stance because the journey in this case must be insistently one of intuitive symbolic knowledge. Since the journey is not a movement to a "strange place" but rather a perceptive transformation of the "real" familiar world of one's ordinary existence, there is no "place" to which Christabel, unlike the Mariner, may return and, consequently, no limit to her experience. Once Christabel leaves the castle to pray by the oak tree and encounters Geraldine there, she is in the perilous land of Faery.

Because the symbolic, consubstantial world exists as the "given" in the poem—the here-and-now world of the opening scenes—we as readers are denied any distance at all. Our identification with Christabel and our concern over the fact that she seems to have wandered into a dangerous situation is immediate and total, and our reaction an interesting one. We take notice of Christabel because we are worried about her, our attitude a combination of protectiveness and exasperation. She is not a poet of whom we should beware, nor is she a Mariner with a glittering eye who holds us spellbound. Rather, she is a young girl, scarcely past childhood. We, as readers, responding to her much as we would to one of our own children under similar circumstances, worry about her and—because she is also we ourselves from long time past— identify with her. It matters to us who Geraldine is. We care about the relationship between Christabel and Geraldine and about its effect. The poem is a hard one; "in a world of sin" (673) it could not be otherwise.

In line with Tolkien's assertion that it is "essential to a genuine fairy-story . . . that it should be presented as 'true' " (14), "Christabel" has no dream frame. The faery world we are given in Part I is the world that *is*, and when Christabel does dream, she dreams

With open eyes (ah woe is me!)
Asleep, and dreaming fearfully,
Fearfully dreaming, yet, I wis,
Dreaming that alone, which is.   (292–95)

"Waking" into the world of Part II, then, the fallen world of death, we are doubly aware of dissention, falsehood, and separation. Christabel wakes in the fallen world of her father but with knowledge of the Other World—and Geraldine—still with her. In effect, the supernatural, or Spirit, world of Faery has entered the fallen world.[5] But Christabel, with her new sight, is the only one who can see it, and she is under spell and has no power to tell. Bracy sees in dream, and he speaks, but to no avail. And, indeed, what would Christabel say and who would hear her? How does one experience symbolic Wholeness in a fallen world? Since divisiveness and separation constitute the fundamental character of our world, resulting in such categories as love and hate, good and evil, dream and reality, and since the fallen world is a "mass of *little things*" apprehended empirically and placed within boundaries, how can the human spirit speak of its origins and its unlimited creative relationship with Spirit? It may be useful to recall Tolkien's injunction: "Faerie is a perilous land, and in it are pitfalls for the unwary and dungeons for the overbold. . . . In that realm a man may, perhaps, count himself fortunate to have wandered, but its very richness and strangeness tie the tongue of a traveller who would report them. And while he is there it is dangerous for him to ask too many questions, lest the gates should be shut and the keys be lost" (3). Christabel's journey is perilous indeed, and her tongue is tied. Coleridge himself can tell her tale only as a symbolic story, and an unfinished one at that.

In "Christabel," the conventions of the folk fairy tale and Coleridge's view of the world as consubstantial merge in the creation of a symbolic tale of Faery of the highest order. The place of exile (the fallen world) and the homeland (the world of Wholeness in which the mother tongue is spoken) with their concomitant "real world" and "Other World" characteristics is made evident in "Christabel" first in the conventions of time and place. In

167

fairy tales, there is a "marvellous independence or true imaginative absence of all particular place & time—it is neither in the domains of History or Geography, is ignorant of all artificial boundary—truly in the Land of Faery—i.e., in mental space," explains Coleridge (*CN* 3: 4501). Fairy tale time is different from ordinary time. Traditionally, "there is an almost world-wide belief that time in Fairyland passes much more quickly [*sic*] than among mortals. In fact, in Fairyland it can hardly be said to pass at all, and the inhabitants partake of the nature of immortality. . . . When we come . . . to the timeless fairyland . . . we are very near to the timelessness of Paradise" (Briggs, *Fairies* 104–06). The most common fairy tale beginning is "Once upon a time," an any-time, or every-time, that is not this-time (but therefore and paradoxically also *not* not-this-time). Fairy tales "open a door on Other Time, and if we pass through, though only for a moment, we stand outside our own time, outside Time itself, maybe" (Tolkien 32). "Christabel" does not even bother with the "Once upon a time" door; we find ourselves immediately in Other Time outside Time.

In this Other Time of mental space, Coleridge creates a symbolic setting which is truly "neither in the domains of History or Geography, is ignorant of all artificial boundary," but which is also the natural world. Christabel leaves the castle of Sir Leoline to pray by the "huge, broad-breasted, old oak tree" (42) in the "midnight wood" (29) and, appropriately, here in this symbolic setting she meets Geraldine. "Nature," declares Coleridge, is a "revelation of God. . . . In its obvious sense and literal interpretation it declares the being and attributes of the Almighty Father." But in addition, "it is the *poetry* of human nature, to read it likewise in a figurative sense, and to find therein correspondencies and symbols of the spiritual world" (*SM* 70).

Nature in its symbolic character is also a kind of poetry, and Coleridge's descriptive, natural details of setting show forth the creative nature of the spiritual world. There is no time in the eternity of Spirit, and the details of the poem of both time and place, one after another, through their very attempt at precision, describe the in-between-ness of the Other World of Part I. The woods themselves represent the mysterious pathless ways that mind and spirit must enter in encounter with Spirit, and the holy, fairy oak trees of that wood are androgynous: the huge and phallic oak is also the broad-breasted and nourishing mother.[6] " 'Tis the middle of night" (1) in the midnight wood, the in-between blink of the eye in which fairies can be seen, neither night nor day but also, mysteriously, both. This "Other Time . . . outside Time itself" (Tolkien 32) is clearly an important natural detail. Coleridge begins with it in lines 1–4, comes back to it almost immediately in 9–10—"She [the mastiff bitch] maketh answer to the clock, / Four for the quarters, and twelve for the hour"—and reiterates the "midnight wood" in line 29. Midnight is the most significant of those "lines along which the supernatural intrudes through the surface of existence" (Rees 94); and the repeated, connecting detail underscores the time of Spirit, since the mastiff bitch is said to see "my lady's shroud" (13), a detail with further implications. The dog moans again when Christabel and Geraldine pass, bringing an awareness of both the ambiguous nature of Geraldine and her relationship with the spirit of Christabel's mother and indicating that this present occurrence is an event of Other Time. There is no time in the eternity of Spirit.

The refusal to put even the natural details into neat categories continues as the narrator asks, "Is the night chilly and dark?" (13). The expected answer is yes or no, but the actual answer is "The night is chilly, but not dark": that is, yes and no, a yes and no that in both cases affirms an in-between state: it is not warm, nor is it cold; it is night, but it is not dark night. The explanation of the lack of darkness continues in the same vein:

The thin gray cloud is spread on high,
It covers but not hides the sky.
The moon is behind, and at the full;
And yet she looks both small and dull.   (16–19)

The full moon should be large and bright, but because it is behind a cloud—which is neither black nor white but gray, neither thick nor absent but thin, covering the sky but not hiding it—it looks small and dull. Still, there is enough light so that the night is not dark. All possibilities exist. The narrator emphasizes the point by repeating, "The night is chill, the cloud is gray" (20) and then extends the description to the season: " 'Tis a month before the month of May" (21). May, the last spring month, is evoked only to be negated; May is named explicitly, but it is actually a month before that—April, the middle month—and since "Spring comes slowly up this way" (22), there is a March chill in the air.

The qualifications make the details almost painfully precise, but it is a precision based on ambiguous reconciliation. The setting is "ignorant of artificial boundary." It is as though we are being shown the Other World of Faery or Spirit through the symbolic presentation of the natural world. Just so. Coleridge does not remove us to another place and time in the poem; rather, the poem changes our perception of the natural world—that event in itself, a symbolic experience. We *see* differently—"the soul of man awakes and starts up"—and we see truly. Because our experience, like that of Christabel, is of the fallen world, the place of possibility and wholeness seems a paradise or a fairy tale, a tale that describes "events that took place when a different range of possibilities operated in the unidentified long ago" (Opie and Opie 18).

Iona and Peter Opie observe that fairy stories "would, curiously, not be so believable if the period in which they took place was specified, or if the place where they occurred was named. In the history of 'Jack and the Giants' it comes as a jolt when an actual location is mentioned ('a Market-town in Wales'), the tale thereafter seems a foolish tale, the spell has been broken" (19). In the opening lines of "Christabel," Part II, just such a breaking of spell occurs. The "matin bell . . . / Knells us back to a world of death" (332–33): the specified, named world of Bratha Head and Wyndermere, Langdale Pike and Witch's Lair and Dungeon-ghyll. We are back in the familiar fallen world in places we can visit on a Sunday afternoon. Just as the introductory details of Part I function as reconciled symbols of Spirit, admitting the reader into a world of Life, so the introductory details of Part II mock that reconciliation and lead the reader into a world of death. In the first six lines of Part II, the fallen world of death is shown to move back each morning to the day Sir Leoline "found his lady dead" and forward to his "dying day." Death pervades each day of his life and the lives of those who inhabit his world. There is no escape—"not a soul can choose but hear" the "warning knell" (342–43). All time and all places are included, but instead of making creative reconciliation possible, this fact binds the listener and participant into limiting juxtaposition. The living brother, the "drowsy sacristan" (346), sounds the death strokes, and the "space between" (349) is filled by the "death-note[s]" that the "three sinful sextons' ghosts . . . give back . . . to their living brother" from "Langdale Pike and Witch's Lair, / and Dungeon-ghyll" where the "ghosts are pent" (350–55). The ghosts pull immaterial "ropes of rock and bells of air" (352), while the sacristan "duly pulls the heavy bell" (340), but this is no reconciliation of spirit and matter. The living brother is the counterpart of the sinful sextons; their notes peal in alternation, not harmony; and their notes are death-notes. The two are one, but the one is a death-mockery of Life, presided over by the devil who "mocks the doleful tale / With a merry peal from Borodale" (358–59). The opening scene of Part II reestablishes the fallen world in which Geraldine "awakens the lady Christabel" (367). And yet they, and we, are in the same place; the castle has not disappeared. It is perception and, consequently, language that have shifted. Though the castle of Part I is the castle of Part II and Christabel and Geraldine are the central figures of both parts, the Faery world is not the fallen world, and the poem shows that symbolic encounter has consequences in the world of Sir Leoline.

The fairy tale conventions of time and place suit Coleridge's purpose in "Christabel" admirably, as do the conventions that have to do with the land of Faery itself. As noted above, critics are in agreement that "fairy-stories are not in normal English usage stories *about* fairies or elves, but stories about Fairy, that is *Faërie*, the realm or state in which fairies have their being. *Faërie* contains many things besides elves and fays, and besides dwarfs, witches, trolls, giants, or dragons: it holds the seas, the sun, the moon, the sky; and the earth, and all things that are in it: tree and bird, water and stone, wine and bread, and ourselves, mortal men, when we are enchanted" (Tolkien 9). Luthi explains that fairy tale "embraces in its own way the world: nature both dead and living, man and the works of man, and the supernatural." Encompassing such diverse things as the elements—earth, air, fire, water—plants, animals, material objects, human emotion, the fairy tale is a "universe in miniature" (*Once upon a Time* 25). The "way" of the fairy tale is the way of specific detail, details that are sometimes ordinary, sometimes extraordinary, carrying strong symbolic associations: "Fairy tale figures have an immediate appeal. The king, the princess, a dragon, a witch, gold, crystal, pitch, and ashes—these things are, for the human imagination, age-old symbols for what is high, noble, and pure or dangerous, bestial, and unfathomable; what is genuine and true, or what is sordid and false. . . . This clear portrayal of objects together with their mysterious, unaccountable properties is characteristic of fairy tale style" (Luthi, *Once upon a Time* 138, 68). The details in "Christabel" are precise and compelling: the owl and the crowing cock, the mastiff bitch, the moon "both small and dull," the chilly night and "thin gray cloud," the "huge, broad-breasted, old oak tree," the "one red leaf," the "fit of flame," Geraldine's gems, the wine of "virtuous powers," the silver lamp, the lady's "moist, cold brow," Christabel's "large tears that leave the lashes bright." These details embrace the world: "nature both dead and living, man and the works of man, and the supernatural."[7]

The creation of a "universe in miniature" is important because one of the primordial human desires that fairy tales satisfy is the desire "to converse with other living things":

On this desire, as ancient as the Fall, is largely founded the talking of beasts and creatures in fairy-tales, and especially the magical understanding of their proper speech. This is the root, and not the "confusion" attributed to the minds of men of the unrecorded past, an alleged "absence of the sense of separation of ourselves from beasts." A vivid sense of that separation is very ancient; but also a sense that it was a severance: a strange fate and a guilt lies on us. Other creatures are like other realms with which Man has broken off relations, and sees now only from the outside at a distance, being at war with them, or on the terms of an uneasy armistice. (Tolkien 66)

Or, as Luthi puts it, the mixtures of "human, animal, vegetable, and mineral . . . bring all things into relationship with one another" (*Once upon a Time* 146):

> The fairy tale sees man as one who is essentially isolated but who, for just this reason—because he is not rigidly committed, not tied down—can establish relationship with anything in the world . . . not just the earth, but the entire cosmos. . . . The fairy tale hero also does not perceive the world as a whole, but he puts his trust in and is accepted by it. . . . He is isolated and at the same time in touch with all things. The fairy tale is a poetic vision of man and his relationship to the world . . . isolated, yet capable of universal relationships. (*Once upon a Time* 143–44)

The idea of "universal relationships" is a familiar one to any reader of Coleridge. The speaker in "The Eolian Harp" posits "one intellectual breeze, / At once the Soul of each, and God of all" that sweeps across all "animated nature" (47–48, 44). Through his voyage, the Mariner learns that he is related to the world of "man and bird and beast," since "the dear God who loveth us, / He made and loveth all" (Rime 613, 616–17). This, too, is Christabel's journey, the symbolic journey into mystery to experience the Spirit that reconciles the world. As fairy tale heroine, she is isolated—in the traditional ways of young girls in fairy tales who are orphaned or have only ineffectual fathers, and also in the necessary stance of spirit to Spirit. For contrary to most fairy tale heroines, not only does Christabel put her trust in the "world as a whole," but her primary task is the perception of that Wholeness.

Christabel is, in many ways, an archetypal fairy tale character, and parallels with traditional tales are numerous in her story: her isolation through the death of her mother, the presence of the dead mother, the ineffectual father, the desire to marry the lover who is far away, the use of spell—such details recall "Snow White," "Sleeping Beauty," and "Cinderella," among others. Iona and Peter Opie list several conventions of fairy tales and their central characters, the first being that "usually the tale is about one person, or one family, having to cope with a supernatural occurrence or supernatural protagonist during a period of stress." Christabel, longing for her lover and meeting Geraldine instead, surely qualifies on this count. "The hero is almost invariably a young person, usually the youngest member of a family, and if not deformed or already an orphan, is probably in the process of being disowned or abandoned," a precise description of what happens to the motherless Christabel in Part II as her father turns away from her. "The characters in the stories are, nevertheless, stock figures. They are either altogether good or altogether bad, and there is no evolution of character." Some readers of the poem would want to take issue with this point, but it seems to me, when the argument is all said and done, that it is most in keeping with the story and its tone to see Christabel as "good" and remaining so.[8] Finally, archetypal fairy tale characters, as has been noted, "are referred to by generic or descriptive names, as 'Jack' (for lad), 'Beauty', 'Snow White', 'Silver Hair', 'Tom Thumb', 'Red Ridinghood', 'Cinder-girl.' Fairy tales are more concerned with situation than with character" (18). The name "Christabel," associated with the suffering Christ and sacrificial Abel and their implied opposites Satan and Cain,[9] is a descriptive name in the best fairy tale tradition.

Fairy tale heroes and heroines are stock figures with generic or descriptive names because their significance is greater than themselves; in Coleridgean terms, they are symbolic. In "Christabel," the central character has a double significance. We do care about Christabel in the way the author of the London Times essay of 20 May 1816 indicates. We are concerned about her and the situation in which she finds herself because there is a sense in which we identify with her. Our "affections have . . . been kindled," and we, like little Johnny Wordsworth, want to know why she had to leave the castle to pray. It matters to us who Geraldine is, and we care about the effect of her relationship with Christabel. All of this because Christabel is also we ourselves. She does, as Coleridge explains in the Biographia, "transfer from our inward nature a human interest," and she does engage our affections because her emotional responses seem natural and true to us.[10] Thus, while we do care about the character Christabel, we do so primarily because she "partakes of the Reality which [she] renders intelligible." At this level, the Reality that Christabel symbolizes is the psychological reality of the human condition,[11] and in this way she functions as does Sleeping Beauty:

> The characters of the fairy tale are not personally delineated; the fairy tale is not concerned with individual destinies. Nor is it the unique process of maturation that is reflected in the fairy tale. The story of Sleeping Beauty is more than an imaginatively stylized love story portraying the withdrawal of the girl and the breaking of the spell through the young lover. One instinctively conceives of the princess as an image for the human spirit: the story portrays the endowment, peril, paralysis, and redemption not of just one girl, but of all mankind. The soul of man again and again suffers convulsions and paralysis and, each time—with luck—it can be revived, healed, redeemed. With luck! (Luthi, *Once upon a Time* 24)

Clearly, at another level, the psychological reality shifts into a Reality of Spirit, and Christabel, like Sleeping Beauty, symbolizes the condition and journey of each human soul. She matters to us in a way very profound because we also, in our peril in this world, wish not to remain paralyzed but to be redeemed. As with "The Rime of The Ancient Mariner," Coleridge, in "Christabel," has made the fairy tale "a vehicle of Mystery."

The symbolic import of fairy tales in general, and "Christabel" in particular, determines the stylistic character of the narrative; that is, fairy tales tend to

> transform everything internal into something external, to portray the intimate relationship between two people in an image. . . . The fairy tale likes to portray external happenings. It does not portray feelings, moods, inner conflicts, and thought processes, but strives to translate everything into action. . . . And precisely because the fairy tale does not psychologize but portrays external happenings truly and clearly, these actions acquire a transparency and brilliance which one seeks in vain in other types of narrative. The fairy tale depicts external events, but these events seem to become spiritualized and sublimated almost by themselves. (Luthi, *Once upon a Time* 74, 124–25)

The actions and details, particular unto themselves but stripped of limiting analysis and commentary, are symbolic, precisely in Coleridge's own definition of the term: "A Symbol . . . is characterized by a translucence of the Special in the Individual or of the General in the Especial or of the Universal in the General. Above all by the translucence of the Eternal through and in the Temporal" (*SM* 30). The narrative of "Christabel" begins with stark, almost abbreviated, descriptive detail. The narrator then asks the question, "What makes her in the wood so late, / A furlong from the castle gate?" (25–26). The answer comes in terms of obvious externals:

> She had dreams all yesternight
> Of her own betrothéd knight;
> And she in the midnight wood will pray
> For the weal of her lover that's far away.   (27–30)

Christabel has dreamed of her lover; he is far away; she has come to the woods to pray for his welfare. There is no explanation of the dream or why Christabel is concerned.[12] We *infer* from her actions—the prayer and her sighs—that she is troubled. And the narrative continues in the same manner. Christabel hears a moan on the other side of the tree, sees a "damsel bright" who is "beautiful exceedingly" (58, 68), and listens to Geraldine's story. Christabel says, "Mary mother, save me now!" (69), but we are given no explanation for the prayer; whatever explanation there is lies in the description of Geraldine and her story. Christabel invites her home and lifts her across the threshold; the mastiff bitch moans, and the dying firebrands burst into a "fit of flame" (159) when Christabel and Geraldine pass them; but we receive only the narrator's question, "What can ail the mastiff bitch?" (153). And so it is through the scene in Christabel's room—action, details, brief conversation between Christabel and Geraldine, but no analysis of the inner thoughts of either character. The internal is transformed into the external, and the "intimate relationship between the two people [is shown] in an image," the image of the mother and child. The interested questions of the narrator are never answered; they, and many more, simply become the questions of the critics and readers of the poem. The events have become "spiritualized"; the Temporal is translucent, and the Eternal shines through it.

The external happenings of the fairy tale are most often constructed around a task, or series of tasks; "one of the most common is the quest. . . . What the hero goes in quest of again may vary from type to type. . . . It is always something very concrete, a woman, the ideal woman, of course, a wonderful horse, a wonderful bird, the water of life . . . or, maybe, an answer to some puzzling question" (Krappe 23). Christabel initially thinks her task, or quest, is to leave the castle to pray for her distant lover. While praying for her lover, however, she encounters Geraldine, and the nature of the task shifts. Christabel's true task is to discover, through symbolic encounter, the nature of Love. Love/Spirit/God is the ongoing creative reconciliation of opposing qualities or forces: that is, Wholeness. God exists eternally as an act of Love; the "action of God is love" (*CL* 2: 634). And human love symbolizes Divine love. Therefore, it is a natural extension of Christabel's ostensible task that her real task be an encounter with Love. For Coleridge, the task and joy of the soul is symbolic knowledge, made possible only through the act of imagination: "[Symbolic knowledge] is not only extolled as the crown and honor of a man, but to seek after it is again and again commanded us as one of our most sacred duties" (*Friend* 1: 104). Symbolic knowledge is knowledge of Love. Christabel, encountering Love through Geraldine, is under spell not to speak:

> In the touch of this bosom there worketh a spell,
> Which is lord of thy utterance, Christabel!
> Thou knowest to-night, and wilt know to-morrow,
> This mark of my shame, this seal of my sorrow:
> > But vainly thou warrest,
> > > For this is alone in
> > Thy power to declare,
> > > That in the dim forest
> > Thou heard'st a low moaning,
> And found'st a bright lady, surpassingly fair;
> And didst bring her home with thee in love and in charity,
> To shield her and shelter her from the damp air. (267–78)

In this case, the spell does not disguise, as is usual in fairy tales; instead, it prevents the telling of what has already been made clear (though it does simultaneously disguise from the rest of the world that which has been made known). This then becomes the second part of Christabel's task: to reenter the fallen world of Part II with her knowledge of Spirit. "Intimately connected," in fairy tale structure, "with the number [of tasks] is the gradual intensification of the action, the centre of gravity of which lies on the third as it were" (Krappe 31). Appropriately, therefore, Christabel's task in Part II will be more difficult than the encounter with Geraldine in Part I.

The spell over Christabel's speaking is connected with two common fairy tale motifs, the first being that of the power of the name. To know someone's name gives one power over that person. In Part I, Geraldine speaks her name directly to Christabel: "My name is Geraldine" (80)—thus giving Christabel power of knowledge. The God of the Israelites called himself the I AM—a "name" for God that Coleridge often uses, and there is a connection, I think, between the I AM and Christabel's dreaming, in the Conclusion to Part I, of that which *is*. (Coleridge italicizes *is* in the Hinves copy of the first edition.) In the *Biographia*, he argues that Absolute Truth, or Spirit, is immediate, not derived from some other truth; it is "self-grounded, unconditional, and known by its own light"; it "*is*, simply because it *is*" (*BL* 1: 268). And finally, one might also say that just as Cinderella is "under spell" when she is dressed in rags and marked by the cinders signifying the ashes of death, so too is Christabel under spell in her father's castle before she encounters Geraldine. In this case, one could also argue that Geraldine's mark of shame and seal of sorrow are similar to the cinders: that is, evidence of the mortal nature of the fallen world. Christabel has been given Geraldine's name and knowledge of her shame and sorrow, but they are not hers to reveal. The second motif is that of prohibition or taboo, here intimately connected with the spell that leaves Christabel no power to speak. "The many prohibitions, stipulations, and precisely stated tasks are again primarily just an element of fairy tale *style*. They help to give the tale conciseness,"

says Luthi. If Sir Leoline—or the mastiff bitch, for that matter—
were to wake up, Christabel's first task would be a failure. "But
underlying these severe prohibitions and commands, one senses a
way of thinking similar to that in the taboos of primitive peoples"
(*Once upon a Time* 78). Similarly, prohibitions are probably pre-
served in fairy tales "because of the great mythical significance of
prohibition. A sense of that significance may indeed have lain
behind some of the taboos themselves. Thou shalt not—or else
Thou shall depart beggared into endless regret" (Tolkien 32). Thus,
Christabel is prohibited from speaking her knowledge.

Christabel is the fairy tale heroine of her story. Who, then, is
Geraldine? The question stands as the most important though most
perplexing one of the poem. Christabel is the heroine, but Geraldine provides the key to meaning. While putative answers abound,
there has seemed to be no truly adequate answer. The question of
whether she is good or evil, a debate that goes back to the disagree-
ment between Dr. Gillman and Derwent Coleridge about Coleridge's intention, has most often been decided against her. G.
Wilson Knight calls her a "nameless obscenity" (93), and Edward
E. Bostetter says she is an "incarnation of sadism" (*"Christabel"*
192). James Gillman, in his biography of Coleridge, writes: "The
story of the Christabel is partly founded on the notion, that the
virtuous of this world save the wicked. The pious and good Christabel suffers and prays for 'The weal of her lover that is far away,'
exposed to various temptations in a foreign land; and thus she
defeats the power of evil represented in the person of Geraldine.
This is the main object of the tale" (283). Derwent Coleridge, on
the other hand, in his edition of Coleridge's poems, asserts the
contrary: "The sufferings of Christabel were to have been represented as vicarious, endured for her 'lover far away'; and Geraldine, no witch or goblin, or malignant being of any kind, but a
spirit, executing her appointed task with the best good will, as she
herself says:

All they who live in the upper sky,
Do love you, holy Christabel,
And you love them, and for their sake

And for the good which me befel,
Even I in my degree will try,
Fair maiden, to requite you well.   (xiii)

In addition to the discrepant accounts of Coleridge's inten-
tions, the debate about whether Geraldine is evil or good has its
roots in the ambiguity of her words and actions within the poem
itself.[13] The discussion generally centers on Geraldine's unwillingness to perform her task—and rightly so, I think. I argue that
Geraldine is, in fact, the symbolic manifestation of Spirit in the
poem and is, therefore, necessarily both ambiguous and good. She
symbolizes the impossible union that is Spirit, and it is within this
mystery that her "contradictions" are reconciled. My view that
Geraldine functions as not only a beneficent spirit but, more
important, a symbol of Spirit is reinforced by an early copy of
"Christabel," containing notes and textual alterations otherwise
unrecorded, in the Cambridge University Library.[14] Two items are
of particular interest in the question of the nature of Geraldine.
The first is a note on page 2 of the book, signed S. T. Coleridge and
dated 3 February 1819, which reads in part:

> I still cherish the hope of finishing this poem, and if by any means I
> can command two months' actual leisure at the sea side, I hope to
> finish it in the course of the present year. Enough at present to assure
> you, that Geraldine is *not* a Witch, in any proper sense of that word—
> That she is a man in disguise, is a wicked rumour sent abroad with
> malice prepense, and against his own belief and knowledge, by poor
> Hazlitt. Unhappy man! I understand that when one of his Faction
> had declared in a pamphlet ("Hypocrisy unveiled") the Christabel
> "the most obscene poem in the English language" he shrugged himself
> up with a sort of sensual orgasm of enjoyment, and exclaimed—How
> he'll stare! (i.e. meaning *me*) Curse him! I *hate* him.

It would be difficult for Coleridge to be more emphatic. The second item of note is a textual alteration on page 18, referring to
Geraldine:

> A woman she: and in her mood
> Still wrought the soul of Womanhood.

180

That Geraldine embodies the "soul of Womanhood" and is "*not a Witch, in any proper sense of that word,*" leaves open and indeed makes plausible the possibility that, as Derwent Coleridge says, she is "a spirit executing her appointed task with the best good will."

Far from being an evil and malignant being, Geraldine is the primary agent of Spirit, or Faery, in "Christabel." That she is the symbolic representation of the world of Spirit is shown by her androgynous nature and by her words and actions.[15] Thomas McFarland's comment that one of the chief illustrative images of the Romantic theories of polarity was "that of the division of human sexuality into male and female" and that one of the major variations on the sexual metaphor was that of the androgyne (324–27) is apt, as is Owen Barfield's discussion of polarity as the creative process of Life:

> Polarity is dynamic, not abstract. It is not "a mere balance or compromise" but "a living and generative interpenetration." Where logical opposites are contradictory, polar opposites are generative of each other—and together generative of a new product. Polar opposites exist by virtue of each other *as well as* at the expense of each other; "each is that which it is called, relatively, by predominance of the one character or quality, not by the absolute exclusion of the other." Moreover each quality or character is present *in* the other. We can and must distinguish, but there is no possibility of *dividing* them. . . . The apprehension of polarity is itself *the basic act of imagination* (36).

Geraldine is a person in whom there is a "predominance of the one character or quality [but] not . . . the exclusion of the other." For Coleridge, what is called for in the androgynous nature is not the obliteration of gender but a reconciliation of the two sexes that yet recognizes the individualizing tendency toward one sex or the other. What is wanted is not annihilation but ongoing creative process: simultaneous difference and identity—Life. As the discussion of androgyny in Chapter 1 shows, the androgynous nature, like Spirit itself, is the "manifestation of one power by opposite forces" (*Friend* 1: 479). The androgynous Geraldine symbolizes

God/Spirit/Truth both in her person and in her actions—a bold and risky venture into mystery on Coleridge's part.

Although the feminine is certainly predominant in Geraldine, as the initial description of her as a "damsel bright . . . beautiful exceedingly!" makes clear, still there is that about her which makes Hazlitt's "malicious" remark—that she is "a man in disguise"—strike a note of truth, even if it is inaccurate. It acquires additional interest in conjunction with Dr. Gillman's repetition of the motif: he suggests that Coleridge intended eventually to have Geraldine disguise herself as Christabel's absent lover. Whatever credence we give this purported ending, the recurrence of the idea of disguise and the fact that it does not seem entirely implausible attest to the strength of the masculine side of the polarity that Geraldine's nature encompasses. Geraldine plays the "masculine" role in the relationship with Christabel in a number of ways. She is a parallel figure for Christabel's lover, appearing from far away just as Christabel is praying for the lover who is far away. She becomes the aggressor in the seduction; it is she who takes Christabel in her arms as would a male lover with a woman—though equally, of course, as would a mother with a child—and it is she who dominates the relationship with Christabel. Most obviously, her name shows androgynous reconciliation, being the feminine form of the masculine "Gerald." Similarly, the masculine side of Christabel's androgynous nature can be seen in the doubly masculine referents for her name—Christ and Abel—and in her initiatory invitation to Geraldine to enter the castle and share her bed. Although the "masculine" seems less emphatic in Christabel than in Geraldine, it is still clearly present.[16] Geraldine, however, even more strongly than Christabel, conveys an aura of masculinity which neither dispels nor is dispelled by the distinctly feminine description of the "girded vests" that "grew tight beneath her heaving breasts" (379–80) and which is incorporated in the description of her as "the soul of Womanhood," since that soul, manifesting its one power by opposing forces, would necessarily be androgynous. The androgynous Geraldine represents the essence of Life and Spirit.

Geraldine "partakes of the Reality which [she] renders intelligible." Again and again in the poem, her description, words, and actions emphasize her role as a symbol of Spirit. Geraldine exists as the "soul of Womanhood" within the Temporal, but she is also the means by which the Eternal is made translucent. She herself looks almost translucent as Christabel first beholds her:

> There she sees a damsel bright,
> Drest in a silken robe of white,
> That shadowy in the moonlight shone:
> The neck that made that white robe wan,
> Her stately neck, and arms were bare;
> Her blue-veined feet unsandal'd were,
> And wildly glittered here and there
> The gems entangled in her hair.
> I guess 'twas frightful there to see
> A lady so richly clad as she—
> Beautiful exceedingly! (58–68)

Geraldine seems suffused with inner light, as though a halo or glory shines by means of a light from within. Her white robe looks wan in comparison with her bright skin. The white of her robe and the blue of her blue-veined feet recall the Virgin; and Christabel's first words, "Mary mother, save me now! / (Said Christabel,) And who art thou?" (69–70), which are usually read as a prayer on Christabel's part to be saved from Geraldine, can just as easily be read as addressed to Geraldine, whom Christabel takes to be the spirit of the Virgin. The plausibility of this reading is enhanced by Geraldine's reassurance that she is not a disembodied vision: "Stretch forth thy hand, and have no fear!" (75)—the same command that the risen Christ gives the doubting Thomas. Geraldine's association with "Mary mother" anticipates the Conclusion to Part I, in which Geraldine "holds the maiden in her arms" and slumbers "still and mild, / As a mother with her child" (299–300). Mary is also Queen of Heaven, an association called forth by the glittering gems that sparkle like a crown of diamonds in Geraldine's hair. Geraldine's silken robe of white is the color of stainless purity.[17] "Richly clad" and "beautiful exceedingly," she seems an awesome heavenly spirit. The later description is similar:

The lofty lady stood upright:
She was most beautiful to see,
Like a lady of a far countrée.   (223–25)

This is the same "far countrée" of the Mariner's experience, and Geraldine's true father is "of a noble line" (79) indeed.

Within the fairy tale structure of the poem, Geraldine's far countrée is the Other World of Faery, and she is one of "the heroic fairies" who "are of human or more than human height. They are the aristocrats among fairy people . . . riding in procession on white horses" (Briggs, *Puck* 13). White is a fairy color, and though sometimes thought to be unlucky, white horses were usually lucky " 'provided certain very necessary conditions were complied with.' Bad luck followed if they were not complied with" (Adlard 233). H. W. Piper agrees with Adlard that "Geraldine comes from the old world of Fairy. . . . Geraldine then is eldritch . . . dangerous to mortals" but not "simply evil" ("Disunity" 219).[18] The land of Faery is always perilous.

Geraldine has been brought forcibly from the far countrée. The journey has been difficult and long—"And once we crossed the shade of night" (87), a phrase more in keeping with the tale of Faery than with calendar counting. Geraldine says she doesn't know who the warriors were or where they have gone, but there is clearly some purpose operating. Specifically, Geraldine was seized on the "yestermorn" after the "yesternight" on which Christabel dreamed of her betrothed knight, who seems to be in some kind of difficulty. Geraldine was brought to the very tree where Christabel comes to pray for her lover. She was brought and left and has "lain entranced" (92) until the moment of Christabel's arrival at the tree. The emphasis in Geraldine's story lies in her unwillingness to be there; she would prefer to be in the far countrée where she lives. Here, she becomes a "weary woman, scarce alive" (95); the burden of assuming mortal form is a heavy one. It is small wonder that Geraldine is so weary. Her journey began in the land of Spirit; she was forced to ride across the shade of night into the natural world which, though symbolic, is nonetheless mortal; and now she must move from the symbolic world of nature into Sir Leoline's castle of death. Christabel uses the key to go through the castle door, leaving the world of Faery and passing through the same gate where death-dealing armies "in battle array had marched out" (128). Geraldine's spirit of Life might well sink "through pain" at having to cross this threshold on her journey into the castle itself. Just as she was abducted by the five men, she is now aided by Christabel who has "lifted her up, a weary weight" (131). Geraldine has entered the fallen world unwillingly, but she carries out her appointed task. The conclusion of that task is foreshadowed as Christabel says:

> Praise we the Virgin all divine
> Who hath rescued thee from thy distress!
> Alas, alas! said Geraldine,
> I cannot speak for weariness. (139–42)

Geraldine has not been, and will not be, rescued from the true cause of her distress, and that truth brings her weariness.

The deathly quality of the Baron's world is emphasized by the fact that he is "weak in health" (118); the mastiff bitch is now a "mastiff old" (145); and "the brands were flat, the brands were dying, / Amid their own white ashes lying" (156–57). Each responds to the Life within Geraldine: the Baron "[forgets] his age" (431); the mastiff old, who "sees my lady's shroud," moans at Geraldine; and the brands come to life for a moment in a "fit of flame" (159). Nevertheless, as Christabel and Geraldine "steal their way from stair to stair, / Now in glimmer, and now in gloom," they must "pass the Baron's room, / As still as death, with stifled breath!" (168–71). Paradoxically, at what seems to be the center of this world of death is Christabel's room:

> The chamber carved so curiously,
> Carved with figures strange and sweet,
> All made out of the carver's brain,
> For a lady's chamber meet:
> The lamp with twofold silver chain
> Is fastened to an angel's feet. (179–83)

The room is a place of motion and imagination with its "figures strange and sweet, / All made out of the carver's brain," a place of light presided over by an angel. Geraldine, "in wretched plight" from her journey through Sir Leoline's castle and the rest of the mortal world, sinks "down upon the floor," as Christabel turns up the lamp, and leaves it "swinging to and fro" (186–89).

Geraldine's journey from the far countrée to Christabel's bed comes very close to being the story of Christ's life and passion. The son of God assumes mortal flesh and is born of woman. Geraldine has an unnamed sire of "noble line," and she assumes the form of a "weary woman" (95), "a maid forlorn" (82) taken from her former home in a violent seizure that ends abruptly after a long and laborious ride—a birth into the mortal world. Geraldine seeks pity and release from her task when Christabel says:

> O weary lady, Geraldine,
> I pray you, drink this cordial wine!
> It is a wine of virtuous powers;
> My mother made it of wild flowers. (190–93)

Accepting the wine, Geraldine asks if Christabel's mother will "pity" her, again, "a maiden most forlorn" (194–95). And when Christabel exclaims: "O mother dear! that thou wert here!" Geraldine responds: "I would, said Geraldine, she were!" (202–03). Geraldine, wanting this cup to pass from her, is utterly sincere, but the cup containing the wine of virtuous powers is one from which she must drink, as Christ accepted the suffering which was the will of the Father. And so,

>   soon with altered voice, said she—
> "Off, wandering mother! Peak and pine!
> I have the power to bid thee flee."
> Alas! what ails poor Geraldine?
> Why stares she with unsettled eye?
> Can she the bodiless dead espy?
> And why with hollow voice cries she,
> "Off, woman, off! this hour is mine—
> Though thou her guardian spirit be,
> Off, woman, off! 'tis given to me." (204–13)

Acceptance of suffering is a weary burden whose end is shown as Christabel

> knelt by the lady's side,
> And raised to heaven her eyes so blue—
> Alas! said she, this ghastly ride—
> Dear Lady! it hath wildered you!
> The lady wiped her moist cold brow,
> And faintly said, "'Tis over now!"   (214–19)

There are strong echoes of the crucifixion scene in which the women kneel with their eyes on the Christ who is the hope of heaven. Moist, cold mortality lies on the brow of the two sufferers, and Geraldine faintly repeats Christ's words, "It is finished." In preparation, "again the wild-flower wine she drank" (220), and as she does so, she rises in strength and beauty:

> Her fair large eyes 'gan glitter bright,
> And from the floor whereon she sank,
> The lofty lady stood upright:
> She was most beautiful to see,
> Like a lady of a far countrée.   (221–25)

No longer a weary woman but a lofty lady, Geraldine announces the purpose of her entry into the fallen world, the reason she has been sent as a messenger of Love:

> And thus the lofty lady spake—
> "All they who live in the upper sky,
> Do love you, holy Christabel!
> And you love them, and for their sake
> And for the good which me befel,
> Even I in my degree will try,
> Fair maiden, to requite you well."   (226–32)

This is no ironic or covertly malignant statement. It is the simple truth, and the actions of the poem follow from it, actions that are grounded in Love. The "holy Christabel," loving the spirits of the "upper sky," acts with charity toward Geraldine. Geraldine, in her turn, is a messenger, a symbol of the God of Love, sent by those spirits because they love Christabel and Christabel loves them. The reconciling "action of God is Love" (CL 2: 634), writes Coleridge; and Geraldine, partaking symbolically in that action of Love, has the task of rendering it intelligible to Christabel.

Difficult as the tasks may seem in fairy tales, there is almost always help available to the hero or heroine. The help comes because of his or her "unconsciously correct behavior. . . . The hero and heroine in the fairy tale do the right thing, they hit the right key; they are heaven's favorites" (Luthi, *Once upon a Time* 142–43). Christabel's task is an encounter with Love. Geraldine has come to aid Christabel, to "requite [her] well." Because Christabel loves the spirits of the upper sky, they love her and in turn send Geraldine as a messenger; because Christabel, out of love, goes to pray for her lover, she meets Geraldine; and because Christabel acts "in love and in charity" (277) toward Geraldine, she can experience the message of Love. It is her own "correct behavior" that initiates the aid she receives. Luthi's commentary on "Cinderella" is an apt parallel: "Cinderella is helpless, forsaken, and alone, like so many other heroes and heroines in the fairy tales. . . . Precisely as an outcast can man hope to find help. The fairy tale is an initiation. Man is cast into suffering and want, evidently destined to endure privation, misunderstanding, and malice, and yet summoned to a regal existence. Man is surrounded by hostile and helpful forces; but he is not entirely at their mercy: through his own attitude—perseverance, humility, and trust—he can be supported through the help of nature and the enduring, strengthening love of the deceased mother and can thus be led to the light" (*Once upon a Time* 61). Christabel's spirit is summoned to a "regal existence" with Love; life in the fallen world of Sir Leoline is that of an "exile in a far distant land" (*SM* 24), away from her rightful heritage; she is indeed a princess needing to be restored to her kingdom in the "light." And for her, restoration can occur only in surroundings of "privation, misunderstanding, and malice," as her father's response to her in Part II shows. However, because Christabel acts in humility and trust and love, she receives aid from Geraldine, who functions as another aspect of the "strengthening love of the deceased mother."

Apprehension of the creative polarity of God occurs as the fundamental act of imagination. That act is intuitive self-knowledge, self-knowledge that speaks the "language of Sight." Love that is God/Spirit/Truth is knowable as intuitive self-knowledge made manifest through symbolic experience. Geraldine, as symbol of Love and Spirit, makes the Unity knowable to Christabel through Christabel's symbolic experience of Geraldine. That the relationship between the two manifests self-knowledge explains two otherwise puzzling parts of the poem: the sexual and, more specifically, lesbian nature of the encounter and the Christ motif associated with Geraldine, as well as Christabel.

Sexual encounter is the traditional metaphor for knowledge. For Coleridge, given his belief in the doctrines of polarity and consubstantiality, sexual encounter will likely also be symbolic. One of the most precise presentations of this symbol of Love would be the sexual joining of two androgynous beings, as exemplified in the husband-wife marriage relationship described previously in relation to the poem "Love." But in "Christabel," Coleridge's primary concern is to emphasize the self-knowledge inherent in symbolic experience and the personal implications of such an experience for the individual soul within a fallen world. Therefore, he uses as central characters two people, each of whom within her own person is androgynous. The male and female are both present within each of the women, Christabel and Geraldine, so that the sexual encounter encompasses both the masculine and the feminine. But since the androgynous nature, while exemplifying the polar unity of both sexes, still has an individualizing tendency toward one sex or the other, Coleridge must choose male or female characters for his poem. He chooses the female because the traditional association of women with the creative *anima* emphasizes the fact that the apprehension of unity *is* the act of imagination. In addition, he chooses to portray a same-sex love relationship because the symbolic experience is one of self-knowledge: when Christabel comes to know Geraldine, there is a sense in which she comes to know herself. Because she understands the mystery that inheres in Geraldine, she understands the same mystery within herself: the mystery of Spirit. The Christ identification motif that operates for both Geraldine and Christabel underscores and extends the symbolic experience. Christ, as son of God, is Spirit, but

Spirit made flesh, as also is Geraldine—and Christabel, and the reader. The androgynous Christ is male, whereas Geraldine and Christabel are female; thus, the identification of Geraldine and Christabel and Christ, through the figure and name motif, is generative polarity in action. The female and the male interpenetrate, become the other, while retaining integrity. In addition, since Christabel and Geraldine share the same Christ associations, the knowledge of the one becomes even more intensely the knowledge of the other: intuitive self-knowledge. And "whatever is conscious *Self*-knowledge is Reason" (*Friend* 1: 156).

The dual identification with Christ also prepares for the suffering that accompanies knowledge in the fallen world. Innocence is the necessary sacrifice for knowledge in this world. The slaying of the innocent Abel makes necessary the sacrifice of the Christ, and behind the lives of Christ and Abel are the agency of Satan and Cain. In the fallen world, there is no knowledge of the Unity of the Godhead without the accompanying knowledge of the partial and particular, and for this reason—to avoid the inevitable betrayal of Christabel into suffering—Geraldine wishes the spirit of the mother present. No mother wants to be the bearer of suffering to her child. One of the sorrows of motherhood is the fact that despite our desire to preserve the innocence of our children, we have no choice but to participate in initiating them into an awareness of the fallen world. Thus, Geraldine *must* bid the guardian spirit flee. The relationship between Geraldine and Christabel's mother is one of the most puzzling yet interesting relationships in the poem. Geraldine and the mother are one, here split (in contrast with the mother in "The Three Graves") as they often are in fairy tale into the "good" mother who only protects and shelters and the "bad" mother who must discipline or lead the child into growth.[19] Thus, the "strengthening love of the deceased mother" is evident in the poem in the mother's spirit, but it is also evident in Geraldine, as she comforts Christabel after her initiation into experience. "The deceased in the fairy tales are not ghostly, like those in local legend, but enter into the play of forces" (Luthi, *Once upon a Time* 61). Clearly, Geraldine is well acquainted with the spirits of the upper sky who love Christabel; and just as clearly, the mother is one of those spirits. Christabel offers, and Geraldine twice drinks, the mother's wine of virtuous powers. When Christabel exclaims, "O mother dear! that thou wert here!" Geraldine answers immediately and truly, "I would . . . she were!" (202–03). Yet "soon with altered voice" she says, "Off, wandering mother! Peak and pine! / I have power to bid thee flee" (204–06). As other passages of the poem indicate, Geraldine and the mother are one. They are the mother who loves and protects from harm, but they are also the mother who brings the daughter into the world of experience, the fallen world. Only through knowledge can the daughter become the mother herself. To remain without knowledge is to remain a child. So, for one hour, the mother who would *only* protect must be banished while the mother who initiates into self-knowledge tries to requite Christabel well.

Because of the mark of the shame and sorrow of the fallen world that she bears, Geraldine is the "mother" who must aid Christabel in her task of self-knowledge of Love. Geraldine says to Christabel, "But now unrobe yourself; for I / Must pray, ere yet in bed I lie" (233–34). Christabel obeys,

> But through her brain of weal and woe
> So many thoughts moved to and fro,
> That vain it were her lids to close;
> So half-way from the bed she rose,
> And on her elbow did recline
> To look at the lady Geraldine. (239–44)

Eager for knowledge, for the apprehension of Reality, Christabel watches Geraldine undress and sees

> full in view,
> Behold! her bosom and half her side—
> A sight to dream of, not to tell!
> O shield her! shield sweet Christabel! (251–54)

Geraldine's mark of shame and seal of sorrow, wounds of the fallen world, cannot be shielded from Christabel, since they are the price of imaginative knowledge for her. The fallen world is sealed in sorrow, and it is a mark of shame for one's spirit to have to bear the print of death with the grace of Wholeness, but this knowledge, self-knowledge, will belong to Christabel on the morrow: "Thou knowest to-night, and wilt know to-morrow, / This mark of my shame, this seal of my sorrow" (269–70).

Geraldine "seeks delay," but in the end, she acts in Love:

> Yet Geraldine nor speaks nor stirs;
> Ah! what a stricken look was hers!
> Deep from within she seems half-way
> To lift some weight with sick assay,
> And eyes the maid and seeks delay;
> Then suddenly, as one defied,
> Collects herself in scorn and pride,
> And lay down by the Maiden's side!—
> And in her arms the maid she took,
>   Ah wel-a-day!   (255–64)

Geraldine's reluctance to be Christabel's initiator out of innocence and into knowledge of the fallen world is very strong, but there is no relenting in the necessity of her role. Thus, her desire for the avoidance of harm having been defied, Geraldine asserts her regal "scorn and pride" in the face of the defiance and lies down "by the maiden's side." Geraldine acts out of Love as she tries to requite Christabel well. But Christabel lives in a fallen world. She must wake in the morning to her father's world, a world characterized by death rather than life, a world which, by its very nature, does not have whole vision, does not speak the language of Sight. In other words, the world in which Geraldine's symbolic act of love occurs is, as the Conclusion to Part II laments, a "world of sin" (673). Because this is so, and because the fallen world speaks the language of the Understanding rather than the Reason, Christabel will have no power to tell what she knows. Instead, she, like Coleridge in writing a symbolic poem, will only be able to tell a story:

> And with low voice and doleful look
> These words did say:
> "In the touch of this bosom there worketh a spell,

Which is lord of thy utterance, Christabel!
Thou knowest to-night, and wilt know to-morrow,
This mark of my shame, this seal of my sorrow;
  But vainly thou warrest,
   For this is alone in
  Thy power to declare,
   That in the dim forest
  Thou heard'st a low moaning,
And found'st a bright lady, surpassingly fair;
And didst bring her home with thee in love and in charity,
To shield her and shelter her from the damp air."   (265–78)

Christabel will be able to tell a story about an act of love and charity, a symbolic story. In the fallen world, this is the only speech possible; the language of Sight is under spell.

The Conclusion to Part I constitutes, first, the narrator's re-iteration of the story of Part I and, then, the presentation of the fact of symbolic experience—not the experience itself, since the Holy Word is forbidden, but the external, physical details that symbolize the spiritual knowledge encountered:

With open eyes (ah woe is me!)
Asleep, and dreaming fearfully,
Fearfully dreaming, yet, I wis,
Dreaming that alone, which is—
O sorrow and shame!   (292–96)

Christabel, with open eyes and yet asleep, dreams the reconciliation that is Wholeness. It is a fearful thing, fearful not only in the negative sense but also in the positive sense of full-of-awe. With knowledge, however, comes the burden of sorrow and shame, so that when Christabel dreams "that alone, which is," she encounters the truth of Wholeness and the fact of its existence in a fallen world. As Christabel dreams, Geraldine combines in her person the two parts of the mother:

And lo! the worker of these harms,
That holds the maiden in her arms,
Seems to slumber still and mild,
As a mother with her child.   (298–301)

She has had her hour as worker of harms—giver of knowledge of the fallen world. But she also has her hour as the mother of protection and comfort. Holding Christabel in her arms "as a mother with her child"—in an image reminiscent of Mary, the mother mild, holding the Christ both as infant and crucified sufferer—Geraldine, like Christabel, sleeps, and the two are joined in the dream.

Christabel's response to the dream embodies the reconciliation of opposites that is the nature of the Reality of Love and Spirit. The scene is strangely peaceful and quiet, gentle and mild:

> Her limbs relax, her countenance
> Grows sad and soft; the smooth thin lids
> Close o'er her eyes; and tears she sheds—
> Large tears that leave the lashes bright!
> And oft the while she seems to smile
> As infants at a sudden light!
>
> Yea, she doth smile, and she doth weep,
> Like a youthful hermitess,
> Beauteous in a wilderness,
> Who, praying always, prays in sleep. (313–23)

The smiling and weeping are two parts of a whole. Christabel, within the mother-child comparison, becomes an infant who smiles in pleasure at the light of new knowledge. There is no fear or protestation or repulsion on Christabel's part. Instead, the tears she sheds are "large tears," shed softly and slowly; leaving the "lashes bright," they also hold some of the quality of the light. The tears are simultaneously tears of happiness and tears of sorrow— happiness for knowledge of Love, sorrow for knowledge of separation. She is like a "youthful hermitess, / Beauteous in a wilderness": that is, a hermitess committed to holiness but thus necessarily separated from the rest of the world. Though inevitable, the separation seems touching because of her youth. She is "alone, alone" in a wilderness that makes her beauty even more apparent and more poignant in contrast. Like the hermit and the Wedding-Guest of "The Rime," she has had an encounter with the world of Spirit which changes her life. The Wedding-Guest's silent "sadder but wiser" state parallels Christabel's dreaming response. The sense of utter aloneness she experiences in Part II recalls the Mariner's terror lest his sighting of the land be an illusion. The narrator assumes that Christabel is having a "vision sweet" of her guardian spirit/mother, perhaps; and truly both mothers are present. Geraldine works "harms" in the "prison" of her arms, a prison much like the "prison-house" of mortality of Wordsworth's "Immortality" ode. But her arms also shelter and protect as she gives self-knowledge to Christabel. The "blue sky" that "bends over" the sleeping Christabel further shelters her, performing a motherly watchfulness in its benediction.

Christabel awakens in "a world of sin," and immediately speech and action become distorted into the divisive categories of the fallen world: " 'Sure I have sinn'd!' said Christabel" (381), with her new awareness of the shame of the Fall which she, as a mortal, possesses. Geraldine apparently becomes merely the daughter of Sir Leoline's estranged friend; Christabel's knowledge of mortality—rather than remaining unified with light and smile—becomes separated from the "vision blest" (464); it now seems a "vision of fear . . . and pain" (453), which she expresses in a hissing sound. Although "the vision blest, / Which comforted her after-rest" immediately follows the "vision of fear," bringing "smiles like light" (464–65, 469), the two are separate, not commingled. In the world of death, the division will lead to the predominance of the vision of fear. Geraldine, seeing what is happening, asks Sir Leoline for leave to go:

> Yet he, who saw this Geraldine,
> Had deemed her sure a thing divine:
> Such sorrow with such grace she blended,
> As if she feared she had offended
> Sweet Christabel, that gentle maid!
> And with such lowly tones she prayed
> She might be sent without delay
> Home to her father's mansion. (474–82)

When read as devoid of any ironic intent, the passage reveals the true state of affairs. Geraldine, a "thing divine," blends within herself sorrow and grace, in a Christlike manner. Having come with the intention of requiting Christabel well, she now sees that in Sir Leoline's world, she can only serve to harm and offend Christabel. The longer she stays, the more distorted the true state of affairs will become. Echoing Christ's words "in my father's house are many mansions," Geraldine prays to be sent home immediately to her father's mansion. Her concern for Christabel and her request seem perfectly sincere. If Sir Leoline had not imposed his "Nay, by my soul!" (483), Christabel's "All will yet be well!" (472) might well have been the case:

> Sin is Behovely, but
> All shall be well, and
> All manner of thing shall be well.   ("Little Gidding," 3)

As it is, things only get worse.

Geraldine, listening to Sir Leoline's false interpretation of Bard Bracy's dream, "looked askance at Christabel" (581):

> A snake's small eye blinks dull and shy;
> And the lady's eyes they shrunk in her head,
> Each shrunk up to a serpent's eye,
> And with something of malice, and more of dread,
> At Christabel she looked askance!   (583–87)

Christabel, with her new awareness both of Love and of the fallen world, sees in Sir Leoline's court of death the "bad" mother, the worker of harms, whose mark of shame and seal of sorrow are imaged in the snake eyes of the tempter in the garden. Christabel, because she is human, sees the "something of malice" in Geraldine's eye and knows she herself also embodies the "world of sin." Like Geraldine, Christabel now wears a mark of shame. Still, although Geraldine's look has "something of malice," it has "more of dread." The dread emerges from Geraldine's fear that her desire to requite Christabel well will be lost in Christabel's inability to come to terms with the fallen world and her place in it: that is, with the necessity imposed on the human spirit to affirm its consubstantiality with Spirit while existing in a fallen world.[20] Totally disoriented, seeing only the snake's eyes, which become the visible emblem of the mark and seal, Christabel stumbles "on the unsteady ground" (590) and falls into a mimetic trance. Geraldine is horrified but helpless:

And Geraldine again turned round,
And like a thing, that sought relief,
Full of wonder and full of grief,
She rolled her large bright eyes divine
Wildly on Sir Leoline.   (592–96)

Full of wonder and grief at Christabel's response and herself almost disoriented by the fallen world and lack of perception that surrounds her, Geraldine seeks "relief" or help from a father who reputedly loves his daughter well. But there is no salvation from grief in the person of Sir Leoline, and he completes the actions of separation and division of Part II by abandoning his daughter and leading Geraldine from the hall. Christabel cannot speak, and the narrator's question, "And wouldst thou wrong thy only child, / Her child and thine?" (634–35), falls on deaf ears.

"Christabel" is an incomplete and unfinished fairy tale; nor, given the symbolic experience of mystery which is the burden of the story, could it be otherwise. The happy ending of a fairy tale is traditional and close to obligatory, although one can think of tales in which the ending is not happy, such as "The Red Shoes" or Perrault's "Little Red Riding Hood." But "everything usually comes out all right in the end—for the hero and heroine at least" (Luthi, *Once upon a Time* 59). Alexander Krappe puts it even more strongly: "In his task, the hero is invariably successful [and there is a] happy ending, without which a fairy tale is unthinkable" (22). At the least, a happy ending is expected. This point could hardly have been lost on Coleridge and could well account for Gillman's assertion that the poet toyed with a suitable fairy tale ending in which, after much delay and disguise, Christabel and her lover are married and live, presumably, happily forever after. But this is not an ending that Coleridge wrote. If he is to be believed—and I think he is—Coleridge knew, as he asserted many times, how he wanted to complete the poem. But given the "extremely subtle and difficult" (*TT*, 6 July 1833) idea of the poem, what could the ending have been? If, as I have argued, it is Christabel's first task to encounter symbolically the world of Spirit and Love (which she does successfully in Part I) and her second task to reenter the fallen world with her knowledge (the task she begins in Part II), there are a limited number of options for her third and culminating task, none of which would lead to an entirely satisfactory fairy tale ending. She could learn to live successfully and happily in the fallen world with her knowledge, reject her knowledge, try to return to the Faery world, or go mad.

Coleridge had already used one of these possibilities in "The Rime." The Mariner lives, though how successfully or happily is debatable, in the "real" world after his voyage. His experience with Spirit, however, differs from that of Christabel in two significant ways. First, the Mariner's understanding of the experience he has had is not nearly as total as Christabel's. For this reason, his penance—one sufficient for his knowledge—is to tell his story; that is, he tells the *story* of the encounter, not the experience itself. Christabel has a story to tell also, but "there worketh a spell" in the "touch of [Geraldine's] bosom" (267) which renders Christabel powerless to convey the knowledge of symbolic encounter: "For what she knew she could not tell, / O'er-mastered by the mighty spell" (619–20). The second difference is that the Mariner's journey—though, at its most profound level, spiritual in nature—is at least on one level a physical, geographical journey. He goes through the door to the Other World beyond kirk, hill, and lighthouse and returns. But for Christabel, there is no geographical "place" to which she can return. She has seen the Reality of the Other World of Wholeness, but she cannot return to it, because it exists now only perceptually, in her knowing. And knowing also that she is in exile from a far countrée, how can she live happily in the world of Sir Leoline? The poet's attempt in "Kubla Khan" to ignore the fallen world will not work for Christabel. Madness as a "way out," posited in "The Fable of the Madning Rain," avoids the problem rather than solving it.

There is, finally, *no* adequate ending for "Christabel" because there is no adequate way to overcome the fallenness of this world and our knowledge of that Fall. Even the fairy tale structure, which works so well up to the final point, will not suffice in this case. The only ending possible is the one we have in the Conclusion to Part II:

> A little child, a limber elf,
> Singing, dancing to itself,
> A fairy thing with red round cheeks,
> That always finds, and never seeks,
> Makes such a vision to the sight
> As fills a father's eyes with light;
> And pleasures flow in so thick and fast
> Upon his heart, that he at last
> Must needs express his love's excess
> With words of unmeant bitterness.
> Perhaps 'tis pretty to force together
> Thoughts so all unlike each other;
> To mutter and mock a broken charm,
> To dally with wrong that does no harm.
> Perhaps 'tis tender too and pretty
> At each wild word to feel within
> A sweet recoil of love and pity.
> And what, if in a world of sin
> (O sorrow and shame should this be true!)
> Such giddiness of heart and brain
> Comes seldom save from rage and pain,
> So talks as it's most used to do.   (656–77)

The Conclusion shows explicitly what happens to reconciling Love in a fallen world. When the world is not perceived as whole or as consubstantial, opposing primary principles become simply two coexisting contradictory forces, each battling for the annihilation of the other. "Thoughts so all unlike each other" are forced together, not interfused and reconciled. Excessive love can be countered or opposed only by bitterness, even though unmeant. Bitter, wild words then recoil to love and pity. The first thing we are told about Christabel is that she is one "whom her father loves so well" (24), words reminiscent of those of the Father at Christ's baptism: "This is my beloved son, in whom I am well pleased"

(Luke 3.22). But even the love of parent and child, which should symbolize the Love of God, becomes distorted in the fallen world. Love must be betrayed, and innocence must be sacrificed. This "little child" of the Conclusion, which Coleridge deliberately makes neither "he" nor "she" but, rather, an androgynous "fairy thing," "a limber elf, / Singing, dancing to itself," is a being of Spirit—vital, active, creative—containing within itself the source of song and dance and, therefore, having no need to seek outside itself for that which it always finds within. This vision of wholeness is betrayed because in a world of sin, extreme pleasure finds its expression as a counter-balance to "rage and pain." We talk as we are "most used to do," and what we speak is the fallen word. The anguish in the voice of the narrator of the Conclusion— "O sorrow and shame should this be true"—arises from the despondent surmise that no other speech may be possible in this "world of sin." The little child is inevitably betrayed by the father into its own knowledge of sorrow and shame. Faery is in truth a Perilous Realm, "and while [one] is there, it is dangerous for [one] to ask too many questions, lest the gates should be shut and the key lost."

"And There Is Only the Dance"

" *Time present* and time past," writes T. S. Eliot, "Are both perhaps present in time future, / And time future contained in time past."

> Dry the pool, dry concrete, brown edged,
> And the pool was filled with water out of sunlight,
> And the lotos rose, quietly, quietly,
> The surface glittered out of heart of light,
> And they were behind us, reflected in the pool.
> Then a cloud passed, and the pool was empty.
> Go, said the bird, for the leaves were full of children,
> Hidden excitedly, containing laughter.   ("Burnt Norton," 1)

The dry pool in Eliot's rose-garden is for a moment "filled with water out of sunlight" so that the surface glitters "out of heart of light," reflecting simultaneously the echoes of the past and the moving present—and in that reflection enclosing, again for a moment, the speaker and the future. The hidden children, laughing with glee, fill the leaves. And so it is in Coleridge's "Garden of Boccaccio."

Written in 1828 and arguably Coleridge's last great poem, "The Garden of Boccaccio" has as its theme the ability of symbolic poetry to give entrance to the garden, the garden of Faery which is also the garden of Eden and the garden of the reconciling imagination—the garden of Creation and the Creator. The poem is about the relationship of past, present, and future—in other words, about the passing of time in the fallen mortal world—but it is also about the eternal, though always developing and never static, place that is out-of-time: the place of Spirit and Love. It does not attempt to solve the problems of the soul's existence in this world, nor does it ignore them. Rather, the poem and the speaker move in the course of the poem from a mood of "dreary" isolation and "vacancy" (3, 8) to a mood of quiet anticipation and participation. The poem acknowledges that life does not always have the shape of a story with a happy ending, but "The Garden of Boccaccio" also affirms that "story" itself—tales of Faery—can be a gift, a moment of grace. These stories, or gifts, come unexpectedly but continuously, and, taken together, they give a language for the story of the human spirit. The poet in "The Garden of Boccaccio" speaks in a voice that is full and patient and knowing, a mature and gentle voice. It is the voice of a poet who has come to terms with life and, having done so, still retains an almost impish sense of delight, a puckish curiosity, and a childlike ability to meet "elfin playfellows" (55) on their own ground.

The poem begins with the speaker sitting, in effect, by the "dry pool," as imaginatively parched as a soul walking through "the fearful desert" (*BL* 1: 244). He feels alone, without companionship and without emotion. He has the sense of being outside even himself; as if from a distance, he watches his "own vacancy" and "dull continuous ache" (8–9). Separation from all sense of the "genial powers" of life leaves the poet almost without life itself. Like the becalmed Mariner, he has tried to bring himself out of this state, but to no avail: "Call'd on the Past for thought of glee or grief. / In vain!" (6–7). At this juncture, then, he is given the unexpected and unasked-for gift of grace, a tale of Faery:

Boccaccio's Garden and its faery,
The love, the joyaunce, and the gallantry!
An Idyll, with Boccaccio's spirit warm,
Framed in the silent poesy of form.   (15–18)

The "exquisite design" (14) that the poet calls a "silent poesy of form" is an illustration, "a tapestry depicting scenes from Boccaccio" (Beer "Supernatural" 87), but the picture merges immediately with the poetry of Boccaccio to become the inner pictures of Boccaccio's stories brought to the poet's mind's eye. Boccaccio's garden is the garden of Faery, and it contains everything that has been absent from the vacant heart of the poet: love, joyance, gallantry, companionship. Boccaccio's warm spirit touches the heart of the illustrator who, himself having been given an entrance into story and Faery, transforms Boccaccio's art into another form, which in turn can touch the heart of the speaker: "A tremulous warmth crept gradual o'er my chest, / As though an infant's finger touch'd my breast" (25–26).

"The Garden of Boccaccio" is very much a poet's poem about the role of poetry for the poet, a personal statement about the power of poetry to generate, bring into new existence, other poems. Symbolic poetry opens the door to the garden of Faery, the garden of creative reconciliation, so that another symbolic poem can be created. The poem nourishes poetic genius which in turn creates another poem, and so forth, so that in effect the souls of the poets become united in their diverse individuality, and symbolic poems become metaphors for each other. This is the context within which Coleridge in another place can assert that he reads Plato by anticipation. "Boccaccio's Garden and its faery" belong to all symbolic poets. Here Poesy, the "faery child" (48), lives alongside her more conscious self, Philosophy. Here the "lute's love-echoing strings" (67) are played. Here are clear fountains, "green arches," and the "high tower" of romance (61, 70). Here, the speaker exults, "with old Boccaccio's soul I stand possest, / And breathe an air like life, that swells my chest" (71–72). And here he sees Boccaccio himself:

See! Boccace sits, unfolding on his knees
The new-found roll of old Maeonides;
But from his mantle's fold, and near the heart,
Peers Ovid's Holy Book of Love's sweet smart!   (97–100)

Boccaccio lives in the garden, but he does not live alone. Here he "unfolds" the poetry of Homer, for himself and others. And closest to his heart he carries "Ovid's Holy Book of Love's sweet smart!"

At the most personal level of this poem, Coleridge is claiming his place in the garden of Boccaccio. Very early in his poetic career, he listens to the songs of the pixies and inscribes his name in their "parlour." Now, long years of life later, he writes a tale of Faery which gathers together and reconciles his past, present, and future right to belong with the company that inhabits the garden. The poem itself makes the case for inclusion. Lines 19–56 recount the poet's youthful nurturance by story and song, by Poesy. In lines 57–100 the poet, finding himself in Boccaccio's garden, proceeds to re-create that garden. Lines 101–09 move into the future. With this temporal frame, Coleridge affirms the nature of the garden, acknowledges the Spirit which the garden of Faery symbolizes, and brings in echoes of his previous poetry to reconcile them with this present creation. In "The Garden of Boccaccio," Coleridge sums up his life and validates his claim to a place in the garden.

The movement into Faery begins in the space between lines 18 and 19 as the picture steals upon the poet's "inward sight"

Like flocks adown a newly-bathéd steep
    Emerging from a mist: or like a stream
Of music soft that not dispels the sleep,
    But casts in happier moulds the slumberer's dream. (19–22)

One might say, as Schulz does (*Poetic Voices* 102), that the poet here moves into a dream state, and, of course, in some sense that is true. In another way, however, the reverie awakens him to another place, the "Land of Faery," which is always available through a shift in perception.

Within the poem, the natural world and music explain the shift. White emerges from white as the flocks, which have seemed nonexistent but have really only been hidden, take shape again. Influenced by soft music, the sleeper is moved to a happier dream. Touched by the warm spirit of Boccaccio, the poet is visited once again by the "spirits of power" that have attended his life: stories and legends of the Scalds, the hymns of "prophetic maids," "minstrel lay[s]," rhymes of the whole panoply of society—"monk and priest, / Judge, mayor, and many a guild in long array, / To high-church pacing on the great saint's day" (28, 35–42). The stories of long ago are themselves the spirits of power. They led him from infancy through the fancies of "selfless boyhood"; they "charmed" his youth, kindling "from above" the ability to love even before there was an object of love; and they "lent a lustre" to the moral thoughts of manhood (29, 31, 33). As the spirits of power—the creations of earlier poetic imaginations—reemerge in this poet's memory, they once again activate his imagination. His soul has been nurtured and continues to be nurtured by spirits of power. Through their agency, he sang his own verses "That woke the tear, yet stole away the pang / Of hopes, which in lamenting I renew'd" (44–45), verses that reconciled hopes and tears.

The last spirit of power who visits him allows the speaker to re-create in past and present the garden of Faery he inhabited as an innocent:

> And last, a matron now, of sober mien,
> Yet radiant still and with no earthly sheen,
> Whom as a faery child my childhood woo'd
> Even in my dawn of thought—Philosophy;
> Though then unconscious of herself, pardie,
> She bore no other name than Poesy;
> And, like a gift from heaven, in lifeful glee,
> That had but newly left a mother's knee,
> Prattled and play'd with bird and flower, and stone,
> As if with elfin playfellows well known,
> And life reveal'd to innocence alone.   (46–56)

The "faery child," coming "like a gift from heaven," is at first named Poesy and later Philosophy. The two are the same, the latter only more conscious of itself. Gift from heaven, the faery child woos the speaker-child to experience and play with Faery. Like the "little child, a limber elf" in the Conclusion to Part II of "Christabel," this faery child quite bubbles over with "lifeful glee," the exuberance of Life before the Fall.

Two interrelated things are noteworthy here. The glee comes from within the faery child, who is, of course, our own innocence as well as that of the speaker. In addition, she has "but newly left a mother's knee." The heavenly mother, as parent of the child, is source and teacher of the lifeful glee. The concept of God the Father has expanded to include God the Mother, and the analogy of God the parent/faery child/human soul is complete. What is revealed is Life. The faery child brings—and simultaneously becomes—a symbolic encounter with Life by prattling and playing "with bird and flower, and stone, / As if with elfin playfellows well known." The individual things of nature—bird, flower, stone— are equally symbolic and just as real in Faery as the faery child and the speaker-child. They are all elfin playmates and well known to each other as they reveal Life.

Coleridge's earlier encounters with the faery child provide him with the means and occasion for a present symbolic encounter: a vision in the mind, a poem conveying the vision, and a renewed entry into Faery. Nor is he unaware of what has happened.

> Thanks, gentle artist! now I can descry
> Thy fair creation with a mastering eye,
> And all awake! And now in fix'd gaze stand,
> Now wander through the Eden of thy hand. (57–60)

The "gentle artist" is, first of all, the creator of the "exquisite design" that has awakened the past. But Boccaccio is also the artist, and behind him is the Creator of all, so that each of the artists' gardens of imagination symbolizes the Eden of the Creator. As the speaker sings his praises, he becomes no longer an observer but a participant:

> I see no longer! I myself am there,
> Sit on the ground-sward, and the banquet share.
> 'Tis I, that sweep that lute's love-echoing strings,
> And gaze upon the maid who gazing sings:

Or pause and listen to the tinkling bells
From the high tower, and think that there she dwells.
With old Boccaccio's soul I stand possest,
And breathe an air like life, that swells my chest.   (65–72)

The garden is the same garden in which Poesy, the faery child, plays; and the speaker-Coleridge, entering the Faery world, participates in its creative energy as he re-creates both Boccaccio's garden in Florence and his own past poetic gardens of Faery. Possessed of Boccaccio's soul, the speaker, through verbal and associational echoes, re-enters Kubla's garden, plays on the "lute's love echoing strings" the songs of the Eolian Harp, and accompanies the song of the Abyssian maid. *Purchas's Pilgrimage* and the exquisite design and Boccaccio's poetry all become one as "the storied halls" (84) tell of fountains and castles and gardens where "Love lies listening" (85). Sitting "on the ground-sward," sharing in the banquet he is creating, the speaker sees, "Mid gods of Greece and warriors of romance" (96), Boccaccio sitting in the same position reading Homer and holding Ovid next to his heart.

Coleridge has himself become a symbolic artist as he re-creates the garden, a place already known, a place where he is at home, a Faery place he now embraces as that place becomes a symbol of Spirit. Boccaccio sits

Where many a gorgeous flower is duly fed
With its own rill, on its own spangled bed,
And wreathes the marble urn, or leans its head,
A mimic mourner, that with veil withdrawn
Weeps liquid gems, the presents of the dawn;—
Thine all delights, and every muse is thine;
And more than all, the embrace and intertwine
Of all with all in gay and twinkling dance!
Mid gods of Greece and warriors of romance.   (88–96)

The symbolic garden encompasses and reconciles: flowers weep liquid gems, presents of the mortal world of morning; delight lives there, all "animated nature . . . at once the Soul of each and God of all" (EH 44, 48), as do all muses who embrace and intertwine. This time, Coleridge is at ease with a multiplicity of manifestations of Spirit, gods and goddesses as well as God. Ovid's Book of Love becomes a Holy Book. Human love symbolizes the God of Love. In the Faery world of Infinite Possibility, the poet delights in the gardens of Boccaccio and Ovid, the "all-enjoying and all-blending sage" (101):

> Long be it mine to con thy mazy page,
> Where, half conceal'd, the eye of fancy views
> Fauns, nymphs, and wingéd saints, all gracious to thy muse!
> Still in thy garden let me watch their pranks,
> And see in Dian's vest between the ranks
> Of the trim vines, some maid that half believes
> The vestal fires, of which her lover grieves,
> With that sly satyr peeping through the leaves! (102–9)

The eye of Boccaccio's muse, which encompasses equally and joyously fauns and nymphs and wingéd saints, becomes analogously the speaker-poet's muse. Boccaccio's garden belongs to him also. His eye sees the vestal maid and her lover and the passion that will result in unifying love. Thus, Coleridge once again plays the lute for the "coy maid half yielding to her lover" (EH 15) in the garden of Faery. Their story is yet to happen, but when it does, Coleridge, like the "satyr peeping through the leaves," claims his right to tell it.

> In that open field
> If you do not come too close, if you do not come too close,
> On a summer midnight, you can hear the music
> Of the weak pipe and the little drum
> And see them dancing around the bonfire
> The association of man and woman
> In daunsinge, signifying matrimonie—
> A dignified and commodious sacrament.
> Two and two, necessayre coniunction,
> Holding eche other by the hand or the arm
> Whiche betokeneth concorde. ("East Coker," 1)

As with Boccaccio, "the embrace and intertwine / of all with all in gay and twinkling dance" belongs also to Coleridge. He has risked enchantment. He has entered the Perilous Land. And he has told its tale in this world.

Notes

Introduction

1. Madam d'Aulnoy's *Contes des fées* was published in 1698 and translated into English in 1699; a three-volume edition of her works in 1721–22 brought into English "The White Cat," "Finetta the Cinder-Girl," and "The Yellow Dwarf." The eight tales of Charles Perrault's 1727 collection, published in English in 1729, were "Sleeping Beauty," "Little Red Riding Hood," "Bluebeard," "Puss in Boots," "Diamonds and Toads," "Cinderella," "Riquet a la Houpp" (the story of a deformed prince's romance with a princess who is lovely but witless), and "Hop o' My Thumb." In 1756, clearly influenced by Sarah Fielding, Madame Leprince de Beaumont published *Magasin des enfans* in London; the 1761 translation contained "Beauty and the Beast" and "The Three Wishes."

The English attitude toward fairy tales as dangerous to the rational mind shifted abruptly with the publication in 1823 of the Grimm brothers' collection, and by the time Hans Christian Andersen's stories appeared in 1846, the acceptability—indeed, desirability—of fairy tales was firmly established. But Grimm and Andersen and the new attitude toward fairy tales were still in the future when Coleridge was growing up and when "Christabel" was published in 1816, and Coleridge's poetry and theories of the creative imagination did much to prepare the way. For a thorough account of the appearance of fairy tales in English, from which I have taken much of my information, see Opie and Opie.

2. See Pickering for an informative account of the influence of John Locke on theories of childhood reading.

3. See Darton; Meigs et al.; Muir; Pickering; and Thwaite.

4. See Wooden 97–120.

5. Notebook 37, f.82v (British Museum Add MS 47532) provides an interesting commentary in this regard: "In the fourth Verse of the first Chapter of Daniel a Critic who had made up his mind to the *popellar* Birth and Parentage of the six first Chapters would seem to himself to find a confirmation of his hypothesis—for tho' by widening the sense of the word Children, so as to include young men therein, his reasons might be blown back upon him by a single puff from the mouth of the Orthodox. But certainly ~~primo~~ aspectu primo et festinanti Children of spotless beauty, skilful in all wisdom, cunning in knowledge and understanding Science, and of fit and sufficient ability for the acquirement of the Chaldean Language and Learning, does seem very like—Ane Newe, Trewe, and very Auncyent Historia of the Prophet, Merlin, of his marveylouse Childehoode, &c. &c.——and other such that piled among Comfits and Lollipops in one well-remembered Booth at Ottery Fair perplexed my infant choice, the formidable Rivals to Gilt Gingerbread.—For even then I, like Daniel, discovered a fitness for the Learning of the Chaldeans!" (quoted with the kind permission of Mrs. A. H. B. Coleridge).

6. Sara Coleridge, in her *Memoir and Letters*, describes her father's attempts during this visit to win her affections away from her mother, Sarah Fricker Coleridge, from whom Coleridge was separated.

7. Hartley Coleridge's fairy tale, "Adolph and Annette," first published in 1986, is discussed by Judith Plotz.

8. Anya Taylor notes this lack of attention to Coleridge's study of magic and his use of magic—of spells, in particular—in his "prose writings . . . crammed with references to magic" and his poems, "over a third" of which contain magical references ("Magic" 76).

9. Taylor provides an appropriate context for my study: "Coleridge's concern with spirits is not theoretical or archaic—something childish or merely poetical that he wishes to purge himself of—but is at the core of his own personal energy and artistic creativity. He must solve the problem of spirits and ghosts, as he solves the problem of being a more than material substance. If we are in some sense spirits, passing in and out of unions and connections beyond the visible world, our element is not matter or air or anything else measurable by the senses. Our element, Coleridge writes in *Biographia* (1: 244), is freedom: 'The medium by which spirits understand each other is not the surrounding air, but the freedom which they possess in common, as the common ethereal element of their being, the tremuluous reciprocations of which propagate them-

selves even to the inmost soul.' Such intercourse of spirits haunts Coleridge in minor poems, in philosophy, and in the hidden connections of science, as well as in the obvious hauntings of the major poems; these 'tremulous reciprocations' are an essential indication for him of our more than animal nature" (*Defense* 111).

10. As McFarland notes, questions about the immortality of the soul "obsessed Coleridge for forty years and more. In its intent of form, the *magnum opus* was to be the *systematic* terminus for all Coleridge's intellectual strivings to supply a positive answer to that great question. . . . To utilize an organic analogy that Coleridge himself might have found congenial, it was as though a stalk called *magnum opus* grew up out of the deepest concerns of Coleridge's life, but then kept dividing into subsidiary branches that bore blooms and foliage and were harvested before the trunk itself matured" (353–54).

11. Kessler—who quotes Eliot: "The sad ghost of Coleridge beckons to me from the shadows"—devotes the Afterword of *Coleridge's Metaphors of Being* to a discussion of Coleridge and Eliot: "Both desperately needed an absolute power to give meaning to the random fragments of living that some accept as life, but neither felt able to celebrate the Christian mystery without first evolving his own particular form that could incorporate both doubt and belief. At the same time, each needed to create a new self capable of living the Christian paradox of Being-in-Time" (184–85).

Chapter One

1. All poetry is cited by line number (rather than page number) except *Four Quartets*: see n. 3 below.

2. See esp. Bostetter, *Ventriloquists*; Fields; and Magnuson on the strength of the dark side of this tension. Bostetter argues that although Coleridge believed poetry should be morally affirmative, "he was increasingly frustrated in trying to write the kind of poetry he thought he ought to write. His imagination simply would not respond; it demanded a world more complex; left to its own devices it betrayed him by reveling in the 'sensual dark.' Horrified by what he found as he looked within, unable to control or force the imagination in the direction he wanted to go, Coleridge after 1800 almost gave up the writing of poetry" (99).

3. Quotations from T. S. Eliot's *Four Quartets* are identified by section title—"Burnt Norton," "East Coker," "The Dry Salvages," "Little Gidding"—and internal part number.

4. The translation of T. Barnet's Latin is from Perkins 405.

5. I will let Coleridge speak for himself frequently in this chapter, a

practice he defends: "That our elder writers to Jeremy Taylor inclusive *quoted* to excess, it would be the very blindness of partiality to deny. . . . On the other hand, it seems to me that we now avoid quotations with an anxiety that offends in the contrary extreme" (*Friend* 1: 52).

6. See, e.g., Appleyard; Barfield; Barth, *Christian Doctrine*; Bate; Harding; and Kessler.

7. In *Coleridge and Christian Doctrine* and in *The Symbolic Imagination*, Father Barth establishes the centrality of the concept of consubstantiality for Coleridge. I am greatly indebted to his work. Barth's distinction between the poetry of reference/metaphor and the poetry of encounter/symbol is accurate, I think, and useful for my present study. See also Schulz ("Enchantments" 116–59) for a discussion of Coleridge's efforts "to link the divine nature of eternity-infinity to the transitory earth" (129).

8. A good deal of critical attention has been given to Chapter 12, dealing especially with the direct translation and close paraphrasing of many passages from Schelling's *Abhandlungen*, in particular, as well as Coleridge's use of others' work. See *BL* (Engell-Bate edition), and *CN* 3: 4265n for Coburn's comparison of the chapter with the relevant Schelling passages. See also Barfield 6–7; and Lockridge 23–55.

9. Many critics have, of course, discussed at length Coleridge's idea of the reconciliation of opposites, since it is so central to his thought. See Fogle; Barfield; and, more recently, "A Complex Dialogue: Coleridge's Doctrine of Polarity and Its European Contexts" (McFarland). McFarland objects to Barfield's book because Barfield stresses the importance of Chapter 12 of the *Biographia*, which by 1834 Coleridge described as "unformed and immature" (*TT*, 28 June 1834), and because Barfield ignores the "historical ecology of [Coleridge's] thought" (McFarland 308). Barfield's introduction makes clear the deliberateness of his choice, and neither objection holds if one is relating the statements in *BL* to the early poetry. In addition, it seems relevant to see how Coleridge continues in 1834: "It contains the fragments of the truth, but it is not fully thought out. It is wonderful to myself to think how infinitely more profound my views now are, and yet how much clearer they are withal. The circle is completing; the idea is coming round to, and to be, common sense." There is no rejection here of earlier statements, only acknowledgment of fragmentariness.

10. See Barth, *Symbolic Imagination*; also the introduction to *BL* Shawcross. For a different view about Coleridge's claims for the symbolic imagination, see Appleyard.

11. See Taylor's commentary on this section of *C&S* (*Defense* 183–90). In addition, cf. McFarland 382–418. The yearning or longing that we

feel is for a "realm simultaneously *present as home and origin and empty of all content*"—i.e., it is real, but devoid of tangible form—"but the sense of the void is also the sense of origin: we are, as Baudelaire says, exiled in the imperfect; we do not really belong here" (McFarland 398–99).

12. Similarly, Tolkien says: "Fantasy, of course, starts out with an advantage: arresting strangeness. But that advantage has been turned against it, and has contributed to its disrepute. Many people dislike being 'arrested.' They dislike any meddling with the Primary World, or such small glimpses of it as are familiar to them" (47).

13. Cf. McFarland: "If the approach to 'true being' can only be through the symbol, it is also the case that the gap between phenomenal existence and true being is abridged by human awareness of transcendence. . . . 'But we remain in the world and find ourselves again, not in transcendence but in heightened awareness'" (402–03). We desire and yearn for wholeness, and "the whole thus striven for is a *transcendentally constituted whole*. It is also the one true whole. We achieve it only in epiphanies—those of art or those of philosophy and love—and as a consequence the consciousness of the actual life we lead is irrevocably, in Hegel's pregnant phrase, an unhappy consciousness" (409). Coleridge characterizes "the *leit-motif* of Platonic thought as a 'thirst for something not attained, to which nothing in life is found commensurate and which still impels the soul to pursue' [*Philosophical Lectures* 158]"; through different ways, meontic poetry "*restores* the wholeness of existence" (414). "Symbol and transcendence [are] the referents of the fact that 'we live in a place that is not our own,'" and this is the realization of all great meontic poetry. That "to which all meontic art aspires . . . is a wholeness and a transcendence, shimmering before us as the goal of all strivings. It alleviates the burden of incompleteness, fragmentation, and ruin. And if we could enter rather than glimpse it, all strivings would cease; for there could be no need of art in paradise" (417–18).

14. Coleridge typically uses the masculine "Father" when ascribing any gender to God, as he typically describes the soul as feminine, so that the self-conscious participation of the individual soul in God can be imaged as the mingled meeting of feminine and masculine. However, Coleridge is not asserting that God is male and the soul female. Rather, he makes it clear that he considers each to be the reconciliation of masculine and feminine. Thus the soul symbolizes God's androgynous wholeness. God is total Possibility, existing eternally as an act of Love; creation is the giving of the reality of that existence to things. Because of this, the soul participates symbolically in the being of God.

15. McFarland states that "the sexual, and even the androgynous,

illustration of polarity, though not a large factor in the thought of Coleridge and of Wordsworth, was not entirely absent even in their minds" (326–27), but Coleridge's use of androgyny as an illustration of polarity is more pervasive than this would indicate. For a more complete discussion, see Watson, "Coleridge's Androgynous Ideal."

16. This summary is drawn in part from Krappe; Luthi, *Once upon a Time* and *Fairytale*; Opie and Opie; Sale; and Tolkien.

Chapter Two

1. What was true of Coleridge's sense of obligation to his readers when he began publishing *The Friend* in 1809 would only have been even truer earlier in his career: "In spite of [Coleridge's] frailties, it was hard not to think of himself as one of the elect, and he assumed the role of the righteous man exultingly contemplating virtue or mourning over the fallen, pouring indignant scorn upon the wicked of the world, overflowing with love for the innocent and oppressed. This was the role that he felt was necessary and proper to the poet-seer he aspired to be; this was, therefore, the role he cultivated in the political and philosophical poems of 1794–98 . . . . He believed that one should label clearly what was morally good and what was morally bad, and that poetry should be the instrument of the former" (Bostetter, *Ventriloquists* 93, 99). Even if one takes the lines of argument developed by Bostetter and Magnuson, which explore Coleridge's decreasing ability to write unambiguously affirmative poetry, the tales of Faery—in their very fragmentariness and setting in the fallen world—affirm a faith in the soul's symbolic existence.

2. In his chapter on "The Method of *The Friend*," Christensen observes that *The Friend* deals with "the difficulty of bringing the truth into the everyday" (193) and that, at a first level, "The Fable of the Madning Rain" is concerned with whether or not some way can be found to communicate truth to an uncomprehending audience. He notes: "In part, the fable is itself an attempted solution to the problem it presents: by fabulizing the message the foreign is made familiar" (190).

3. The actions of the pixies are very similar to those of the Witch of Atlas, Shelley's figure of creative imagination. See Watson, "Shelley's Witch."

4. For discussion of the ending of "The Eolian Harp," see, e.g., Gérard; Haven; Paris; and Wendling.

5. For discussion of sources for the poem, whether literary or experiential, see, e.g., Berkoben; and Fruman 26–30. Schulz deals rather extensively with the poem as poem, noting that the natural imagery provides "an emblem of the poet's consciousness" (*Poetic Voices* 44).

6. As Taylor points out, miracles are "supernatural breaks" that interrupt the "continuities of nature." In them, "we encounter . . . what Coleridge calls the essential problem of philosophy—how the phenomenal and noumenal can cohere, a problem that takes its sacramental form in the mysteries of the Eucharist." Miracles, then, like encounters with Faery, may be seen as instances of spirit in the ordinary, everyday world: "Love is a miracle" (*Defense* 176, 180).

7. In critical discussion of "Kubla Khan," issues concerning the nature of the creative process, the role of the poem's Preface, and the question of the poem's fragmentary status are almost inevitably linked. From an abundance of criticism, one might look at, e.g., Chayes; Purves; Schneider; and Suther, "Interpretation of 'Kubla Khan'" and *Visions of Xanadu*. Milton's essay on "Kubla Khan" in her annotated bibliography summarizes the critical issues raised from 1935 to 1970.

8. Wheeler argues that "the preface is to be intimately associated with the poem in an aesthetic sense" by noting the "creation of personas and the addition of details . . . which turn the preface into literary prose" and by showing the ways in which the Preface is connected with the last eighteen lines of the poem. As she argues, both of these are "meditations on visionary activity itself" (24). The use of a persona in the Preface who seems to assume a divine vision and a correlation between that persona and the speaker-poet in the last eighteen lines allow Coleridge to imply that "Kubla Khan" is divinely inspired without claiming the inspiration for himself; it is, rather, the persona-poet speakers who have had the vision.

9. In discussing the Abyssinian maid, Suther comments appropriately on Coleridge's poetic method as well: "By this stage of the poem it becomes very difficult to talk about the images one by one, for one begins to sense the amalgamation of them all. Since one must both be and not be something else in order either to love it or experience it poetically, and since this contradiction is not to be reconciled logically, amalgamation *in a poem* is the only solution, and the multiple identities gradually make themselves felt. The poet *is* the maid; the maid *is* her instrument (in 'The Eolian Harp'), just as all of animated nature may be thought of as organic harps played upon by an intellectual breeze; her music is *like* the mount she sings of ('The Stranger Minstrel' and 'Hymn before Sunrise'); the poet both creates the mount and *becomes* it ('Effusion at Evening' and 'Hymn before Sunrise'). And so one might go on until one had identified all of the major objects of the poem with one another" (*Visions of Xanadu* 269).

10. Piper notes that she sings of "Mount Abora, the mountain of the primal paradise. The damsel associated with paradise on earth sings of the earthly paradise in Eden. . . . The primal eden, human pleasure, and the

paradise to come are all aspects of the same 'strange bliss,' the joy that Coleridge was always seeking in a threatening world" (*Mount Abora* 69, 72).

11. For further discussion of "The Rime" as fairy tale, see Watson, "Coleridge's Rime" and "Coleridge's Mariner." For discussions of the use of the ballad genre, see, e.g., Coffin; and Kroeber.

12. Wheeler's discussion of the relationship of the Argument and gloss to the verse of "The Rime" emphasizes the concern of the former with specificity of time, space, causality, and moral conclusion as distinct from the breaking down of these absolute boundaries that characterizes the imaginative, psychological, and metaphysical experience of the Mariner—and by extension the experience of the speaker-poet and the reader as we encounter the verse narrative. The verse narrative is the world of the Reason and of Faery. "The sense of being poised or balanced on the boundary of two worlds (a familiar world perhaps, and an unfamiliar one) is one of the primary features of the suspense that an imaginative narrative can induce. It can be related to the anxiety in ordinary life of border crossing. It can also provide a definition of metaphor, as the mode of moving the mind to the border of the familiar by inducing a connection with the unfamiliar, or of causing changes in consciousness from unimaginative to imaginative perception" (46–47).

13. Since the publication of Warren's influential essay, much has been written about the symbolic significance of the sun and the moon in "The Rime." For examples of critics who reject Warren's equation of the moon with redemptive imagination and the sun with punitive understanding, see House; and Adair.

14. Wheeler calls this particular gloss passage "one of the most interesting" of "The Rime"; it is, she says, "a moment of high poetry in the gloss (rare enough to count as a marked exception)" (57–58), but her explanation of its obtrusiveness sounds forced. Perhaps the gloss narrator is more complex a person than it would at first appear, with the capacity for symbolic encounter and awareness.

Chapter Three

1. Suther (*Dark Night*) comments on the interconnections within these poems, along with "Kubla Khan," in his discussion of Coleridge's search for a love relationship in which there would be "a lovely maid to read his visage in his mind" and his longing "for something like the beatific vision, a complete presence and union in full knowledge" (33, 27): "The theme is thus a recurrent one in Coleridge's poetry, and some significance may be seen in the fact that in every instance it occurs in a

'fragment.' Perhaps Coleridge was never able to work it out in poetry because he never worked it out in his own experience—it always remained one of the *Magna mysteria*" (43).

2. Yarlot plays up both the autobiographical context and the sentimentality when he comments that "Love" is about a "guilty love affair," which "opens with what seems like a defiant vindication of promiscuity. . . . It is a tragic story of romantic love . . . though marred occasionally by sentimentality" (318–19). Oswald Doughty's tone is similar; he calls the poem a "romantic, pseudomedieval ballad" in which "Sara as Genevieve and Samuel as a medieval minstrel, have been reborn in the never-never land of sham romantic dream" (192).

3. Although he ignores the emotional and psychological force of the poem, Suther notes its relationship to "Kubla Khan" and "The Rime" and gives Coleridge the benefit of the doubt concerning the poem's significance: "The Dark Ladié, by her very cognomen, immediately suggests the woman wailing for the demon-lover. . . . Here, at any rate, there can surely be no doubt as to the 'fragmentary' character of the poem, and it is hard to see, judging by what exists of it, what Coleridge might have meant by suggesting that it should have more nearly realized his ideal than 'The Ancient Mariner.' Yet we should not suppose he made such a statement carelessly, and the 'Kubla Khan' elements in it suggest, at least, the depth at which it was conceived" (*Visions of Xanadu* 128, 130).

4. Tinker (incorrectly, I would argue) sees Henry Lord Falkland—like the "Fiend" in "Love," the demon lover in "Kubla Khan," the power that possesses the Mariner, and Geraldine—as "one of the powers of evil, a creature of the dark, who acquires hold of a human victim, and pursues him to his ruin" (19).

5. Kessler says of the scene, "Opposites are balanced in an 'intense repose' that is not a passive dream state but a dynamic act of Being" (34).

6. See Bostetter, *Ventriloquists* 104–08, for a discussion of the poem's dual authorship; see also Jacobus 224–32.

7. As Taylor puts it, "The resemblances between ['The Three Graves']—with its curses, hypnotic silences, and perverse sexuality—and 'Christabel' are striking. . . . [Coleridge] explores a world of frighteningly primitive energies, only occasionally relieved by calm and patient reason" (*Defense* 107, 109).

8. It is inadequate to say, as Everest, e.g., does, that "the sexually and morally perverse mother of *The Three Graves* destroys the happiness of her children" (48). John Beer comes much closer to the mark when he comments that the power of cursing "worked by summarily breaking the magnetic connections that link human beings to one another, causing certain subtle faculties that otherwise minister to life and health to

wither at their roots. It would follow from this that the most effective malediction, severing the most powerful unconscious link of all, would be that of a mother cursing her child" (*Poetic Intelligence* 220).

9. The evidence for Coleridge's and/or Wordsworth's knowledge of the story of Snow White as a source for "The Three Graves" is conjectural, based on literary developments in the late eighteenth century, and textual, based on what I would conclude are too many parallel details of character, imagery, and thematic significance in the two stories to ignore. The first question is whether or not there would have been any English versions of "Snow White"—or the German "Schneewitchen"—available at the 1897–98 time of composition. Steven Jones, who has done extensive research on the tale, is inclined to think that although some published versions were available in French, Italian, or German, they would have been unlikely sources for Wordsworth or Coleridge (personal conversation). A stronger hypothesis is that the story, while not as common in England as in other parts of western Europe, had become available as part of the oral tradition. Coleridge calls "The Three Graves" a "common Ballad-tale" in much the same way that he describes "Christabel" as a "common Faery Tale." Gibson, without any documentation, notes: "In *Cymbeline* Shakespeare turned his attention to an old and honoured fairy story, *Schneewitchen or Snow-White*. This accords very strikingly with what we have already seen as to Shakespeare's evolution. His last years bring him back to the themes of his early days. The story tells us how 'Snow-white was dead and remained dead. The dwarfs laid her upon a bier, and wept three long days. Then they were going to bury her, but she still looked as if she were living, and still had her pretty red cheeks.' Surely this is the foundation for the death and re-awakening of Fidele, and the sorrow of Arviragus, Guiderius and Belarius in IV.ii" (140). Whether Gibson is quoting a chapbook or some other written or oral source, or is simply conjecturing, is unclear. Whatever the case, I am assuming Coleridge's acquaintance with the tale of Snow White, whether through some written source or the oral tradition. If he did not know it, he was writing an uncannily parallel story for which "Snow White" can serve as an enriching gloss.

10. See Rose for a discussion of retelling mother-daughter tales so that the mother continues to be nurturing.

Chapter Four

1. The assumption that "Christabel" is a fairy tale has remained strong enough that Harold Bloom, in his review of Bettelheim's *Uses of Enchantment*, can argue for his interpretation of "Snow White"—and

against Bettelheim's—by adducing a comparison of the fairy tale with "Christabel" to make his point. For commentary on the review, see Sale 40–41.

2. William Hazlitt, *Examiner*, 2 June 1816 (qtd. in Jackson 205–09). Hazlitt seems not to understand much of anything about "Christabel" except that "this woman [Geraldine] is a witch." Josiah Condor, in the *Eclectic Review*, June 1816 (qtd. in Jackson 209–13), also finds the elves incomprehensible: "The Conclusion to Part the Second, is, we suppose, an enigma. It is certainly unintelligible as it stands." Thomas Moore, in *Edinburgh Review*, September 1816 (qtd. in Jackson 226–36), professes, "We are wholly unable to divine the meaning of any portion of it."

3. Schwartz attributes this review to Charles Lamb, an attribution that would partially explain its sympathetic understanding and tone.

4. It is interesting that Tolkien also uses the clothing metaphor in speaking of fairy tales: "It may be better for [children] to read some things, especially fairy-stories, that are beyond their measure rather than short of it. Their books like their clothes should allow for growth, and their books at any rate should encourage it" (44).

5. Jane Nelson discusses the positive effects of Geraldine's actions in the course of tracing "the complex of surface oppositions."

6. "The holiness of the oak is of course not merely a Somerset tradition. All over England we have Gospel Oaks. Oaks that had been sacred to Thor were re-sanctified by the carving of crosses on them. The oak was early regarded as the tree of Mary. But here in *Christabel* the belief seems to be that condensed in a rhyme quoted by Dr. Katherine Briggs: 'Fairy folks / Are in old Oaks.' 'Even in England,' wrote a Mrs. Philpot in 1897, 'especially in Devon and Cornwall, there still exist people who believe that oaks are inhabited by elves'" (Adlard 231–32). Beyond the obvious point that oaks are fairy trees, two things seem significant. First, the tree of the male god of thunder and power is also the tree of the mother of the God of Love; thus, the tree symbolizes the truth of reconciliation. Second, the sacred tree has been resanctified. Spirit is unchanging; the story of Spirit is what is created anew. Thus the Christian myth respeaks Faery.

7. Adlard's essay, in particular, explains the supernatural character of many details of the poem; see also Liggins.

8. As for the other characters, Sir Leoline hardly deserves to be called good or bad. He is wrongheaded throughout; the only thing that changes is the object of his wrong thinking. Bard Bracy is good but unable to make his goodness active.

9. See Fruman 362; and Nelson.

10. The Opies provide corroborative commentary: "Fairy tales are thus more realistic than they may appear at first sight; while the magic in

them almost heightens the realism. The magic gets us wondering how we ourselves would react in similar circumstances. It encourages speculation. It gives a child license to wonder. And this is the merit of the tales, that by going beyond possibility they enlarge our daily horizon" (20).

11. Bettelheim explores at length the psychological significance of fairy tales, as does Luthi (*Once upon a Time*). Spatz's essay is based on a psychological reading of the poem.

12. In terms of fairy tale structure, there is no need for explanation: "The true fairy-tale princess acts out of inner necessity. She need not explain her actions. . . . The events and characters in the genuine folk fairy tale have such a strong symbolic appeal [because] the principal actors in the fairy tale are neither individuals nor character types, but merely figures, and for just this reason can stand for a great many things. One can view them as representatives of cosmic or psychic forces just as easily as real people" (Luthi, *Once upon a Time* 126).

13. The two views remain essentially antithetical, although a few critics have attempted to reconcile them: "The inconsistency could be resolved if it were recognized . . . 'that the power of evil' (Gillman) might in some perplexing way turn out to be 'her appointed task' (Derwent). . . . Far from being a simple evil, Geraldine might be seen as representing something like the seemingly ominous and demonic, but nevertheless necessary forces of life that lie beneath the peace of the Khan's garden" (Edwards and Emslie 238, 241). Barth suggests: "Geraldine is not wholly in the power of the flesh; spirit already works in her. The two forces must aim at integration; neither can have its genuine fulfillment without the other. The spirit without the flesh has no true place in the temporal, mortal world, and flesh without spirit is selfish and ignoble" (*Power of Love* 82). A small minority of critics have viewed Geraldine in a positive light: e.g., Preston argues that Geraldine is the instrument for Christabel's union with God; and John Beer (*Visionary*) sees Geraldine as a force of love. Delson provides a nice summary of criticism.

14. I am grateful to John Beer for calling this copy to my attention.

15. Geraldine's androgynous nature has been noted—mostly in passing or in puzzlement—by several critics. Nelson, e.g., notes that there are several "bisexual indications" in the central characters: "Christ and Abel appear in female form; Geraldine evokes by her actions, her form, and her name, the powerful suggestions of masculinity" (381). Basler, comments Delson, "hints that Geraldine has a touch of the 'androgynous' in her make-up" (132).

16. Both women at one time or another perform both the masculine and feminine roles. According to Spatz, Christabel "temporarily plays the male role to push the incident quickly to its climax, but, as she lies with

Geraldine afterward, she has become a deflowered but grateful female"
(112).

17. Sara Coleridge writes, "My father admired white clothing, because he looked at it in reference to woman, as expressive of her delicacy and purity" (1: 21).

18. Adlard writes: "Dr. Briggs, in the *Anatomy of Puck*, has stressed the 'mingling of the ghosts, devils, and fairies of popular belief.' To identify Geraldine as a fairy is thus not as limiting as it may sound. 'Ever since the first traceable beginnings of fairy beliefs,' Dr. Briggs writes, 'the dead have been curiously entangled with fairies in popular tradition.' This would account for Geraldine's relationship with Christabel's dead mother" (235).

19. Many of the psychoanalytic readings of "Christabel" also describe the relationship between the mother and Geraldine in terms of a good mother/bad mother split, although they do not do so in fairy tale terms, and they tend to oversimplify the actual psychological—not to mention spiritual—complexity inherent in the characters of Geraldine and Christabel. While I do not entirely agree with Schapiro, she has built usefully on earlier studies, and her reading and mine are in fundamental agreement as far as the good/bad character of the mother/Geraldine relationship and the nature of Geraldine and Christabel are concerned. That is, in addition to the absent mother's being "good" and Geraldine "bad," Geraldine is both "good" and "bad." Schapiro also notes the mother-within-the-daughter identity: "As Geraldine embodies both the desired and ideal good mother and the feared and vengeful bad mother, so the mother-image is split generally between the good and bad throughout the poem. Christabel frequently appeals to the image of the idealized good mother to defend her from the bad. She is threatened not only by the bad mother in Geraldine, but by the bad mother within herself" (73).

20. Schapiro comments: "Christabel, like the mother-image, is split between the ideal and the malevolent, divided by her ambivalent feelings. . . . The bad mother's glance . . . contains only 'somewhat of malice' but 'more of dread.' She is less terrible than terrified herself. It is Christabel's, or the child's, own violent and destructive feelings that are the real source of dread; she fears most the serpent within herself" (80, 82).

Works Cited

Adair, Patricia M. *The Waking Dream: A Study of Coleridge's Poetry*. London: Harvester, 1967.

Adlard, John. "The Quantock *Christabel*." *Philological Quarterly* 50.2 (1971): 230–38.

Aiken, Lucy, ed. *Poetry for Children*. 2nd ed. London, 1803.

Allsop, Thomas. *Letters, Conversations, and Recollections of S. T. Coleridge*. New York: Harper, 1834.

Andersen, Hans Christian. *Wonderful Stories for Children*. [London]: Howitt, 1846.

Appleyard, J. A. *Coleridge's Philosophy of Literature*. Cambridge, Mass.: Harvard UP, 1965.

Aulnoy, Marie Catherine. *Contes des fées*. 1698. Trans. as *Tales of the Fairys*, 1699.

Barfield, Owen. *What Coleridge Thought*. Middletown, Conn.: Wesleyan UP, 1971.

Barth, J. Robert. *Coleridge and Christian Doctrine*. Cambridge, Mass.: Harvard UP, 1969.

———. *Coleridge and the Power of Love*. Columbia: U of Missouri P, 1988.

———. "Coleridge's Ideal of Love." *Studies in Romanticism* 24 (Spring 1985): 113–39.

———. *The Symbolic Imagination: Coleridge and the Romantic Tradition*. Princeton, N.J.: Princeton UP, 1977.

Works Cited

Basler, Roy P. *Sex, Symbolism, and Psychology in Literature*. New Brunswick, N.J.: Rutgers UP, 1948.

Bate, Walter Jackson. *Coleridge*. New York: Macmillan, 1968.

Beagle, Peter S. "Tolkien's Magic Ring." *Fantasists on Fantasy*. Ed. Robert H. Boyer and Kenneth J. Zahorski. New York: Avon, 1984. 128–36.

Beer, John. "Coleridge and Poetry: 1. Poems of the Supernatural." *S. T. Coleridge*. Ed. R. L. Brett. Athens: Ohio UP, 1972. 45–91.

———. *Coleridge's Poetic Intelligence*. London: Macmillan, 1977.

———. *Coleridge the Visionary*. London: Chatto & Windus, 1959.

Berkoben, L. D. "The Composition of Coleridge's 'Hymn Before Sunrise': Some Mitigating Circumstances." *English Language Notes* 4 (1966): 32–37.

Berman, Morris. *The Reenchantment of the World*. Ithaca, N.Y.: Cornell UP, 1981.

Bettelheim, Bruno. *The Uses of Enchantment*. New York: Knopf, 1976.

Bloom, Harold. Rev. of *The Uses of Enchantment*, by Bruno Bettelheim. *New York Times Book Review*, 15 July 1976.

Bostetter, Edward E. "*Christabel*: The Vision of Fear." *Philological Quarterly* 36.2 (1957): 183–94.

———. *The Romantic Ventriloquists: Wordsworth, Coleridge, Keats, Shelley, Byron*. Seattle: U of Washington P, 1963.

Briggs, Katherine. *The Anatomy of Puck*. London: Routledge, 1959.

———. *The Fairies in English Tradition and Literature*. Chicago: U of Chicago P, 1967.

Campbell, Joseph. *The Masks of God: Occidental Mythology*. New York: Viking, 1964.

Chayes, Irene H. "'Kubla Khan' and The Creative Process." *Studies in Romanticism* 6 (1966): 1–21.

Christensen, Jerome. *Coleridge's Blessed Machine of Language*. Ithaca, N.Y.: Cornell UP, 1981.

Coffin, Tristram P. "Coleridge's Use of the Ballad Stanza in *The Rime of The Ancient Mariner*." *Modern Language Quarterly* 12 (1951): 437–45.

Coleridge, Derwent, ed. *The Poems of Samuel Taylor Coleridge*. London: Maxon, 1871.

Coleridge, Hartley. "Adolph and Annette." Ed. Judith Plotz. *Children's Literature* 14 (1986): 151–61.

Coleridge, Samuel Taylor. *Aids to Reflection*. Ed. H. N. Coleridge. New York: Harper, 1884. Vol. 1 of *The Complete Works of Samuel Taylor Coleridge*. Ed. W. G. T. Shedd. 7 vols.

———. *Biographia Literaria*. Ed. James Engell and W. Jackson Bate. 2 pts. Princeton, N.J.: Princeton UP, 1983. Vol. 7 of *The Collected Works of Samuel Taylor Coleridge*. Bollingen Series 75.

———. *Biographia Literaria.* Ed. J. Shawcross. 2 vols. Oxford: Oxford UP, 1907.

———. *The Collected Letters of Samuel Taylor Coleridge.* Ed. Earl Leslie Griggs. 6 vols. Oxford: Oxford UP, 1956–71.

———. *The Complete Poetical Works of Samuel Taylor Coleridge.* Ed. E. H. Coleridge. 2 vols. Oxford: Oxford UP, 1912.

———. *The Friend.* Ed. Barbara E. Rooke. 2 pts. Princeton, N.J.: Princeton UP, 1969. Vol. 4 of *The Collected Works of Samuel Taylor Coleridge.* Bollingen Series 75.

———. *Hints towards the Formation of a More Comprehensive Theory of Life.* New York: Harper, 1884. Vol. 1 of *The Complete Works of Samuel Taylor Coleridge.* Ed. W. G. T. Shedd. 7 vols.

———. *The Notebooks of Samuel Taylor Coleridge.* Ed. Kathleen Coburn. 5 vols. to date. Princeton, N.J.: Princeton UP, 1957–   .

———. *On the Constitution of Church and State.* Ed. John Colmer. Princeton, N.J.: Princeton UP, 1976. Vol. 10 of *The Collected Works of Samuel Taylor Coleridge.* Bollingen Series 75.

———. *The Statesman's Manual. Lay Sermons.* Ed. R. J. White. Princeton, N.J.: Princeton UP, 1972. Vol. 6 of *The Collected Works of Samuel Taylor Coleridge.* Bollingen Series 75.

———. *The Table Talk.* New York: Harper, 1884. Vol. 6 of *The Com͵lete Works of Samuel Taylor Coleridge.* Ed. W. G. T. Shedd. 7 vols.

Coleridge, Sara. *Memoir and Letters of Sara Coleridge.* Ed. Edith Coleridge. 2 vols. London: King, 1873.

Cook, Elizabeth. *The Ordinary and the Fabulous.* London: Cambridge UP, 1967.

Cooper, Susan. "Escaping into Ourselves." *Fantasists on Fantasy.* Ed. Robert H. Boyer and Kenneth J. Zahorski. New York: Avon, 1984. 280–87.

Darton, F. J. Harvey. *Children's Books of England: Five Centuries of Social Life.* Cambridge: Cambridge UP, 1966.

Delson, Abe. "The Function of Geraldine in *Christabel*: A Critical Perspective and Interpretation." *English Studies* 61 (1980): 130–41.

De Selincourt, Ernest. *Wordsworthian and Other Studies.* New York: Russell, 1964.

Doughty, Oswald. *Perturbed Spirit: The Life and Personality of Samuel Taylor Coleridge.* Rutherford, N.J.: Fairleigh Dickinson UP, 1981.

Duffy, Maureen. *The Erotic World of Faery.* London: Hadder, 1972.

Edwards, Paul, and MacDonald Emslie. " 'Thoughts So All Unlike Each Other': The Paradoxical in *Christabel*." *English Studies* 52 (1971): 236–46.

Eliot, T. S. *Four Quartets.* New York: Harcourt, 1943.

Works Cited

Everest, Kelvin. *Coleridge's Secret Ministry: The Context of the Conversation Poems, 1795–1798.* Sussex: Harvester, 1979.

Fielding, Sarah. *The Governess; or, Little Female Academy.* Juvenile Library. London: Oxford UP, 1968. Facsimile reproduction of first edition of 1749, with introduction and bibliography by Jill E. Grey.

Fields, Beverly. *Reality's Dark Dream: Dejection in Coleridge.* Kent, Ohio: Kent State UP, 1967.

Fogle, Richard Harter. *The Idea of Coleridge's Criticism.* Berkeley: U of California P, 1962.

Fruman, Norman. *The Damaged Archangel.* New York: Braziller, 1971.

Frye, Northrop. *Anatomy of Criticism: Four Essays.* Princeton, N.J.: Princeton UP, 1971.

Gérard, Albert. "The Systolic Rhythm: The Structure of the Conversation Poems." *Essays in Criticism* 10 (1960): 307–17.

Gibson, J. Paul S. R. *Shakespeare's Use of the Supernatural.* Cambridge: Deighton Bell, 1908; Folcroft Library Editions, 1973.

Gilbert, Sandra M., and Susan Gubar. *The Madwoman in the Attic: The Woman Writer and the Nineteenth Century Literary Imagination.* New Haven, Conn.: Yale UP, 1979.

Gillman, James. *The Life of Samuel Taylor Coleridge.* London: Pickering, 1838.

Grimm, Jacob, and Wilhelm Grimm. *German Popular Stories.* Trans. Edgar Taylor. 1823–26. New York: Scholar Press, 1971. Facsimile of 1823 edition.

Harding, Anthony J. *Coleridge and the Inspired Word.* Montreal: McGill-Queen's UP, 1985.

Haven, Richard. *Patterns of Consciousness: An Essay on Coleridge.* Amherst: U of Massachusetts P, 1969.

House, Humphrey. *Coleridge: The Clark Lectures, 1951–52.* London: Hart-Davis, 1953.

Jackson, J. R. de J., ed. *Coleridge: The Critical Heritage.* New York: Barnes, 1970.

Jacobus, Mary. *Tradition and Experiment in Wordsworth's "Lyrical Ballads" (1798).* London: Oxford UP, 1976.

Jung, C. G. *Collected Works.* Ed. Herbert Read, Michael Fordham, and Gerhard Adler. London, 1953– .

Kessler, Edward. *Coleridge's Metaphors of Being.* Princeton, N.J.: Princeton UP, 1979.

Kilner, Dorothy. *The Histories of More Children than One.* London, 1783.

Knight, G. Wilson. *The Starlit Dome.* New York: Barnes, 1960.

Kotzin, Michael C. *Dickens and the Fairy Tale.* Bowling Green, Ohio: Bowling Green U Popular P, 1972.

Krappe, Alexander Haggerty. *The Science of Folklore*. Strand, Eng.: Methuen, 1962.

Kroeber, Karl. *Romantic Narrative Art*. Madison: U of Wisconsin P, 1960.

Lamb, Charles. *The Letters of Charles Lamb*. Ed. E. V. Lucas. 3 vols. London, 1935.

Langton, Jane. "The Weak Place in the Cloth." *Fantasists on Fantasy*. Ed. Robert H. Boyer and Kenneth J. Zahorski. New York: Avon, 1984. 165–79.

Le Guin, Ursula K. "From Elfland to Poughkeepsie." *Fantasists on Fantasy*. Ed. Robert H. Boyer and Kenneth J. Zahorski. New York: Avon, 1984. 195–209.

Leprince de Beaumont, Jeanne. *Magasin des enfans*. London, 1756. Trans. as *Young Misses Magazine*. London: Nourse, 1761.

Liggins, Elizabeth M. "Folklore and the Supernatural in 'Christabel.'" *Folklore* 88 (1976): 91–104.

Lockridge, Laurence S. "Explaining Coleridge's Explanation." *Reading Coldridge: Approaches and Applications*. Ed. Walter B. Crawford. Ithaca, N.Y.: Cornell UP, 1979.

Luthi, Max. *The Fairytale as Art Form and Portrait of Man*. Trans. Jon Erickson. Bloomington: Indiana UP, 1984.

———. *Once upon a Time: On the Nature of Fairy Tales*. Trans. Lee Chadeayne, Paul Gottwald, and Max Luthi. Bloomington: Indiana UP, 1970.

MacDonald, George. "The Fantastic Imagination." *Fantasists on Fantasy*. Ed. Robert H. Boyer and Kenneth J. Zahorski. New York: Avon, 1984. 14–21.

McFarland, Thomas. *Romanticism and the Forms of Ruin: Wordsworth, Coleridge, and Modalities of Fragmentation*. Princeton, N.J.: Princeton UP, 1981.

Magnuson, Paul. *Coleridge's Nightmare Poetry*. Charlottesville: UP of Virginia, 1974.

Meigs, Cornelia, Anne Eaton, Elizabeth Nesbitt, and Ruth Hill Viguers, eds. *A Critical History of Children's Literature: A Survey of Children's Books in English from Earliest Times to the Present*. 4 pts. New York: Macmillan, 1953.

Milton, Mary Lee Taylor. *The Poetry of Samuel Taylor Coleridge: An Annotated Bibliography of Criticism*. New York: Garland, 1981.

Muir, Percy. *English Children's Books, 1600 to 1900*. New York: Praeger, 1969.

Nelson, Jane. "Entelechy and Structure in 'Christabel.'" *Studies in Romanticism* 19 (1980): 375–93.

Opie, Iona, and Peter Opie. *The Classic Fairy Tales*. New York: Oxford UP, 1974.

Works Cited

Osborne Collection of Early Children's Books: A Catalogue. Ed. Judith St. John. Intro. Edgar Osborne. 2 vols. Toronto: Toronto Public Library, 1975.

Paris, Bernard J. "Coleridge's 'The Eolian Harp.'" *Papers of the Michigan Academy of Sciences, Arts, and Letters* 51 (1966): 571–82.

Perrault, Charles. *Histoires ou contes du temp passé: Avec des moralités.* Paris, 1727. Trans. Robert Samber as *Histories; or, Tales of Times Past.* London: Pote, 1729.

Perkins, David, ed. *English Romantic Writers.* New York: Harcourt, 1967.

Pickering, Samuel F., Jr. *John Locke and Children's Books in Eighteenth Century England.* Knoxville: U of Tennessee P, 1981.

Piper, H. W. "The Disunity of *Christabel* and the Fall of Nature." *Essays in Criticism* 28 (1978): 216–27.

———. *The Singing of Mount Abora: Coleridge's Use of Biblical Imagery and Natural Symbolism in Poetry and Philosophy.* London: Associated UP, 1987.

Plotz, Judith. "Childhood Lost, Childhood Regained: Hartley Coleridge's Fable of Defeat." *Children's Literature* 14 (1986): 133–48.

Preston, Thomas R. "*Christabel* and the Mystical Tradition." *Essays in Studies in Language and Literature.* Ed. Herbert H. Petit. Philological Series 5. Pittsburgh: Duquesne U, 1964. 138–57.

Purves, Alan C. "Formal Structure in 'Kubla Khan.'" *Studies in Romanticism* 1 (1962): 1987–91.

Rees, A. D., and B. F. Rees. *Celtic Heritage.* London: Thames, 1961.

Rose, Ellen Cronan. "Through the Looking Glass: When Women Tell Fairy Tales." *The Voyage In: Fictions of Female Development.* Ed. Elizabeth Abel, Marianne Hirsch, and Elizabeth Langland. Hanover, N.H.: UP of New England, 1983. 209–27.

Sale, Roger. *Fairy Tales and After: From Snow White to E. B. White.* Cambridge, Mass.: Harvard UP, 1978.

Schapiro, Barbara A. *The Romantic Mother: Narcissistic Patterns in Romantic Poetry.* Baltimore, Md.: Johns Hopkins UP, 1983.

Schneider, Elisabeth. *Coleridge, Opium, and "Kubla Khan."* Chicago: U of Chicago P, 1953.

Schulz, Max F. "Coleridge and the Enchantments of Earthly Paradise." *Reading Coleridge: Approaches and Applications.* Ed. Walter B. Crawford. Ithaca, N.Y.: Cornell UP, 1979.

———. *The Poetic Voices of Coleridge.* Detroit, Mich.: Wayne State UP, 1963.

Schwartz, Lewis M. "A New Review of Coleridge's *Christabel.*" *Studies in Romanticism* 9 (1969): 114–24.

Scot, Reginald. *The Discoverie of Witchcraft.* London: Brome, 1584.

Scott, Sir Walter. *The Letters of Sir Walter Scott*. Ed. H. J. C. Grierson. 12 vols. London: Constable, 1932–37; New York: AMS Press, 1971.

———. "Memoir of the Early Life of Sir Walter Scott, Written by Himself." *Memoirs of Sir Walter Scott*. Ed. J. G. Lockhart. 5 vols. London: Macmillan, 1900. 1:1–47.

———. *Minstrelsy of the Scottish Border*. Vol. 2. Ed. T. F. Henderson. 4 vols. Edinburgh: Tweeddale; London: Oliver, 1932.

Spatz, Jonas. "Sexual Initiation in Coleridge's 'Christabel.'" *PMLA* 90.1 (1975): 107–16.

Stone, Harry. *Dickens and the Invisible World: Fairy Tales, Fantasy, and Novel-Making*. Bloomington: Indiana UP, 1979.

Suther, Marshall. *The Dark Night of Samuel Taylor Coleridge*. New York: Columbia UP, 1960.

———. "On the Interpretation of 'Kubla Khan.'" *Bucknell Review* 7 (1957): 1–19.

———. *Visions of Xanadu*. New York: Columbia UP, 1965.

Taylor, Anya. *Coleridge's Defense of the Human*. Columbus: Ohio State UP, 1986.

———. "Magic in Coleridge's Poetry." *Wordsworth Circle* 3 (1972): 76–84.

Thalmann, Marianne. *The Romantic Fairy Tale: Seeds Of Surrealism*. Trans. Mary B. Corcorn. Ann Arbor: U of Michigan P, 1964.

Thwaite, Mary F. *From Primer to Pleasure in Reading: An Introduction to the History of Children's Books in England from the Invention of Printing to 1914, with an Outline of Some Developments in Other Countries*. Boston: Horn Book, 1963.

Tinker, Chauncy B. "Coleridge's 'The Ballad of the Dark Ladié.'" *Yale University Library Gazette* 24 (1949): 17–20.

Tolkien, J. R. R. "On Fairy Stories." *Tree and Leaf*. Boston: Houghton, 1965. 3–84.

Trainer, James. "The Marchen." *The Romantic Period in Germany*. Ed. Siegbert Prawer. New York: Schocken, 1970. 97–112.

Warren, Robert Penn. Essay. *The Rime of the Ancient Mariner*. By S. T. Coleridge. Ed. Warren. New York: Reynal and Hitchcock, 1946. Rpt. as "A Poem of Pure Imagination: An Experience in Reading." *Selected Essays*. New York: Random, 1958. 198–305.

Watson, Jeanie. "Coleridge's Androgynous Ideal." *Prose Studies* 6 (1983): 35–56.

———. "Coleridge's Mariner in the Perilous Land." *Charles Lamb Bulletin* ns 64 (1988): 270–76.

———. "Coleridge's *Rime of the Ancient Mariner*: An Encounter with Faerie." *Children's Literature Association Quarterly* 11.4 (1987): 165–70.

Works Cited

———. "Shelley's Witch: The Naked Conception." *Concerning Poetry* 10.1 (1977): 33–43.

Wendling, Ronald C. "Coleridge and the Consistency of 'The Eolian Harp.'" *Studies in Romanticism* 8 (1968): 26–42.

Wernaer, Robert M. *Romanticism and the Romantic School in Germany.* New York: Appleton, 1910.

Whalley, George. *Coleridge and Sara Hutchinson.* London: Routledge, 1955.

Wheeler, K. M. *The Creative Mind in Coleridge's Poetry.* Cambridge, Mass.: Harvard UP, 1981.

Wooden, Warren W. "A Child's Garden of Sprites: English Renaissance Fairy Poetry." *Bulletin of the West Virginia Association of College English Teachers* 6 (1981): 37–54. Rpt. in *Children's Literature of the English Renaissance: Essays by Warren W. Wooden.* Ed. Jeanie Watson. Lexington: UP of Kentucky, 1986. 97–120.

Woodring, Carl R. *Politics in the Poetry of Coleridge.* Madison: U of Wisconsin P, 1961.

———. "Sara *fille*: Fairy Child." *Reading Coleridge: Approaches and Applications.* Ed. Walter B. Crawford. Ithaca, N.Y.: Cornell UP, 1979.

Wordsworth, William. *The Letters of William and Dorothy Wordsworth: The Middle Years.* Ed. Ernest De Selincourt. 2 vols. Oxford: Oxford UP, 1937.

———. *The Poetical Works of William Wordsworth.* Ed. Ernest De Selincourt and Helen Darbishire. 5 vols. Oxford: Oxford UP, 1940–49.

———. *The Prelude: 1799, 1805, 1850.* Ed. Jonathan Wordsworth, M. H. Abrams, and Stephen Gill. New York: Norton, 1979.

Yarlot, Geoffrey. *Coleridge and the Abyssinian Maid.* London: Methuen, 1967.

Zipes, Jack. *Breaking the Magic Spell.* Austin: U of Texas P, 1979.

Index

Index

Index